This Other Eden

This royal throne of kings, this scepter'd isle,
This earth of majesty, this seat of Mars,
This other Eden…

William Shakespeare, *King Richard the Second*, Act II, Scene 1

This Other Eden

Paintings from the Yale Center for British Art

Catalogue

Malcolm Warner

Julia Marciari Alexander

Introduction

Patrick McCaughey

YALE CENTER FOR BRITISH ART

YALE UNIVERSITY PRESS

NEW HAVEN & LONDON

Published on the occasion of a traveling exhibition
from the Yale Center for British Art
New Haven, Connecticut, USA, to

The Art Gallery of New South Wales
Sydney, Australia
May 2 to July 5, 1998

Queensland Art Gallery
Brisbane, Australia
July 16 to September 6, 1998

Art Gallery of South Australia
Adelaide, Australia
September 17 to November 15, 1998

Library of Congress Cataloging-in-Publication Data
Yale Center for British Art.
This other Eden : paintings from the Yale Center for British Art /
catalogue, Malcolm Warner, Julia Marciari Alexander;
introduction, Patrick McCaughey.
p.   cm.   Includes bibliographical references.
ISBN 0-300-07498-0 (alk. paper).
ISBN 0-930606-86-8 (pbk. : alk. paper)
1. Portrait painting, English – Catalogs. 2. Portrait painting –
17th century – England – Catalogs. 3. Portrait painting –
Connecticut – New Haven – Catalogs. 4. England – Biography –
Portraits – Catalogs. 5. Yale Center for British Art – Catalogs.
I. Warner, Malcolm, 1953-
II. Alexander, Julia Marciari, 1967-   . III. Title.
ND1314.3.Y36   1998
757´.0942´0747468–dc21   98-10586 CIP

A catalogue record for this book is available
from the British Library.

The paper in this book meets the guidelines for permanence and
durability of the Committee on Production Guidelines for Book
Longevity of the Council on Library Resources.

Design and composition by Julie Lavorgna
Photography by Richard Caspole
Printed in Italy

Front cover: William Bell Scott, *Ailsa Craig* (detail), no. 65
Back cover: Yale Center for British Art, south side
              © Grant Mudford, Los Angeles, CA
Frontispiece: George Stubbs, *Zebra* (detail), no. 42

10 9 8 7 6 5 4 3 2 1

Contents

Foreword

THE YALE CENTER FOR BRITISH ART opened in April 1977. The building and the collections, together with an endowment to operate a fully-staffed center, was entirely the gift of Paul Mellon to Yale University, from which he graduated in 1929. The building was designed by Louis I. Kahn and, although completed posthumously, closely followed his original plans. The architecture of the Center with its naturally lit galleries and rich and restrained palette drawn from the materials of the building itself—travertine marble, steel, concrete, and white oak—mark the building as a landmark of modern architecture.

The Center's collection extends from Tudor times to the present day and encompasses paintings, sculpture, drawings, watercolors, rare books, and manuscripts—the largest and most comprehensive collection of British art ever assembled outside the United Kingdom. It was personally acquired by Paul Mellon, who has added to it over the past twenty years both through gifts of works of art and the provision of acquisition funds.

The Center has a dual function: it plays an integral part in the teaching and research life of Yale University and operates as a public art museum. Regularly it brings scholars to New Haven from around the world. It offers educational programs, lectures, seminars, and conferences and sponsors musical performances and film series related to the program of changing exhibitions.

The Center mounts exhibitions on a regular basis and often circulates these to other museums both nationally and internationally. Its mission is to spread knowledge about British art and add to its wider appreciation in the United States.

Patrick McCaughey, Director
Yale Center for British Art

Fig. 1. Tessa Pullan, *Paul Mellon*, 1984, bronze, 14⅛ x 9 in (inc. base), Yale Center for British Art

Paul Mellon and the British Imagination

P AUL MELLON was christened in St. George's Chapel at Windsor Castle in 1907 and so "foreshadowed," as he remarked years later, "my later addiction to English life and English places."[1] His mother was English and he had a plethora of English uncles and aunts. His childhood, youth, and early manhood were divided between England and Pittsburgh, the city of his father, the legendary banker and financier Andrew W. Mellon. Paul Mellon would draw a sharp contrast in later life between that grim industrial city of western Pennsylvania and the beauty of the English countryside and the grace of English country houses. He would recall, "England had a stillness and deep serenity in those last few years before the First World War…the atmosphere…of that long-lost summer of 1913…had the color and feeling of childhood itself." It is a sentiment that evokes Wordsworth's intimations that heaven lies about us in our childhood. The England of Paul Mellon's early memories was indeed another Eden.

The discovery of the deeper pleasures of English literature and the stimulus of British history at Yale University in the late 1920s buttressed this primal love of England. Gifted and distinguished faculty, including such notable scholars as Chauncey Brewster Tinker and Frederick Pottle, were teaching at Yale (laying the foundations of formidable schools of English and history). The delight in English poetry and the passage of British history went beyond a simple evocation of Englishness. It had a deep emotional resonance, and indeed even the course on Industrial Physiology opened his eyes to "the wonder of the inner man," presaging a theme in Paul Mellon's later life as collector and philanthropist.

In 1929 Paul Mellon went up to Clare College, Cambridge to read history—a mistake, as he later observed. Although Cambridge was not as intellectually stimulating to him as Yale had been, his Cambridge years completed his induction into British life: "I loved the gray walls of Cambridge, its grassy quadrangles, St. Mary's bells, the busy, narrow streets full of men in black gowns, King's College Chapel and Choir and candlelight, the coal fire smell, and walking across the quadrangle in a dressing gown in the rain to take a bath." And, as he would observe laconically in his autobiography, "In my first year at Cambridge, I had discovered foxhunting." It would prove to be one of his greatest interests and pleasures and play an important role in his decision to collect British art. Paul Mellon's interest in and love of horses and the sports associated with the horse invoke a wider world, as he was to reflect in a remarkable memorandum written in 1936, when he was twenty-nine, shortly before his father's death:

I am…partly instinctively English in my love of the country. I have lived in England and tasted English life pretty thoroughly, and it came to me naturally and strongly. It is really in my blood…It explains my addiction to English literature, to the English poets, to descriptions of English life, especially sporting and country life, and to the social and emotional aspects of English history…Hunting is another example of the reaction which has set up inside me against business, the city, modern industrial drabness, the suppression of the natural emotions and feelings…It involves the use of the horse, that instinctive animal, and man's mastery of the horse.

The experience of the life of the landscape—the love of "the natural"—his boyhood memories, and a mind and sensibility shaped by Yale and Cambridge universities formed Paul Mellon's remarkable taste for British art. What has made his taste so distinctive is that the works he has bought and the artists he has pursued in depth are extensions or reflections of his own experience. The work of art must resonate with his own life.

Paul Mellon's collecting began with the acquisition of large color-plate books on foxhunting and horse racing: "From the Robinson Brothers I bought my first illustrated sporting book in 1931—Strutt's *Sports and Pastimes of the People of England.*" The very first oil painting he bought was in 1936 and, presciently, was George Stubbs's *Pumpkin with a Stable Lad* (fig. 2). Paul Mellon has told the story of how he was attracted to the painting:

1

Fig. 2. George Stubbs, *Pumpkin with a Stable Lad*, 1774, oil on panel, 32¾ x 39⅛ in (83.2 x 99.5 cm), Collection of Mr. and Mrs. Paul Mellon

It was during our hunting tour in the Cotswolds back in 1936 that I met Angus Menzies, one of the partners of Knoedler's in London. He told me that the gallery had a beautiful Stubbs, and Mary [Paul Mellon's first wife] and I agreed to go and see it. We were both bowled over by the charming horse, the young boy in a cherry-colored jacket, and the beautiful landscape background. The price was five thousand dollars, and I bought it immediately. It was my very first purchase of a painting and could be said to be the impetus toward my later, some might say gluttonous, forays into the sporting art field.

The beauty of the picture—one of the finest and most distinctively nuanced of all Stubbs's horse portraits—lies in the delicate and unstressed combination of elements. The compact between animal and human, so familiar a theme in Stubbs, is here given a touch of primal innocence, as the stable lad is so young yet so self-possessed. Pumpkin's extended neck as he strains towards the basket of oats animates the relationship. The poetic effect of the milky landscape dissolving into water, cloud, and air behind the figures is neatly braced by the man-made

element of the white fence glimpsed between Pumpkin's back legs. All combine to create a picture which celebrates a famous horse, evokes the English countryside, and has a tantalizingly human presence.

From this first purchase a long sequence of Stubbs's paintings were to enter Paul Mellon's collection. Fifteen oil paintings by Stubbs form one of the central glories of the Yale Center for British Art today and give it the largest representation of this artist to be seen in any public art museum. It also, as Paul Mellon noted, signals his lifelong interest and enthusiasm for British sporting art—in paintings, watercolors, drawings, prints, and illustrated books. This taste has given the Yale collection a distinctive stamp and elevated the reputation of British sporting artists, both those who preceded Stubbs, like John Wootton and James Seymour, and successors such as James Ward, Ben Marshall, and J. F. Herring.

It must, therefore, come as a surprise that Paul Mellon's next passionate interest in an English artist should have been the poet and painter William Blake. The first Blake acquisitions were made in 1941, and over a period

Fig. 3. George Stubbs, *Turf, with Jockey Up, at Newmarket*, no. 43

of thirty years and more a superb collection of Blake was formed, with the illuminated books lying at the heart. Because of the nature of Blake's methods of illuminating his books, great variations are to be found between different copies. Paul Mellon has been an exceptional collector of Blake in adding variant copies of such central works as *Songs of Innocence and Experience*, *The Book of Thel* and *The Book of Urizen*. The climax and center of the collection of illuminated books is unquestionably the unique hand-colored version of *Jerusalem* acquired in 1952.

Just as the acquisition of Stubbs's *Pumpkin with a Stable Lad* had grown from Paul Mellon's vivid experience of the sporting life and the English landscape, so the interest in Blake grew from an intellectually restless, questioning part of his life from the late thirties through the immediate post-World-War-Two period. During this time he had become deeply interested in the work and thought of Carl Gustav Jung. He had begun to read Jung in the early thirties and met him for the first time in New York in 1937. The following year he and his wife paid

their first visit to Jung in Zurich, where they undertook courses and met with Jung in separate sessions. That interest would lead to the creation of the Bollingen Foundation in 1945, funded by Paul Mellon. One of its most ambitious enterprises was the complete translation of Jung's work into English. Paul and Mary Mellon attended the Eranos conferences, which explored themes such as *The Symbolism of Rebirth*, *The Great Mother*, and other topics which bordered on analytic psychology, the study of myth, and the history of religions. Paul Mellon's interests in the more spiritual aspects of analytic psychological theory and Jung's exploration of the world of symbolic archetypes resonated and connected with his interest in the art of William Blake. Here too was an artist whose complex mythology invoked both the world of the spirit and belief in the power of the inner life.

The existence of exemplary holdings of both George Stubbs and William Blake in the same collection—the product of one taste—provokes reflection and consideration. Stubbs and Blake form an Ur-collection before the full strength, range, and diversity of the Paul Mellon

Fig. 4. George Stubbs, *Reapers*, probably 1795, enamel on Wedgwood biscuit earthenware, oval, 30¼ x 40¼ in (77 x 102 cm)

collection of British art became a reality. It is surely extraordinary that these two British artists should have overlapping, if not exactly contemporaneous, careers. (Blake was forty-nine when Stubbs died in 1806.) They belong to different worlds and represent divergent ideas of the nature of the artist, and the contrast between the two provides a notable insight into the British imagination. Although it may be possible to point to equivalent contrasting pairs in other national schools, the comparison of Stubbs and Blake—both unequivocally major artists—etches the national artistic character more keenly.

Stubbs represents the best impulses of the artist of the English Enlightenment. Truthfulness to observation of the natural world is paramount, but observation informed by knowledge. Stubbs the horse painter is also the first artist to undertake a comprehensive anatomy of the horse. The most casual glance at Stubbs's forebears like Wootton or Seymour shows how scientific knowledge transformed the genre of horse portraiture. The anatomically informed horse paintings of Stubbs both

look more true to experience and give to the genre an Augustan *dignitas*. Indeed, what makes Stubbs such a figure of the Enlightenment is that he makes his art seemingly one only of observation, taking the world as it is beheld. The clear focus of *Turf, with Jockey Up, at Newmarket* (fig. 3), for instance, is its chief delight as a painting. Each motif is seen and grasped in separation from all others—the rubbing-down house, the horse, the portrait of the jockey, the course, the marker pole. Stubbs scrutinizes each motif equally, so that the picture seems to read transparently as a product of pure observation without the interference of style or manner.

Stubbs has many characteristics of the Enlightenment artist. His curiosity about natural phenomena allied to his truthfulness of and to observation is borne out in his picture of a zebra (no. 42) probably painted after seeing the animal in Queen Charlotte's menagerie at Buckingham House. The irony is surely not lost on Stubbs of such an exotic beast set in an English wood. Stubbs is ever the Enlightenment artist when he experiments in the new technology of the day in his collaboration with

Fig. 5. George Stubbs, *Two Gentlemen Going a Shooting, with a View of Creswell Crags* (detail), no. 44

Josiah Wedgwood and the production of painted porcelain plaques, of which the Yale Center for British Art's *Reapers* (fig. 4) is perhaps the most beautiful. What fires Stubbs's experiment is the possibility of creating both a more durable work and a more truthful representation as a result. The luminosity of the porcelain ground provides an atmospheric quality hard to match in eighteenth-century landscape painting on canvas.

Stubbs is the *Aufklärer* in image as well as object or attitude. The four-part Shooting Series (fig. 5) is both a testament to friendship and a sporting narrative. The two figures make up their own company for the day together with their dogs—without servants or beaters or loaders. Conversation flows easily between the figures in the first two and concluding works. Human discourse as the basis of the friendship is the easily drawn moral of the series, underscored by the harmonic relationship of the figures to the changing natural world around them, from the faithful depiction of Creswell Crags in the first painting, through the farmland, to the woodland in the concluding scene. Underlying this rhythm is the easy

compact of man and animal. In the Shooting Series this is treated with a gentle humor, as Stubbs rhymes the attitudes of the men with those of their dogs. If a man sits, a dog sits; if a man stands, a dog stands, etc. Through the series Stubbs runs the changing times of the day, adjusting the atmosphere from early morning to dusk. Here again is that Enlightenment view that truth to observation is the single paramount virtue in art.

Could this exemplary eighteenth-century figure contrast more sharply with William Blake, with his disdain, fear, and hostility towards the Enlightenment? "Natural Objects," he once wrote, "always did & now do weaken, deaden & obliterate Imagination in Me."[2] Blake is the apostle of the inward imagination as exemplified in *Jerusalem*:

> …*My great task!*
> *To open the Eternal Worlds, to open the immortal Eyes*
> *Of Man inwards into the Worlds of Thought, into Eternity*
> *Ever expanding in the Bosom of God, the human*
> *Imagination.*[3]

The frequent *terribilità* of Blake's images derived much

Fig. 6. William Blake
"Los howld in a dismal stupor"
from *The First Book of Urizen*, 1794
relief etching color-printed with watercolor

of its power from the trauma of the inner life. "Los howld" (fig. 6) is the image of suffering prompted by the inner imagination, not by external circumstance or event.

Part of Blake's iconoclasm directs itself witheringly at the qualities which make Stubbs such an exemplary artist of the Enlightenment. In his marginalia on Joshua Reynolds's Discourse VIII, Blake says of Bacon, Locke, and Burke: "I felt the Same Contempt & Abhorrence then that I do now. They mock Inspiration & Vision. Inspiration & Vision was then, & now is, & I hope will always Remain, my Element, my Eternal Dwelling place."[4] It is Blake who will further assert, "All Forms are Perfect in the Poet's Mind, but these are not Abstracted nor Compounded from Nature, but are from Imagination."[5]

Observation becomes the enemy of the imagination for Blake as much as the grandiloquence of the Grand Manner which he so despised in the art of Reynolds. One of Blake's most compelling images in *Jerusalem* is the moment when Vala, representing Nature, attempts to clothe and disguise the nude figure of Jerusalem (fig. 7). Nature obscures spiritual truth and hence must be discredited as the guide of art.

The contrast between these two contemporary British artists could hardly be sharper. Stubbs exemplifies the artist faithful to the world of observation, and by this fidelity he fixes the world into lasting and immutable images. He speaks to the present because of that undeviating image of truthfulness which seems to drive out the manners of the eighteenth century and replaces them with an art at once lucid and transparent, poetic and rational. It honors the classic claim of Western art, the abiding alliance between the world of substance and the world of art.

Blake represents the idea of the artist most revered in post-Romantic art and literature: the man who hearkens to the inner voice, feelings, and passions. The truthfulness of the art derives from the life of the imagination, from the unbidden world of feeling and emotion, freed from depicting the world of appearance. As much as an

Fig. 7. William Blake
"Leaning against the pillars"
from *Jerusalem*, c. 1804–20
relief etching with pen and watercolor

opposing aesthetic, these views embody radically different views as to the fundamental nature of the artist.
They provide a dynamic in British art which persists in
different forms to this day.

Stubbs and Blake never met. But Stubbs exhibited a
painting of a tiger in the same building on the Strand
which housed Henry Pars's drawing school when Blake
was a student there. No image is more lasting of Blake
than that of the Tyger — "wiser than the horses of
instruction."[6] In British art, at least, extremes do meet.

Fig. 8. Thomas Gainsborough, *The Gravenor Family,* no. 15

Paul Mellon had made a remarkable start in collecting British art with George Stubbs and William Blake. The drive to form a comprehensive collection, approximately dating from the birth of Hogarth in 1697 to the death of Turner in 1851, took hold in the late 1950s. In 1959 he met Basil Taylor, an English art historian teaching at the Royal College of Art and a connoisseur of distinction who was particularly interested in and knowledgeable about Stubbs. Indeed, the revival of Stubbs's reputation owes much to the combination of the collecting activities of Paul Mellon and the scholarship of Basil Taylor, culminating in the latter's graceful monograph on the artist in 1971. Taylor agreed to act as an advisor to Paul Mellon without a fee.

The collection grew at a spectacular rate. In 1963 the Virginia Museum of Fine Arts mounted an exhibition, *Painting in England, 1700–1850*, drawn entirely from the collection of Mr. and Mrs. Paul Mellon, and it numbered over 400 oil paintings. A large selection was exhibited the following year at the Royal Academy in London and in 1965 at Yale University. Besides oil paintings, watercolors, drawings, prints, and rare books were also acquired to provide a richly textured account of British art through the eighteenth and first half of the nineteenth century. So rich was the collection by the end of the 1960s that special monographic exhibitions drawn from the collection were mounted at the National Gallery of Art, starting with an exhibition of J. M. W. Turner in 1969; successive exhibitions were devoted to John Constable, Joseph Wright of Derby, and William Hogarth. With regard to watercolors and drawings, some entire collections were acquired, most notably those of Martin Hardie and Iolo Williams. But that was not the case with regard to the paintings collection. Paul Mellon would visit London regularly and look carefully and individually at almost every object, taking advice from Basil Taylor in the initial phases and then from John Baskett, a connoisseur who would later become the curator of the Paul Mellon collection. No British collection had ever been formed in this manner before. In less than twenty years it had become the largest and most comprehensive collection of British art outside the United Kingdom.

From the start Paul Mellon shied away from that earlier American taste in British art that prized eighteenth- and early-nineteenth-century full-length portraits of men and women by the familiar roll call of Reynolds and Gainsborough, Romney and Lawrence, Hoppner and Raeburn. The Henry E. Huntington collection in San Marino, California, with Gainsborough's *Blue Boy* and Lawrence's *Pinky* as the emblems of the collection, exemplifies this most spectacularly. It was a taste spurred on by the art dealer Joseph Duveen, a man much disliked by Paul Mellon. Although the collection would add a significant group of full-length portraits from van Dyck to Leighton over the coming years, Paul Mellon's preference from the beginning was for the small informal portrait, the conversation piece, landscape, and genre — while, of course, his interest in sporting pictures continued and deepened.

Typical of Paul Mellon's interest and taste were the early Thomas Gainsborough portraits, both of individual figures and groups, and the conversation pieces of Arthur Devis, Johann Zoffany, Francis Wheatley, Benjamin West, and others. Where the image of British art as demonstrated in an undiluted sequence of full-length portraits becomes stultifyingly tedious, Paul Mellon's eighteenth-century pictures radiate a vital and changing image of civility.

The Gravenor family (fig. 8) may not be the most fashionable in Ipswich, but they are surely the most cheerful. Seated awkwardly but unembarrassedly between their woods and fields, they show an uninhibited sense of belonging to their place, adopting no grand airs of the city but a simple delight in being rooted in their own particular place. The simple dresses and bonnets of the Gravenor daughters, together with the wildflowers they have gathered, and the rustic pose of the youngest daughter seated on the ground at her mother's feet all speak of the unaffected manners of rural society. The natural setting resonates with the naturalness of the daughters. Mr. Gravenor was an apothecary, a member of the merchant classes rather than the hereditary landowning ones. A man of the town rather than the country, he is dressed soberly and unostentatiously, striking a gentleman's pose such as might have been taken by Gainsborough from a guide to gentlemanly decorum. But the overall effect is to suggest the natural man at ease in a setting.

The image of civility quickly carries us into the deeper theme: the image of civilization itself. One of the most delightful examples of this in the Paul Mellon collection

Fig. 9. Francis Wheatley, *The Browne Family*, no. 19

is the contrast between Francis Wheatley showing the Browne family at play (fig. 9) and Benjamin West, the expatriate American painter, depicting his own family in Hammersmith (fig. 10). The worlds of the transplanted American family and the well-to-do English one at play by wood and stream suggest two different civilizations. Mrs. Browne supplies the sporting element with her gentle fishing exercise, and Mr. Browne supplies the attribute of civilized behavior by sketching the scene. The belief was strongly held in the eighteenth century that one literally drew closer to nature by sketching it and thus sharing its qualities. But the picture is more than formulaic. The children are surely bored by this Sunday-afternoon gentility. In a light-handed way there is the suggestion of a difference between the polite pursuits of George and Mary Browne and the natural inclinations of their children. All is held together, however, by the perfect summer day and the idea of a natural civilization.

How differently the stiffness, the silence, and the claustrophobia of Benjamin West's house in Hammersmith strike us. Here indeed is the image of a transplanted American civilization: Puritan in its severity or, more accurately, Quaker in its simplicity. It is a conversation picture without the conversation; the silence is omnipresent compared to the restless movement and chatter of the Browne family. Jules D. Prown, the distinguished historian of American art, has given the most comprehensive and evocative account of this work, and the following owes much to his essay.[7]

The painting commemorates the visit of John West, the artist's father, and Thomas West, his elder son, half-brother to the artist. They are visiting Benjamin and Elizabeth West's house in Hammersmith shortly after the birth of their second child, also named Benjamin. Both John and Thomas West were practicing Quakers, who took their hats off only when praying to God. They are observing a moment of silent meditation before conversation begins. The contrast with the handsomely dressed artist at the right-hand side and his elder son,

Fig. 10. Benjamin West, *The Artist and His Family*, no. 18

Raphael, on the left-hand side clearly reflects a division
between the older way—Quaker and American—and the
newly adopted way of the artist's family—British and
Anglican. The worldliness of the artist (he had recently
received the court appointment of history painter to
George III) and the unworldly austerity of his father
and half-brother are underscored but within a context of
family reconciliation. The tenderness of the painting—
"a nativity in Hammersmith," as Prown calls it—contrasts with the silence and severity of the composition.
In its way the painting is a record of the civilized virtues
as well as family relations. Godliness and human affection are mingled throughout the generations of the West
family.

Fig. 11. Paul Sandby, *Hackwood Park, Hampshire*, no. 25

Fig. 12. J. M. W. Turner, *Inverary Pier*, no. 62

PAUL MELLON has always had a strong predilection for the immediate and the spontaneous in art, a partiality for the sketch or the inspired responsiveness of the great English watercolorist. The central role of certain artists in the transition of British art from the late eighteenth to the nineteenth century coincides with and largely shapes one of the most dramatic and original contributions of British art to the European imagination: the transformation of the natural world. Once familiarly known as "the Romantic revolution," this transition has been much modified and qualified by recent British art history. Nonetheless, it is impossible not to sense an immense change from, say, Paul Sandby at Hackwood Park, Hampshire in the 1760s to J. M. W. Turner at Inverary Pier some eighty years later (figs. 11 and 12). The fundamental way nature is apprehended—that mixture of observation and knowledge—is transformed. We are, quite simply, standing in different worlds. British artists tell that story and mark the change more dramatically than any other national school of the period.

Paul Mellon's resistance to Duveen's taste in British art and his pleasure in the English countryside have led to an impressively large and diverse collection of British eighteenth- and early-nineteenth-century landscape painting, where the transformation of nature takes hold as a theme within the overall collection. There is, however, a paradox to this transformation. The oppositions seem at first sight to suggest a complete renovation of the idea of nature itself. The stability of Paul Sandby's world gives way to Turner's evanescent vision of dawn. Where the settled world is nature for Sandby, Turner's world is barely touched by the hand of man.

Yet British painters had a profound sense of continuity from Gainsborough and Wilson to Turner and Constable. Richard Wilson's admiration for Claude Lorrain—so omnipresent in *Rome from the Villa Madama* (no. 24)—was equaled only by Turner's enthusiasm for Claude and his insistence that a work by himself and one by that artist should stand side-by-side in the National Gallery in London as a condition of his bequest to the nation. Constable admired both Wilson and Gainsborough. The elevation of landscape into a major genre of British art owes itself primarily to these eighteenth-century artists. The very scale of their landscapes gave to casual, unredeemed nature the weightiness of the subject pictures of the past. In many ways Constable

and Turner and the generation of British Romantic artists are the heirs to a tradition already well-established. How are we to resolve this paradox, of a world transformed and yet a pictorial tradition which sees itself in continuity with the immediate past?

The British element plays an important role here in understanding the paradox. As Wilson moved from his early landscapes through his Italian experiences in the 1750s to the monumental landscapes he produced for Sir Watkin Williams-Wynn in the 1770s, topographical facts made their presence felt. Denbighshire cannot readily be mistaken for the Roman campagna nor the ancient fort of Dinas Bran for Tivoli or the Villa of Hadrian. The village and the daily toil of the villagers provide a different, more purposeful human presence than the decorative peasantry of the Italian views. Experience began to correct the Claudean schema. At times the very awkwardness of the larger, later landscapes of Wilson shows an artist emerging from the velleities of convention into a rougher, more naturally recognizable world, just as Constable's memories and evocations of the Stour Valley or his experience of Hampstead released a new and stronger feel for "the low sly lives" of nature.

The gathering specificity of motif in British landscape painting in the eighteenth century combined with an increasing sense of "atmosphere" to become essential ingredients of landscape painting. In early Gainsborough portraits with landscape, such as *The Gravenor Family*, it is common to find the sitters well lit and smiling out at the viewer. Unbeknownst to them, at the back of the picture turbulent storm clouds gather but never quite arrive to drench the sitters. The pictures allude to atmospheric change, but this never actually influences the atmosphere of the work itself. How strikingly different the late Gainsborough, *Landscape with Cattle and Figures* (fig. 13), is from those early essays in natural painting.

Individual motifs are now almost obscured by the swirling, misty atmosphere. What links motif to motif is less the slow meandering activity of the scene and more the brooding environment—unifying figures, livestock, wood, and distant prospect. To be sure, the Claudean vista still opens up to an illuminated middle ground, but the air hangs heavily. Both Wilson and Gainsborough light their landscapes in new and arresting ways. "The sportive light," as William Cowper called it, now falls

Fig.13. Thomas Gainsborough, *Landscape with Cattle and Figures*, no. 28

less steadily across the prospect and spills more erratically from motif to motif. It brings the lively interchange of sunlight and shadow that will flit so continuously across Constable's landscapes. Here again is that restless, indeterminate aspect which will undermine the stately recession of the Claudean vista.

Turner's genius would take these hints of innovation and turn them into the whole principle of the work. In so doing, he transformed forever landscape painting and, however unwittingly, ended the classical or Claudean convention of nature. No greater painting exists in the Paul Mellon collection than Turner's *Dort or Dordrecht: The Dort Packet-Boat from Rotterdam Becalmed* of 1817–18 (fig. 14). The quality of the painting depends on the profound fusion of the specificity of motif and the luminous atmosphere which envelops the packet-boat, the disembarking passengers, the harbor, the bank, and the distant view of Dordrecht. It is early morning, for the sun streams from the east. The packet-boat has just arrived, and the passengers are being taken off in smaller boats to the shore. The oars are suspended over the calm,

reflective waters of the harbor. A bird has just landed. The sails hang listlessly in the brilliant, windless morning. It is a moment in time and place. Yet Turner places this common daily scene in a magnificent universe of air and light, of unceasing change and interaction among the natural elements. By instinct as much as by design, one suspects, Turner has drawn an extraordinarily subtle and far-reaching distinction between the works and presence of man and the works and presence of nature. Everything solid within the painting is man-made—the hull of the boat, the sails, the mast and riggings, the nearby bank, and the sunlit town. Everything insubstantial, changeable, and interactive is natural—the reflections in the water, the high and feathery clouds, the golden light that bathes them, and the glow in the far-off Groote Kerk. The human figure and all his or her works are given full weight and substance, yet they inhabit a firmament of air and light vaster than they and entirely different in its fundamental character. Nature is a series of interchangeable forces which play—here luminously and benignly—on the activities and works of man.

Fig. 14. J. M. W. Turner, *Dort or Dordrecht: The Dort Packet-Boat from Rotterdam Becalmed*, 1817–18, oil on canvas, 62 x 92 in (157.5 x 233 cm)

Fig. 15. Richard Wilson, *Dinas Bran from Llangollen*, no. 26

Herein lies a new and transformative view of nature. For Wilson, working most freely at the end of his life, saw the world as various and vivid because no longer contained within the formula of the classical landscape, but each part solidly and materially realized (fig. 15). The woodsman's ax will ring out on that log. The hilltop fort of Dinas Bran survives in stony ruin. The bridge closes the watery prospect. Everywhere the world is given to us in terms of its material solidity. The world for Wilson is an enduring place.

Turner's instinctive sense of nature as a series of changing and changeable forces which act upon and transform the solid world carries with it a deeper, even allegorical vision of the world. For the forces of nature frequently reveal themselves as exactly that—forces which inflict a heavy, even desperate toll on the human, rendering his or her world dangerous, overwhelming, and destructive in character. If the *Dort* represents an apex in Turner's view of natural beauty and almost supernatural calm enveloping the human, *Wreckers* (fig. 16) presents the other face of nature: a series of forces,

hidden powers, and charges. Here both the human figure and the works of man, whether fragments of the boats being pulled ashore or the ruined castle half obscured by wind and weather, enjoy only the most perilous foothold. To survive involves continuous struggle against the forces of nature. The identity of individual human beings is reduced to a huddled mass. Indeed, we can only just tell men from women, so obliterative is the force of the natural. If the present moment is desperate—at least one ship has foundered, and others are threatened with the same fate—so too is the past. Wind and wave, spray and storm ravage and obscure the bulk and mass of the castle on the shore. All that is solid and enduring is shown as puny, subject to the dynamic and destructive forces unleashed by the storm. The stable is overtaken and invaded by the unstable.

Such a view of nature stands on its head the calm relationship between the natural and the civilized as we have experienced it in the Claudean vision of the eighteenth century. It alters, critically, the relationship of the human to his or her environment. Any sense of

16

GEORGE STUBBS
Horse Attacked by a Lion, probably 1762
Oil on canvas, 96 x 131 in (243.8 x 333 cm)
Gift of Paul Mellon, 1977

References: Egerton 1978, 71–72 (no. 69); Egerton 1984, 92 (no. 60)

Between the early 1760s and the 1790s, Stubbs returned again and again to the theme of a horse stalked or attacked by a lion. Whereas most of his paintings of horses are remarkable for their feeling of keen, objective portraiture, the result of his knowledge of equine anatomy, the horse-and-lion pictures aspire to a more general or "classic" mode: in their muscular beauty and expressiveness these are horses as noble as Michelangelo nudes, a near-human look of terror in their faces, eyes bulging and mouths open as though in a cry of distress. Nowhere have horses ever fallen natural prey to lions. The subject belongs more to the realm of symbol and myth than to that of real life; it represents the more ambitious end of Stubbs's range as an artist, an elevation of animal painting above its usual level — which was as something akin, at best, to human portraiture or genre — toward the status of history painting. Like a classic scene of combat or rape from history, the Bible, or myth, it could suggest high, elemental dramas: good against evil, beauty against ugliness, civilization against savagery. Stubbs's simple, relief-like design brings this out in oppositions of form and tone: placed right above the graceful hind leg of the horse, for instance, the lion's leg reads like a dark, demonic mockery.

One sign of Stubbs's "high" aim in the horse-and-lion subjects is the allusion he makes in the present painting and others to a much admired work of Antiquity. The general arrangement of the animals recalls the sculpture of such a subject at the Palazzo dei Conservatori in Rome, a Roman copy of a Hellenistic original. Stubbs would probably have seen this during his visit to Rome in 1754; it was also readily accessible at home in the form of copies and engravings. According to his early biographer Ozias Humphry, he made observations from nature too, watching and sketching a caged lion at Lord Shelburne's menagerie on Hounslow Heath.[1]

In its violence and horror, the painting reflects a growing interest among artists, writers, and critics in the extreme and awe-inspiring, or "sublime," as the material of art. Edmund Burke gave an account of these qualities and their appeal in his *Philosophical Enquiry into the Origin of Our Ideas of the Sublime and Beautiful* (1757): whereas beauty delights us through its association with pleasant things, he wrote, the sublime delights us through its association with pain and danger, releasing in us the strongest of all emotions. Burke's theories were much discussed; they gave the idea of the sublime a lasting currency, and it is tempting to speculate that Stubbs had them in mind when he developed his horse-and-lion subjects. Certainly Burke used graphic examples and analogies from the animal world: when explaining how mere physical power is not in itself sublime, for instance, he wrote that a domestic animal may be powerful, but can never be sublime as long as it is subservient to mankind and poses no threat; the truly sublime, he added, "comes upon us in the gloomy forest, and in the howling wilderness, in the form of the lion, the tiger, the panther, or rhinoceros."[2]

The present painting is one of Stubbs's earliest essays in the horse-and-lion type of subject, possibly even the first; and at eight feet by eleven it is certainly the largest. It was commissioned by one of the wealthiest British noblemen of the age, the thirty-two year-old Charles Watson Wentworth, 2nd Marquess of Rockingham, for his London residence at 4 Grosvenor Square. Rockingham was a major figure in the worlds of both horse racing and politics. He ran a stud at his ancestral seat of Wentworth Woodhouse in Yorkshire and commissioned Stubbs to paint racehorse portraits, including the monumental *Whistlejacket* (also 1762; National Gallery, London). He was a leading member of the Whig party and was to serve for a couple of brief periods as Prime Minister. From 1765 he employed none other than Edmund Burke as his private secretary, although they seem not to have known each other when he commissioned Stubbs to paint the *Horse Attacked by a Lion*. In 1765–66 Stubbs painted him a pendant to the work, on the same huge scale, showing a lion killing a stag (also Yale Center for British Art).   MW

1   Egerton 1984, 90.
2   Burke, 1:116–17.

J. M. W. TURNER

Wreckers— Coast of Northumberland, with a Steam-Boat Assisting a Ship off Shore, about 1833–34

Oil on canvas, 36 x 48 in (91.4 x 121.9 cm)

Gift of Paul Mellon, 1978

First exhibited: Royal Academy, 1834 (no. 199)

Reference: Butlin and Joll, 206 (no. 357)

Wreckers were gangs who scavenged debris and goods from wrecked ships, often luring them in by setting false lights near dangerous rocks. The theme of shipwreck was a lifelong fascination of Turner's. In an age when sea travel was full of perils, there was no sight more immediately disturbing. It demonstrated the awe-inspiring power of nature and, for Romantic and pessimistic sensibilities such as Turner's, the ultimate helplessness and ignominy of mankind.

The vessel in difficulties on the bleak Northumbrian shore is a two-masted sailing ship, seen in the distance near the center of the composition. Although the title states that the steamship to the right is "assisting," it seems clear that the time for this is past and the ship lost; indeed the implication is that the wreckers in the fore-ground are already dragging in the remains. The castle in the background is identifiable as Dunstanburgh, of which Turner had made drawings and a watercolor (c. 1828; Manchester City Art Gallery). It introduces another of the recurrent themes of his work, the ruin as symbol of transience. The tempestuous sea and sky may be more spectacular in their destructiveness, its presence seems to suggest, but time makes a wreck of everything.

After remaining in the artist's studio for ten years, *Wreckers* was bought from him by one of his most avid and important patrons, the whale-oil merchant Elhanan Bicknell. It entered an American collection around the turn of the twentieth century and remained virtually unknown to the outside world until acquired by Paul Mellon for the Yale Center for British Art in 1978.   MW

J. M. W. TURNER

Dort or Dordrecht: The Dort Packet-Boat from Rotterdam Becalmed, 1817–18

Oil on canvas, 62 x 92 in (157.5 x 233 cm)

Gift of Paul Mellon, 1977

First exhibited: Royal Academy, 1818 (no. 166)

References: Butlin and Joll, 102–4 (no. 137); Cormack 1983

Turner's *Dort* was the jewel in the crown of Paul Mellon's inaugural gift to the Yale Center for British Art and remains the centerpiece of its paintings collection.

The artist visited Dordrecht (sometimes known as Dort) during his tour of the Netherlands and the Rhine in the summer of 1817; he was there for only a day and a half but made numerous pencil sketches, and these served as the basis for the present work. The city is seen from the north, from a point on the river Noord, which connects it to Rotterdam; the skyline is dominated by the famous Groote Kerk, or Church of Our Lady. The direction of the light shows that it is morning. The becalmed packet is more precisely a market-boat or "beurtschip"; the one that sailed between Dordrecht and Rotterdam was traditionally called "De Zwaan" and flew a flag with the emblem of a swan as shown here. While awaiting a change in the wind or tide, the passengers are being sold food and drink by enterprising local people in rowing boats.

Ever matching himself against other landscapists, both ancient and modern, Turner painted the *Dort* as a tribute-cum-challenge to the seventeenth-century Dutch master Aelbert Cuyp. The allusion is especially apt, since Dordrecht was Cuyp's birthplace, and the black-capped painter in the rowing boat may be meant as a jokey portrait of him. The contrasting of dark elements against luminous sky and water in the work are distinctively Cuyp-like, and it recalls in particular that artist's painting of *The Maas at Dordrecht* (then in the collection of the Duke of Bridgewater; now National Gallery of Art, Washington). Turner may also have referred to *The Rotterdam Ferry* (then in the collection of the Earl of Carlisle; now Frick Collection, New York), from which he could have borrowed the swan design on the flag. In subject, composition, and scale his picture also plays competitively off a near-contemporary work, Augustus Wall Callcott's *Entrance to the Pool of London* (collection of the Earl of Shelburne), itself an homage to Cuyp, which Turner had admired at the Royal Academy exhibition of 1816.[1]

Turner measured himself up against Cuyp and Callcott quite knowingly, expecting the informed viewer to call them to mind and, of course, to judge the winner of the contest to be him. In most respects it is. The thrill of space, light, and distance that he conveys in such a work, his mastery of atmospheric perspective, are surely unmatched in the history of painting. Much of this comes from the details: his handling of the Groote Kerk, for instance, imparts quite magically the effect of elaborate stonework seen at a certain distance in a certain light—even the suggestion of details as yet unseen, blended together in the golden haze, that would emerge as we approached more closely. The conjuring of effects of distance was the artist's chief motive in the work, and it is surely no accident that its subject, a becalmed boat, is all about being at some distance from a destination. The incident of the boat also draws attention to the great calmness of the scene as a whole; while on a symbolic level—given Turner's abiding interest in the fate of nations and the rise and fall of empires—it may represent the economic and political state of the Netherlands, glorious in the age of Cuyp but now in the doldrums.

The painting was bought from the Academy exhibition of 1818 by one of Turner's best patrons, Walter Fawkes of Farnley Hall in Yorkshire. As a later watercolor of Turner's shows, it hung over the fireplace in the drawing room, with the light falling from the left as it does in the landscape itself. It was at Farnley more or less without interruption until 1966, when purchased by Paul Mellon, and remains in immaculate condition.   MW

1   Brown, 78–79 (no. 15).

GEORGE STUBBS

Reapers, probably 1795

Enamel on Wedgwood biscuit earthenware, oval, 30¼ x 40¼ in (77 x 102 cm)

Gift of Paul Mellon, 1981

First exhibited: British Institution, 1806 (no. 56)

References: Egerton 1978, 96–98 (no. 95); Egerton 1984, 169 (no. 126); Tattersall, 106 (H)

Stubbs often repeated his compositions in different techniques, and the present work is a version in enamel of an oil painting of 1785 (Tate Gallery). It belongs to a group of three such enamels produced in 1794–95, all about the same size and showing agricultural subjects; the others, which are also based on earlier oils, are scenes of haymaking and haycarting (both Lady Lever Art Gallery, Port Sunlight).

The technique of painting in enamel, which is essentially a kind of glass, was in common use but almost entirely for the decoration of small objets d'art. Stubbs's adoption of enamel for paintings that could be framed and exhibited like oils, sometimes on a fairly large scale, was highly unusual and experimental. He seems to have wished, with a typically Neoclassical regard for posterity, to forge a painting method as rich as oil on canvas but invulnerable to decay, damage, and restoration—one that was hard and durable like the great marble sculptures that had come down from Antiquity. He tried enamels occasionally from the later 1760s, and his first efforts were on pieces of copper. He apparently changed to a ceramic support because he found it more receptive than copper to painterly effects of brushwork and texture.

The enamels on ceramic are part of a fascinating collaboration, beginning in about 1775, with the famous master potter Josiah Wedgwood. Stubbs painted family portraits for Wedgwood, made designs for reliefs to be produced by the Wedgwood factory, and worked with him closely to develop exactly the kind of tablets that he needed for his enamels. Wedgwood would jokingly refer to himself as Stubbs's "canvas maker." The group of three enamels of 1794–95 were the largest such works to result from their collaboration and, with Wedgwood's death in 1795, the last.

Stubbs and Wedgwood worked on the enamel painting at Wedgwood's London premises on Greek Street, where there was an enameling kiln. The most difficult technical challenge for Wedgwood was the firing of a large, regularly-shaped ceramic tablet with a smooth surface; the reason all the tablets are oval is probably that there are no angles where a slight warp would be obvious. On the surface of the tablet he would fire a layer of white enamel, upon which Stubbs painted in special colors suspended in a glassy medium. Then the tablet would be fired again to fuse the image to the ground. Often in traditional enamel technique there would be a further firing to add a glaze, but Stubbs seems to have preferred to leave the surface matte. Despite the care and ingenuity that went into their production, the enamels were received with little enthusiasm by critics and collectors—and Wedgwood's hope that the technique would be taken up by other artists, providing his firm with lucrative business, proved to be completely in vain.[1]

The enamel shows the composition of the original oil painting in contracted form: two reapers are omitted from the center, and the gentleman on the horse and the reaper next to him have been moved from right to left to close the gap. Perhaps Stubbs made the change to suit his design to the proportions of the largest viable ceramic tablet that Wedgwood could provide. In choosing the subject of the wheat harvest, he was following a fashion for picturesque rustic genre established by other painters, including Gainsborough and Wheatley. But he brings to the scene his distinctive taste for the orderly, relief-like composition and for figures who, anonymous though they may be, have the character of portraits observed from the life. Overall, the work suggests the high, dignified view of labor, with an emphasis on good management and productivity rather than sweat and backache. The presence of the church in the background brings to mind both the Christian associations of the harvest and the old saying "laborare orare est" (to work is to pray).   MW

---

1   For further information on Stubbs's relationship with Wedgwood, see Tattersall.

Fig. 16. J. M. W. Turner, *Wreckers*, about 1833–34, oil on canvas, 36 x 48 in (91.4 x 121.9 cm)

mastery or domination over the natural world, of guiding and shaping it on a path of permanence and prosperity—such as Paul Sandby might invite us to believe at Hackwood Park—is here disputed and disproved. The world in which humans find themselves is transformed in Turner and with that transformation goes a radical change in belief about the benign qualities of nature and the power of man within it.

Nature is no less dramatically changed and transformed in the world of Constable. He shares Turner's instinctive sense that nature is essentially volatile and changeable. "Light and shadow never stand still."[8] Again and again Constable shows us sweeping skies with rain and storm, bright light or thunderous darkness about to descend and overwhelm the landscape. Where Turner frequently shows the human struggling to exist within the changeable world, Constable sees the changeable world as a metaphor for the human itself. He was the first major artist to develop "a negative capability," i.e. to let the inanimate landscape evoke the profounder human emotions of longing and aspiration, grief and

despair. The two great six-footers in the Paul Mellon collection show how wide-ranging and subtle a vehicle for human feeling Constable could make the landscape. The lost world of childhood and the agonizing loss of a loved wife are the profound themes animating *Stratford Mill* (fig. 17) and *Hadleigh Castle* (fig. 18).

Stratford Mill is the final oil sketch before Constable painted the finished and more polished version for exhibition at the Royal Academy (now in the National Gallery, London). The Yale picture is much more boisterous, both in its handling and the effect of the image. The London version has the warmth and calm of a golden summer's day. The light sparkles as it passes through the stand of trees, and "the young Waltonians" of the painting's later and more sentimental title are bathed in sunlight. In Paul Mellon's version sunlight and shadow interweave rapidly and disconcertingly. A shadow passes across the young fisherman. The somber colonnade of trees on the left bank of the Stour masks the brilliant shaft of light behind them. The dark reflection on the water and the turbulent sky create a more

Fig. 17. John Constable, *Stratford Mill*, no. 53

restless atmosphere than the high, summery clouds and silvery water of the finished version. Most strikingly of all, Constable alters the figure group. In the Yale version only children fish from the bank. In the final version Constable introduces a man of indeterminate age but hardly a "young Waltonian." The significance of this is to emphasize in the Yale version the division between the world of men and work and the world of children and leisure. For *Stratford Mill* is the world of childhood recalled by Constable in his London studio years after he had visited the area. (He had not sketched the site since 1811.) Malcolm Cormack has suggestively formulated the function of "large-scale preliminary exercises to make the transition from observed facts to remembered reality."[9] The effort of remembering pictorially is central to the *Sturm und Drang* of the Yale version. Constable reaches back into his childhood and remembers the scene in all different manner of weather and season—hence the changeableness and instability of the painting. Eventually, as he worked towards the public piece—the Academy-bound, finished version—he would settle for the

constructed memory of the perfect summer day. But the effort, even the strain, to work himself back into the recollected world of childhood is central in the Yale sketch. He recalls a lost security in the place and haunts of boyhood, and the strain shows.

Hadleigh Castle takes Constable to the other edge of human experience. His deeply loved wife Maria died in November 1828, and in February of the following year Constable was finally elected to the Royal Academy. His grief over the death of his wife can hardly be over-estimated: he would dress in mourning until the end of his life. His delayed and grudging acceptance into the Royal Academy—he was now fifty-two years old—brought him less pleasure and elation than it might have done. By 1829 it was sorely overdue. Yet the combination of agonizing loss and belated acceptance spurred Constable to his most tragic utterance, where the landscape would provide a complete metaphor for human suffering.

Hadleigh Castle, situated on the Essex shore of the Thames estuary, was a fourteenth-century castle of which only the two round towers remained. Landslides

Fig. 18. John Constable, *Hadleigh Castle*, no. 59

had carried off the bulk of the castle down the cliffs to the water below. The motif is literally echoed in the landscape by the tower of St. Clement's at Leigh-on-Sea set against the horizon line. The theme of decline and decay and the melancholy they inspire is clear enough. But the desolation is equally in nature as in the man-made world. The mud flats of the Thames estuary stretch bleakly and tracklessly from the foot of the rough and precipitous cliff. The light which breaks momentarily from the storm-tossed sky falls brilliantly on a distant horizon which we can see rather than approach. It is hope deferred. Rather touchingly, Constable depicts all the ships sailing out to sea towards the light — an obvious but effective metaphor for the soul's departure from the earth. Indeed, he makes the Kent coastline on the southern side of the estuary the distant shore to which all are beckoned.

The interchange between motif and motif, the brilliant river and the gloomy shore, the broken tower and the fugitive clouds, makes *Hadleigh Castle* one of the supreme achievements of the new Romantic landscape.

Nature becomes more than a guide to art or a teacher of artists: it becomes a theater acting out the profoundest human feelings, resonating them into a wider sphere and giving them meaning and resolution. The frail barks on the sunlit estuary of the Thames are freighted with hopes and expectations.

Whether it is Turner's belief that "nature is a Heraclitean fire," to borrow Gerard Manley Hopkins's wondrous phrase, or Constable's that nature sustains and consoles the human, the world in which men and women live is radically changed in British painting at the turn of the eighteenth into the nineteenth century. The new landscape of Romanticism, conceiving of nature as a series of interactive forces and finding in it an echo of human feeling, demonstrably moves closer to the modern experience. English Romantic art, more vividly than any other national school or movement, marks the change.

Fig. 19. Ben Nicholson, *May 1955 (Gwithian)*, no. 81

WHAT ARE Paul Mellon's interests and tastes in British art of Victorian or modern times? Like many of his generation brought up in the aftermath of Victorian taste, he reacted sharply against it, showing little or no interest in Pre-Raphaelitism early or late and clearly preferring French painting in the later half of the nineteenth century. It should never be forgotten that Paul Mellon is as distinguished a collector of Impressionist and Post-Impressionist painting as he is of British art.

His taste in twentieth-century British art is another matter. His interest in sporting art persists with a decided admiration for Alfred Munnings, who painted an equestrian portrait of him in 1932, and, less predictably, John Lavery. He has also been a keen collector of the *animalier* John Skeaping, and it came as something of a surprise to Paul Mellon when he learned that Skeaping was Barbara Hepworth's first husband. Paul Mellon has a particular admiration for both her work and that of her second husband, Ben Nicholson. He tells a story of going into the auctioneers, Phillips, to look at an indifferent Stubbs and catching sight of a painting by Ben Nicholson—then virtually unknown to him—and buying the latter. The other twentieth-century British artists Paul Mellon has collected with some intensity are Walter Sickert and Gwen John. The interest in Sickert has flowered into a fine Camden Town collection at Yale, and Paul Mellon himself has become the leading collector of the horse paintings of the Camden Town painter Robert Bevan. The taste for Gwen John, Ben Nicholson, and Barbara Hepworth, however, reflects a deeper impulse in Paul Mellon's collecting. Each in a different way produces a meditative art, turning on an image of inwardness, as in Gwen John's withdrawn and solitary sitters, or in the detection and demonstration of hidden, secret harmonies in the world of objects so often found in Ben Nicholson (fig. 19). The world is purified, and the resulting work has a pristine quality, a revelation or disclosure of another order. Such an art strikes the same deep chord in the Paul Mellon who at a critical stage in his life turned to the analytic psychology of C. G. Jung. Paul Mellon recounts how Jung's image of "The City that always Sleeps" was to give him "a feeling of immense stillness, a picture permeated with sunlight and lovely late afternoon colors." It is this sensitive-minded man to whom Ben Nicholson appealed so deeply.

The contribution of British art to the twentieth century is still severely underestimated outside of Britain. Of an older generation, the names of Francis Bacon or Henry Moore are familiar, but many of their distinguished contemporaries—Graham Sutherland, Ivon Hitchens, or Peter Lanyon—are all but totally obscure in the United States. Curiously, the closer one draws to the end of the twentieth century, the more distinctive and significant appears to be the role of British artists in contemporary art. The achievements of modern British sculpture from Anthony Caro to Rachel Whiteread are internationally recognized and admired. The individuality of the School of London—Lucian Freud, Leon Kossoff, Frank Auerbach, R. B. Kitaj, and Michael Andrews—has begun to have an impress beyond the British Isles.

The new generation of British artists, with a champion and cheerleader like Damien Hirst, has begun to right ancient wrongs and attract a following of its own both within and outside Great Britain. Whatever judgments we may pass on present productions—major works by both Hirst and Whiteread are in the collection of the Yale Center for British Art—British art continues both to contribute to the central stream of western art and to maintain its sturdy, maverick provincialism energetically and unabatedly into the present.

Patrick McCaughey

1 All quotations of Paul Mellon are taken from his memoir, *Reflections in a Silver Spoon.*
2 Annotations to *Poems* by William Wordsworth (Blake, 783).
3 *Jerusalem. The Emanation of the Giant Albion*, chap. 1, lines 17–20 (Blake, 623).
4 Annotations to Joshua Reynolds's *Discourses on Art* (Blake, 477).
5 Ibid. (Blake, 459).
6 *The Marriage of Heaven and Hell*, plate 9, line 5 (Blake, 152).
7 Prown 1986.
8 Leslie, 7.
9 Cormack 1986, 72.

Court and Country

IN THE SEVENTEENTH CENTURY painting in Britain centered on portraiture, and through this the affirmation of god-given authority, wealth, and grace among the nobility. The pivotal figure in its development was Anthony van Dyck. Before his arrival the court portrait was a rigid, meticulously stitched and laced affair. With his unrivaled painterly brilliance and ability to suggest life and movement, van Dyck gave his noble sitters more, investing them not only with rank, but also with refined feelings and an elegance of deportment—a superiority that seemed to come easily and need no enforcing. His portrait of the Earl of Newport is a case in point; it also serves to remind us that the "other Eden" described by John of Gaunt in his famous speech in Shakespeare's *Richard II* was also a "seat of Mars," the wager of wars both foreign and civil.

We see the importance of van Dyck's example immediately in the work of William Dobson and Peter Lely, taken in a sobering direction on the one hand, and an erotic one on the other. As a painter of distinction who was actually a native, Dobson was exceptional; for the most part British painting in this period is more properly called painting in Britain, dominated as it was by artists from Continental Europe, largely the Low Countries. This is true of not only portraiture but also the budding art of landscape painting, here represented by Claude de Jongh and Jan Siberechts. The latter's "prospect" of Wollaton shows the portraiture of places to be just as closely bound up with concerns of status and social prestige as that of people. If the country was a kind of Eden, as for the landed class it was, then it was one owned and ordered by men.   MW

1   MARCUS GHEERAERTS THE YOUNGER
    Catherine Killigrew, Lady Jermyn, 1614
    Oil on panel, 30¾ x 23 in (78 x 58.5 cm)
    Gift of Paul Mellon, 1981

References: Hearn, 195–96 (no. 132); Millar 1963, 534 (no. 12); Strong, 285 (no. 278)

The sitter in this portrait is traditionally—and probably quite correctly—identified as Catherine Killigrew (?1579 –1640), daughter of William Killigrew, Groom of the Privy Chamber to Elizabeth I. In 1559 she married Sir Thomas Jermyn of Rushbrook, who inherited Rushbrook Park in Suffolk from his father in 1614, and it is possible that he commissioned Gheeraerts to paint his wife on this occasion. In the upper right corner of the portrait an inscription, painted by Gheeraerts himself,[1] reads *Aetatis Suae 35 Anno: 1614* [in the year 1614 at her age of 35]. The portrait was sold from the family collection at Rushbrook in 1919.

Marcus Gheeraerts the Younger moved to London with his family in the late 1560s in the wake of religious persecution in the Netherlands. He was trained as a painter by his father, a printmaker and painter himself, and by Lucas de Heere, another Netherlandish painter who worked for a time in London. Gheeraerts became well known in Elizabethan court circles, primarily through the patronage of Sir Henry Lee, and his most important commission came from Sir Henry in 1592: a full-length portrait of Elizabeth I to mark the occasion of her visit to his estate, Ditchley Park in Oxfordshire. Gheeraerts's portrait of Elizabeth, now known as the Ditchley Portrait (National Portrait Gallery, London), sealed his reputation, and he enjoyed court patronage throughout Elizabeth's reign. After the accession to the throne of James I in 1603, Gheeraerts continued to benefit from royal favor in part because the king's wife, Anne of Denmark, chose to sit to him. His full-length portrait of Queen Anne, painted c. 1611–14, ensured his enduring success at court throughout that decade.

The present portrait of Lady Jermyn displays Gheeraerts's virtuosity in rendering not only the weaves of different fabrics, such as translucent lace, smooth silk, and embroidery, but also the various textures of flesh. It is the sumptuous fabrics of Lady Jermyn's clothing that convey her wealth and status; she wears little jewelry (only a small diamond-set thumb-ring, possibly her wedding ring, and two plain gold loop earrings), which is noteworthy given the Elizabethan and Jacobean predilection for displaying one's finest jewels in one's portrait. In its relative lack of pomp and its attention to the particularity of the sitter's features (such as the line of her nose), *Lady Jermyn* stands in contrast to the hieratic and iconic full-length images typical of late Elizabethan and Jacobean portraiture, as seen in van Somer's *Elizabeth, Countess of Kellie* (no. 2). The directness of Lady Jermyn's gaze, combined with the minute detail of her clothing and face, imparts to the painting a remarkable sense of closeness to and communication with the sitter. In its jewel-like precision the painting resembles a miniature portrait blown up to life-size; indeed, it is possible that Gheeraerts may have been influenced, in both the format of his portraits and their technique, by the work of his brother-in-law Isaac Oliver the miniaturist, who became limner to Anne of Denmark in 1605. The intimacy of the format and the delicacy and detail of the painted surfaces make this work a prime example of Gheeraerts's later style and also of the more private strains of Jacobean portraiture.   JMA

1   Millar 1963, 534.

2　attributed to PAUL VAN SOMER
Elizabeth, Countess of Kellie, about 1619
Oil on canvas, 81 x 48½ in (206 x 123 cm)
Gift of Paul Mellon, 1981

The Countess of Kellie (d. 1622), who is traditionally thought to be the sitter of this imposing portrait, was one of the wealthiest members of noble society in Jacobean England. She was widowed twice before her marriage to Thomas Erskine in 1604. In 1606 Erskine became 1st Viscount Fenton, and in 1615 he was made a Knight of the Garter; four years later he became 1st Earl of Kellie. This portrait may well have been commissioned to mark the sitter's new rank as Countess of Kellie in 1619.

In a manner typical of Jacobean formal court portraiture, in which courtiers wished to stress, above all, their wealth and status, the lady stands before us in all her finery. Women courtiers depended on the ostentatious display of jewels, fashionable dresses made of expensive fabrics, and lush settings to convey their standing in their court portraits since — unlike their husbands, fathers, and brothers — they did not have tokens of office (badges, wands, or sashes that stood as emblems of their court roles and duties).

She wears an elaborately tailored costume that epitomizes high court fashions between 1615 and 1620. Her red damask dress, richly embroidered throughout with patterns of gold and silver threads, has a full skirt and is worn without a farthingale (a wheel-shaped stiff underskirt worn perpendicular to the body at the waist); this type of dress, with matching fabric in all parts, clearly dates the portrait from the late 1610s. The low-cut bodice follows the fashion for daring décolletage made popular by Anne of Denmark, who was extremely proud of her translucent white skin. The long hanging outer sleeves that fall behind her arms are purely decorative; so too are the elaborately cuffed leather, lace, and embroidered gloves that she holds under her left hand — since it is unlikely that she would have worn such large gloves while the intricate lace cuffs remained attached to her sleeves. Especially noteworthy is the delicately patterned yellow lace used at her wrists, in her bodice, and for the standing-falling ruff: in the latter years of James I's reign, yellow lace was highly prized for its appearance and rarity. Her dress, gloves, and lace combine with the exquisitely designed jewels — most obviously the six ropes of pearls strung ostentatiously around her U-shaped bodice — to proclaim boldly her material riches and high rank.

Everything about the sitter and her surroundings indicates the luxury and privilege in which she lived and desired to be remembered. The book on the velvet chair cushion to her left, most likely a bible, may indicate her piety but, with its large format and richly decorated exterior, certainly does not suggest modesty. The domesticated parrot that crawls up her dress to fetch the piece of food she holds loosely in the fingers of her right hand is yet another symbol of her fortune: parrots and other species of exotic birds were prized as housepets and expensive curiosities in early modern England, and their presence in portraits of the period underlined the opulent and rarefied tastes of their owners. In this case, however, the bird's surreptitious feeding also brings a touch of humor to what is otherwise a splendidly iconic and decorative portrait. JMA

3   CLAUDE DE JONGH

The Thames at Westminster Stairs, signed indistinctly 1631 or 1637
Oil on panel, 18¼ x 31½ in (46.4 x 80 cm)
Gift of Paul Mellon, 1973

Reference: Hayes 1956, 4 and 8 (no. 14)

De Jongh's atmospheric view of London looks across the river Thames from its south bank to Westminster. The buildings depicted, from left to right, are St. Stephen's Chapel in the Palace of Westminster (destroyed by fire in 1834), Westminster Hall, the tower of St. Margaret's in front of the north transept of Westminster Abbey, and the Abbey itself. The boats on the water and the low houses whose doors open on to the river are reminders of the crucial role the Thames played in seventeenth-century London life and commerce.

The down-to-earth realism with which de Jongh depicts the dwellings and topography in this painting attests to his awareness of new stylistic developments among his contemporary Dutch landscape painters, especially Jan van Goyen. Yet his attention to detail and perspective camouflages the liberties he has taken with the actual appearance of the place. The painting closely relates to two drawings (Royal Collection), made during his English visit of 1627, that record the scene more or less accurately. In the painted view, however, de Jongh has deliberately altered the topography of the place to create a more compelling composition: the small, tumble-down dwellings on the river contrast with the majesty of the religious buildings beyond, especially the Abbey and St. Stephen's Chapel. Light filters through the gray clouds, mirrored in the river's water, and bathes the blond stones of the buildings in warmth. The varied textures of paint over the surface of the panel—pulled thinly across the water and dabbed thickly in the stone-work of the buildings—impart a jewel-like sparkle that is characteristic of London's river atmosphere.

De Jongh, a Dutchman, never lived in England, al-though—from drawings of English topography dated 1615, 1625, 1627, and 1628—it is apparent that he made frequent visits. Since there is no evidence of his having returned to England in the 1630s, and since his paintings of English subjects date almost exclusively from this decade, he must have executed them, using the drawings he made during his English sojourns as preparatory sketches, in his studios in Haarlem and Utrecht.

Although steeped in the conventions and traditions of Dutch landscape painting, de Jongh was at his best painting views of England. His are the first in a long line of paintings in which successive generations of artists respond to England's rolling, verdant countryside and note with fascination the interdependency of town and river. In his *Thames at Westminster Stairs* he captures the symbiotic junction of land, water, and society in early modern England—city, men, and pastures alike seem to rise out of the Thames.   JMA

4   ANTHONY VAN DYCK
Mountjoy Blount, Earl of Newport, about 1637–38
Oil on canvas, 85 x 51 in (215.7 x 129.5 cm)
Gift of Paul Mellon, 1977

References: Larsen, 2:361 (no. 922); White

In this grand and opulent work van Dyck creates the image of a powerful, confident, and rich military man. Typically for a portrait of the artist's later English period, he has used none of the conventional symbols of allegory to indicate aspects of the sitter's importance. Instead, Newport's wealth and noble status are represented by his rich clothing (especially his intricately painted lace collar and colorful silk gauze sash), his easy yet powerful pose, and his elegant demeanor.

It is likely that the Earl of Newport and van Dyck were well acquainted, since the sitter's wife was the sister-in-law of Endymion Porter, the painter's great friend and patron. Van Dyck painted Newport more than once in the late 1630s; there exist two half-length portraits of him with George, Baron Goring, the noted courtier. In a reference that may be to the present portrait, the seventeenth-century writer Bellori, in his biography of van Dyck, states that the artist painted the Earl of Newport "issuing orders to officers, with two armed figures behind."[1] Certainly, Newport's authoritative manner here would be consistent with his giving orders to his men.

Mountjoy Blount, 1st Earl of Newport (c. 1597–1666), was the illegitimate son of Charles Blount, Earl of Devonshire and 8th Lord Mountjoy, and Penelope Devereux, Lady Rich. Sister of Robert Devereux, 2nd Earl of Essex — the notorious lover and favorite of Queen Elizabeth I — Penelope Devereux had married Robert, Lord Rich in 1581; theirs was an unhappy marriage from its outset, contemporary rumors declaring that it was only Lord Rich's fear of his wife's powerful brother that

tempered his unkind, even ruthless, behavior toward her. Lady Rich found solace outside her marriage: passionate about literature, she maintained a close friendship with the poet Philip Sidney throughout her life. By 1595 she had openly become the mistress of Lord Mountjoy. The lovers had three children out of wedlock; Mountjoy subsequently acknowledged all of them as his own. In 1601 Lord Rich abandoned his wife, and two years later they divorced. Lady Rich and Lord Mountjoy were married in 1605. Newport was thus related by blood to some of the most influential figures of the Elizabethan era, and later his half-brothers Robert Rich, 2nd Earl of Warwick, and Henry Rich, 1st Earl of Holland, played crucial roles in Caroline court politics, both ultimately standing against the Crown during the Civil War.

Like his half-brothers, Newport enjoyed favor with the king and queen throughout the 1620s. In the early years of that decade he was charged with diplomatic affairs in England and abroad. He became an earl in 1628, taking his title from Newport on the Isle of Wight. In August 1634 Charles I appointed him Master of the Ordnance for life, a post in which he made a fortune for himself. At the onset of the Civil War Newport hesitated as to his allegiances but eventually settled his loyalty on the side of the Crown. Van Dyck's portrait suggests none of the sitter's wavering attitudes to the Crown but presents him at his seemingly dauntless prime, a fashionable courtier and imposing military leader of the golden years of Charles I's reign.   JMA

1   White, 385.

Portrait of a Family, probably that of Richard Streatfeild, about 1645

Oil on canvas, 42 x 49½ in (106.7 x 125.7 cm)

Gift of Paul Mellon, 1981

Reference: Rogers, 65–66 (no. 29)

This work is a testament to Dobson's painterly talent and to the promise of a career that would be cut short by his death in 1646. Passed down in the Streatfeild family of Chiddingstone, Kent, it has therefore traditionally been thought to represent Richard Streatfeild (1611–1676), his wife Ann, and three of their children. The Streatfeilds were ironmasters whose financial success had placed them by the mid-seventeenth century among the wealthier members of the region's gentry. Dobson creates a compelling portrait of a family whose destiny is fraught with the uncertainty of living in a nation imperiled and ravaged by civil war. Rich passages of light and shadow, particularly in the dreamy, almost melancholic face of the man, suffuse the canvas with a somber tone.

The father's hand on the head of the boy at the left would designate him as Henry, eldest son and heir (b. 1639). Unfortunately, the identities of the two other children remain shrouded in mystery; following Henry, the Streatfeilds had seven more children, among whom the only four to survive were born after this portrait was painted. The enigmatic allegorical symbols — the three cherries held up by the youngest child to the father; the strangely unclothed, impish, and inexplicable child who smiles mysteriously at the viewer; and the four foreboding skulls piled atop the broken pedestal — compel us to read into the picture meanings of mourning, loss, and even, perhaps, a stoic faith in providence. Ultimately the portrait conveys the realities — both affectionate and disturbing — of family life in mid-seventeenth-century England.

Originally identified as by Dobson in 1957, the portrait is now accepted as one of his relatively few known works. Nevertheless, questions remain as to how much of the extant picture is by Dobson's own hand and which areas belong to his original design. The debate centers on the wide piece of canvas that has been added to the left side of the painting. The seam, clearly visible to the left of the central male figure, runs vertically the height of the canvas, effectively severing the man's right arm from his shoulder and separating the two small children on the left from the other three figures. It was long postulated that this additional section was joined to the canvas after Dobson's death so as to add children to the composition as they came into the family. Certainly, an artist other than Dobson painted these children, who are clearly by a less accomplished hand. But, as Malcolm Rogers has convincingly suggested, Dobson most likely added the strip of canvas himself, designing the present composition but leaving the work unfinished.[1]   JMA

1   Rogers, 65.

6 PETER LELY

Diana Kirke, later Countess of Oxford, probably between 1665 and 1670
Oil on canvas, 52 x 41 in (135.3 x 108.6 cm)
Gift of Paul Mellon, 1981

References: Beckett, 57 (no. 407); Millar 1978, 63–64 (no. 46)

Had we but world enough, and time,
This coyness, Lady, were no crime…
                    Andrew Marvell, "To His Coy Mistress"

The portrait of Diana Kirke (d. 1707) is one of Lely's most sensuous and beautiful. It exemplifies his lush painterly and brilliantly coloristic style, reminiscent of that of Rubens, in which the richly painted surfaces echo and magnify the voluptuousness—and eroticism—of the subject. Like the mistress of Marvell's poem, Diana Kirke exudes provocative intimacy and mystery. With her beguiling stare she coyly commands her viewers, all the while remaining frustratingly silent in her ambiguous gesture. A modern-day Venus, does she proffer her rose to her viewer or deny him its beauty? Languorously posing, breast carelessly exposed by the falling yoke of her silken shift, does she promise or simply tempt? Like a rose herself, will she provide soft comfort or wound with her hidden thorns? Arousing questions and desires, she resists all answers.

The painting was most likely commissioned by Kirke's lover, Aubrey de Vere, 20th Earl of Oxford. Painted in the late 1660s, when Kirke was openly acknowledged at court as Oxford's mistress, the work closely follows the standard pattern used for portraits of "Restoration Beauties," a formula Lely had devised earlier in that decade with his *Windsor Beauties*, a series commissioned by the Duke and Duchess of York (Royal Collection). From early in his career Lely's portraits of women were perceived as deriving from a single facial model, one thought to be fashioned from the features of Charles II's most notorious and powerful mistress, Barbara Villiers, Duchess of Cleveland: a contemporary noted that "Sir Peter Lilly…put something of Clevelands face…her

Languishing Eyes into every one Picture, so that all his pictures had an air of one another."[1] Certainly, Kirke's almond "bedroom" eyes and pursed rosy lips resemble closely those of her rival court beauties. Yet her intimate pose (subtly different from so many of the known, nearly formulaic stances of other sitters) and the careful attention lavished on the portrait by the artist himself set this image apart from the majority of Lely's female portraits of this period, most of which were produced by his studio assistants in an almost assembly-line fashion. Perhaps, in the longstanding tradition of portraits of mistresses commissioned by their royal lovers, Oxford had this picture painted for his own pleasure, keeping it in his private chambers, to be viewed and appreciated only by him and his inner circle of friends and associates.

Kirke belonged to the bevy of beautiful young women so sought after by young courtiers like Oxford who roamed the halls of Whitehall in the 1660s. Second daughter of George Kirke, Groom of the Bedchamber to Charles II and Keeper of Whitehall Palace, she moved in aristocratic circles from an early age. Sometime after the Restoration of Charles II in 1660, an event in which Oxford played a significant role, Kirke and Oxford began their open liaison. They eventually married in April 1673; later, their youngest daughter Diana was—like her mother—renowned at court for her beauty. The family's fate would be forever linked to that of the royal family by the 1694 marriage of the young Diana to the first Duke of St. Albans, Charles Beauclerk, an illegitimate son of Charles II by his infamous mistress, the actress Nell Gwyn. JMA

1 Millar 1978, 63.

Diana Kirke
Cſs, of Oxford.

7   JAN SIBERECHTS

Wollaton Hall and Park, Nottinghamshire, 1697
Oil on canvas, 75½ x 54½ in (191.8 x 138.4 cm)
Gift of Paul Mellon, 1973

Reference: Yale Center for British Art 1979, 22–23 (no. 3)

This painting is of a type known in its time as a "prospect," an extensive bird's-eye view of a country house and its surrounding estates. Prospects are views that tend toward maps, often with different parts seen from different angles, and they demonstrate more of the layout and workings of the given place than any actual viewpoint would reveal. The form was developed by artists of the Low Countries and flourished in Britain from the later seventeenth to the mid-eighteenth centuries. With its comprehensive, godlike perspective, it offered the landowner the pleasure of seeing his property and realm laid out before him as a whole; he might hang a prospect of his estate in the country house itself or perhaps in his London residence, where it would serve the additional purpose of impressing upon visitors the important fact of his owning land. More generally, it gave a delightfully clear expression to the idea of mankind creating order within nature, from the symmetry in the architecture of the house, to the rational plan of the pleasure grounds and gardens attached, to the careful husbandry apparent in the farmlands beyond.

Wollaton Hall, a short distance west of Nottingham, is one of the most important Elizabethan houses in Britain; it dates from the 1580s, and the architect was probably Robert Smythson. It was designed as a grand showpiece, proclaiming the success and status of its owner, Sir Francis Willoughby, a coal magnate-cum-entrepreneur. Its most striking and unusual feature architecturally is the raised central hall with its tall proportions and medievalizing window tracery and turrets. In 1688 Wollaton passed to Sir Thomas Willoughby, Bart., Sir Francis's great-great-grandson, and it was he who commissioned Siberechts to paint this and other views of the estate and neighboring countryside. Though still in his twenties, Sir Thomas

was already a considerable figure in the area, having served as High Sheriff of Nottinghamshire in 1695–96. He was elected Tory Member of Parliament for Nottingham in 1698, later represented Newark, and in 1712 was created 1st Baron Middleton by Queen Anne. He clearly took great pride in Wollaton. He remodeled parts of the interior of the house, commissioned mural decorations, and installed in the park formal gardens in the French style; having inherited some of the scientific interests of his father, who was a famous naturalist, he also created a garden of botanical specimens. (Wollaton is now owned by the Corporation of Nottingham and houses the city's natural history museum.)

The view in the painting, which is from the southeast, gives a fairly faithful account of the appearance of the place, though with the house shown on lower ground, perhaps to lend drama to the hills that rise up in the distance. Like most prospects, it records the owner's improvements to his estate (some of which may have been prospective rather than actual), and the pleasures he could offer his guests there. Fashionably dressed people stroll around the grounds; a game of bowls is in progress on the lawn at lower right; in the foreground the coach and six with escort shows the formal approach to the house, leads the viewer into the scene, and also indicates further luxuries of Wollaton life, those of traveling in style and being attended by an ample household of servants. Elsewhere we see more of the daily workings of the place: to the south of the house, staff at work in the vegetable garden and a man rolling the path of the parterre; to the west a cabbage patch, a bleaching field, and some barns; to the north, between the house and the village of Wollaton, a maid milking a cow in the middle of a field.   MW

Portrait into Genre

I N 1707 THE Act of Union brought England and Scotland together, under a single parliament and flag, as Great Britain. The new Britons felt an urge to national self-definition, and one sign of this was the movement to establish a native school of artists. The most prominent champion of the idea, with his attacks on foreign artists, imported styles, and the patrons and connoisseurs who promoted them, was William Hogarth. Like the popular low-life drama of which he painted a performance in *The Beggar's Opera*, his art stood for British common sense as against European pretensions and sophistry. He was both polemical and practical and took an active part in organizations for the training of British artists and the exhibition of their works.

Among the types of painting commonly practiced in eighteenth-century Britain, there was none more distinctively British in character than the "conversation piece," in which portrait sitters group together in informal situations, enjoying each other's company, playing music, taking pleasure in the outdoors, shooting and fishing, reading and drawing. This was portraiture that tended toward genre, the painting of scenes from everyday life—albeit everyday life at a high social level —and there are fertile interchanges and crossovers between the two types of subject from Hogarth onward. With the spread of the cult of the natural, thanks largely to the writings of the French philosopher Jean-Jacques Rousseau, portraiture could also fuse with landscape. The outdoor conversation pieces of Francis Hayman, the young Thomas Gainsborough, Francis Wheatley, and others show a closeness between society and nature, between the landed and their land, that in the previous century would have been an almost unthinkable breach of decorum. MW

8   WILLIAM HOGARTH
The Beggar's Opera, 1729
Oil on canvas, 23¼ x 30 in (59 x 76 cm)
Gift of Paul Mellon, 1981

References: Bindman, 32–36; Bindman and Wilcox; Paulson 1:180–91; Walker

John Gay's play *The Beggar's Opera*, a satire with songs, premiered at John Rich's Theatre Royal, Lincoln's Inn Fields, on January 29, 1728, and took London by storm. It paints a world turned topsy-turvy, in which highwaymen and robbers, the central, sympathetic characters, conduct themselves in gentlemanly fashion, whereas members of ostensibly respectable professions act like scoundrels. Depicting Act III, scene 11, Hogarth's painting shows the play's climax. The central character Macheath, a notorious highwayman, has been arrested and brought to the Hall Ward at Newgate Prison, from which he will go to his execution. While he stands shackled at hands and feet, his two young and beautiful lovers, Lucy Lockit (left) and Polly Peachum (right), appeal to their fathers—respectively a jailer and a professional informer—for his freedom.

In the three or four years following the opening of *The Beggar's Opera*, Hogarth painted no fewer than five versions of this subject. Recently it has been shown that the present version, which belonged to John Rich, was the fourth.[1] The first three paintings seem to depend on a chalk sketch (Royal Collection) made by Hogarth at an actual performance: the viewpoint is closely cropped around the five actors in the middle ground, and members of the audience are depicted as seated on the stage at the sides of the players and behind. The Center's painting significantly enlarges the scene by reducing the scale of both the central figures and audience and by placing them in a more grandiose setting that looks like a real prison instead of a stage set.

In this and the later versions Hogarth includes two sculpted satyrs that hold up the stage's curtain at the painting's edges; differing only slightly from the actual sculptures on the proscenium arch in Rich's theater, these elements act as visual reminders of the play's first staging. As another allusion to the original staging, he shows identifiable members of the audience who interact with the players; most notably, in the corner seat of the right-hand audience box sits the Duke of Bolton. During the initial run of *The Beggar's Opera*, Bolton became scandalously enamored of Lavinia Fenton, the actress playing Polly, and later publicly kept her as his mistress. Hogarth refers to this notorious affair by showing Polly looking past her father as she sings and locking gazes with the Duke. By describing the picture with the epigram *Veluti in speculum (As in a Mirror)*, inscribed in the banderole at the top of the painting, he invites the viewer to consider the different types of truth the work represents: it holds a mirror up to Gay's play and its relevance to contemporary life; to a particular performance of that play; and even to a compromising relationship between an actress and a prominent member of the audience.

Contemporaries did indeed recognize the play as a thinly veiled lampoon of London society's manners and morals and, more pointedly, as an attack on the Prime Minister Sir Robert Walpole and his government's policies. Although Walpole and members of his party appeared to enjoy themselves at *The Beggar's Opera*, his government actively prevented any performance of its sequel, *Polly*, later that same year. Whatever the political sympathies of Hogarth, it is clear that his painting of a critical scene from *The Beggar's Opera* was part of a larger dialogue about the play and its implications.   JMA

1   Bindman and Wilcox, 20.

9 WILLIAM HOGARTH

Self-Portrait, probably 1730s
Oil on canvas, 21½ x 20 in (54.4 x 51 cm)
Gift of Paul Mellon, 1981

References: Paulson, 1:450 and 556 (note 64) and 2:513 (no. 45 and note 10)

This is Hogarth's earliest-known self-portrait, a work of painterly improvisation that in areas such as the eyes, mouth, and sketchily described cravat seems to vibrate with the traces of his brush. He clearly reworked the portrait constantly, adding and changing details of the composition as he painted. For instance, he originally painted himself wearing a soft cap, the faint outline of which is visible around the crown of his head; the switch to powdered wig may have resulted from compositional requirements, from vanity, or perhaps from a desire on his part to present himself as a fashionable gentleman.

The addition of his palette, awkwardly wedged into the lower right corner of the canvas, clearly articulates his desire to be seen as a painter. Despite his success as an engraver throughout the 1720s and 1730s, Hogarth continually sought to develop his reputation as a leader of the painting establishment. Toward that end, in 1735 he rejuvenated the academy of painting he had inherited earlier that year from his father-in-law, Sir James Thornhill. Through the St. Martin's Lane Academy he endeavored to establish and foster a native school of artists. One of his principal goals was to break British patrons of their habit of employing artists from abroad and to wrest commissions from the clutches of foreigners and British artists working in Continentally-inspired styles. Particularly abhorrent to him was the dominance in artistic circles of the Palladian style promoted by William Kent and his patron, Lord Burlington.

Painted at the height of his success as an engraver and precisely at the moment when he was advancing his fortunes as the leader of a British school of painting, Hogarth's self-portrait is one of his first serious attempts at the genre of full-scale portraiture. Though by no means an aesthetic manifesto like his famous self-portrait of 1745, *The Painter with a Pug* (Tate Gallery), it shows him developing some of the practices and ideals that were to mark his philosophy of art. The dappled paint in his cheeks and the florid brushstrokes around his eyes, for instance, anticipate in paint this commanding passage from his theoretical treatise of 1753, *The Analysis of Beauty*:

> *Recollect that in the disposition of colours as well as of forms, variety, simplicity, distinctness, intricacy, uniformity and quantity, direct in giving beauty to the colouring of the human frame, especially if we include the face, where uniformity and strong opposition of tints are required, as in the eyes and mouth, which call most for our attention. But for the general hue of flesh… variety, intricacy and simplicity, are chiefly required.*[1]

JMA

1 Hogarth, 128.

10 WILLIAM HOGARTH

William Cavendish, Marquess of Hartington, later 4th Duke of Devonshire, 1741
Oil on canvas, 29¼ x 24¼ in (76 x 63.5 cm)
Gift of Paul Mellon, 1981

Reference: Paulson, 1:448

William Cavendish was born in 1720, the eldest son of the 3rd Duke of Devonshire. In 1729 he became Marquess of Hartington and in 1741, the year of his coming of age, he was elected to the House of Commons as MP for Derbyshire. It was in that same year that Hogarth painted this portrait, inscribed "W. Hogarth Pinxt 1741" and "The Right Hon.ble The Marquess of Hartington."

Hogarth regarded portraiture as a lesser branch of the art of painting, and the arrival in England in 1737 of the French portraitist Jean-Baptiste van Loo prompted him to combine, with particular venom, his criticism of portraiture with his contempt for foreign artists and styles. Reflecting upon van Loo's overwhelming success with English patrons, he wrote in his autobiographical notes:

> Portrait Painting…[is] a branch [of painting] that depends cheifly on much practice and an exact Eye as is plain by men of very midling natural parts haveing been at the utmost hights of it [—it] hath allways been engrossed by a very few Monopelisers whilst many others in a superior way more desirving both as men and artists are every were [sic] neglected… Vanloe a freinch portrait painter…with his…Puffing mono[po]lised all the people of fasheon in the kingdom…so that all our [artists] down went at once…into utmost distress and poverty.[1]

When he undertook portraits himself, it was partly in a spirit of defiance and competition, challenging his foreign rivals like van Loo and those who did not consider him capable of "face painting." From 1738 until the mid-1740s he painted portraits on a fairly regular basis, although he never established a proper practice. In contrast to most portrait painters, who often employed a battery of other artists to paint drapery and backgrounds, Hogarth always painted all parts himself.

The *Marquess of Hartington* is a prime example of Hogarth's abilities as a portraitist. The thick impasto on the Marquess's face and in the gold, silver, and red braid on his vest and jacket shows particular confidence and flair. Such vivacious passages of paint and color, in which one can almost sense the hand of the artist jabbing at the canvas, lend a liveliness to his portraits that definitively sets them apart from the work of van Loo, in which a smooth — or "licked" — surface gives the sitter an elegant, polished veneer.

As a nobleman the Marquess stands out among Hogarth's sitters, most of whom were from the gentry or upper-middle class. Even he appears primarily as a wealthy gentleman; he clearly possesses grace and bearing, and his clothes are fine and expensive, but no symbols overtly proclaim his rank.

The Marquess, who became Duke of Devonshire in 1755, played a large role in Hogarth's later artistic career. In 1757, after he had become Lord Chamberlain, he appointed Hogarth to the post of Sarjeant Painter to George II (a position for which the artist had been passed over twenty-four years before when Sir James Thornhill stepped down to be succeeded by his son John). The post was extremely lucrative and therefore perfect for the aging, embittered, and increasingly ailing painter. JMA

1 Hogarth, 216–17.

11 ARTHUR DEVIS

Children in an Interior, about 1743
Oil on canvas, 39 x 49¾ in (99 x 125.5 cm)
Gift of Paul Mellon, 1978

Reference: D'Oench, 46–47 (no. 8)

Children in an Interior is an early example of Devis's work as a painter of conversation pieces, the genre of informal domestic portraiture in which he made his reputation and career. The four children playing in a monumental interior convey a touching and somewhat enigmatic picture of domestic life in the eighteenth century. They seem resigned to entertaining themselves and have found ingenious ways to play within the strict and forbidding confines of the great gallery of their house. Particularly touching is the young boy at the left, who has converted an ornamented walking-stick into his hobby horse. The games the children play are ultimately in vain: the older boy's kite is grounded, and the younger girl builds a fragile house of cards. The conceit of children occupied in fruitless activity was common in French Rococo painting of the period (one has only to think of paintings by Chardin, for instance), the themes of which were popularized in England by artists such as Philippe Mercier and Hubert Gravelot.

Devis found inspiration in the work of his French contemporaries and in Dutch seventeenth-century interior scenes. Having had little formal training as a portraitist, he used his knowledge of topographical landscape painting to render architecturally accurate interiors, compensating for his moderate talent at figure painting. The contrasting wooden and stone surfaces, the varied textures of the children's clothing, and the velvet and gilt furnishings join with still-life elements such as the sewing basket on the table to create an enchanting, albeit deceptive, vision of this interior playground.

Almost doll-like in appearance, the young sitters seem stiff and overwhelmed by the accoutrements of their surroundings. Devis's practice of using lay figures (wooden mannequins measuring about thirty inches high) frequently gave such a stultified look to his paintings. He relied on these figures throughout his career, as did many of his contemporaries, since their use reduced the number of hours a sitter would have to spend posing in the painter's studio. We know that he had a number of costumes for his lay figures, both male and female (a few are now in the Harris Museum in Preston), and he obviously recycled the same costumes, since many appear in portraits of different sitters. In addition to using lay figures and stock costumes, he also depended on architectural pattern-books, designs from which he would often select for use in the settings of his portraits. Contrary to our preconceptions of portraiture as an intensely personal genre, he often did not paint his subjects in their own homes and would repeat architectural forms and details in numerous portraits of the same period. Some of the setting of *Children in an Interior*—particularly the decorative pilasters, the half-visible pictures on the wall, the perspectival sequence of rooms, and the Serlian window—are virtually identical to ones used elsewhere. Devis's use of such regularized poses, settings, and costumes gives to this painting an airless, slightly eerie atmosphere that, ironically, undermines the ostensibly jovial pursuits of the young sitters.

Neither the artist nor probably his patrons denied or disliked the stage-like quality of his portraits. By including a teal velvet curtain drawn back at the upper right of this picture, he reinforces rather than repudiates the artificiality of the image. His early patrons may have consciously sought to have their portraits emphasize the material, as opposed to psychological, aspects of their lives. The use of stock elements was not an unusual practice in seventeenth- or eighteenth-century portraiture, and to members of the gentry, anxious to be perceived as socially acceptable through their material wealth and good breeding, appearance would have been more important than truth.   JMA

12 PHILIPPE MERCIER

The Sense of Hearing, about 1744
Oil on canvas, 52 x 60½ in (132 x 153.6 cm)
Purchased through the Paul Mellon Fund, 1974

Reference: Ingamells and Raines, 62 (no. 264)

This work is from a series representing the five senses; the other subjects—also in the collection of the Yale Center for British Art—are sight, smell, taste, and touch. In each painting a group of four or five people, generally young, attractive, and flirtatious, act out a scene involving the given sense: music-making for hearing; looking into a mirror and through a telescope and magnifying glass for sight; sniffing flowers and a melon for smell; eating and drinking at a banquet for taste; embracing and being scratched by a cat for touch. Mercier took more or less all of these ideas from long-established iconographic traditions, the chief models being paintings and engravings by seventeenth-century artists working in the Low Countries. As a painter whose sensibilities were rooted in the French Rococo, and especially in the work of Watteau, he imparted to three of his senses—smell, taste, and touch—the look of *fêtes galantes*, with young men and women clearly pairing off and amorous possibilities in the air. His casting in the scenes for hearing and sight is less predictable. Although both feature young women, the males in the sight subject are an old man and a boy, and in *The Sense of Hearing* the characters are all female. But even when removed from the image, the male presence remains—in the person of the assumed viewer, with whom the beautiful harpsichordist makes titillating eye contact. Mercier's interest in all the senses was largely in sensual pleasure and, with the present work, in music as the food of love.

If not musically, then certainly as far as beauty and grace are concerned, the elderly lady playing the cello and the girls playing the flute and violin are the harpsichordist's mere accompaniment. Mercier paints the immature looks of the girls, presumably her younger sisters, in passages of looser, duller brushwork that make them seem all the more unformed; by contrast the harpsichordist's features are both fine in themselves and finely painted, set off by touches of sparkle in the eyes and the earring. The elderly lady is also loosely painted. It is difficult to guess what relation she may be to the others, but certainly she appears in the role of the chaperone, severely dressed and placed close to the viewer in a slightly barrier-like way. Even the instruments seem distributed according to how fetching they are: whereas the harpsichordist is free to look alluringly out at us, the flautist puffs her cheeks, the violinist cranes her neck, and the elderly lady holds her cello, inevitably with a hint of the indecorous, between her knees.

The scores on the harpsichord are marked "Hendel Operas" and "Geminiani's Sonates." Both the German-born George Frideric Handel and the Italian violinist and composer Francesco Geminiani were living in London at this time, and Mercier—as a foreigner striving for success in the British art world—may well have chosen these names to make a point: if foreigners could take the lead in music in Britain, why should not foreign painters, such as he, take the lead in art? More particularly, it seems at least possible that the rather unusual combination of instruments comes from Geminiani's instructional *Rules for Playing in a True Taste on the Violin, German Flute, Violoncello and Harpsichord... Exemplify'd in a Variety of Compositions on the Subjects of English, Scotch and Irish Tunes*, which was issued in parts from about 1739 to about 1745.

Mercier painted his series of the senses in the 1740s while living in York. The paintings are difficult to date exactly and may have been done over a protracted period, which might explain the differences in technique between the hearing and sight subjects on the one hand, and the smell, taste, and touch subjects on the other. The date given above seems reasonable for the present work since a reproductive mezzotint by John Faber was published, under the ungainly title of *Musical Family Concert of Ladies*, in 1744. According to the diarist George Vertue, the artist brought the whole series with him to London in 1747 and sold them for £100.[1]   MW

1 Vertue, 3:135.

Portrait of an Elderly Lady and a Girl, 1747
Oil on canvas, 50 x 40 in (127 x 102 cm)
Gift of Paul Mellon, 1976

Reference: Surry, 32–33 (no. 28)

George Beare's distinctive *Portrait of an Elderly Lady and a Girl* is unquestionably his masterpiece. Of the relatively small number of paintings known to be by him (between fifty and seventy-five in all), this is the only double portrait. By bringing together in one image two sitters of greatly differing ages, he creates not only a touching portrait of what must be a grandmother and grandchild, but also a study in contrasts in which his eye for subtleties of texture and color is shown to full advantage.

Beare makes the most of the visual possibilities inherent in the depiction of young with old. The thick strokes of paint that describe the old woman's wrinkled face stand out against the smooth surfaces of the creamy pink flesh of the young girl; similarly the deep grays of the older sitter's silver silk-damask dress provide a rich contrast to the milky-white linen of the grandmother's cap and the handkerchief draped over her shoulders. The pink silk underneath the white cloth of the young girl's dress reinforces the tonalities of her youthful and vibrant complexion, while the grays and whites of the old woman's dress emphasize her advanced age and heighten the pictorial impact of her slackening and yellowed skin. By placing the sitters against a darkened background, Beare draws our attention immediately to the heads of the women, particularly that of the elderly sitter who candidly engages us with her slightly wizened yet still vibrant eyes. The sumptuous fabrics in the portrait suggest that the sitters belonged to one of the wealthier families of the Salisbury region where Beare had his practice, and it has been suggested that they were members of the Grove family of Ferne House, Berwick St. John, Wiltshire. Most of Beare's patrons were from the upper-middle classes living in or around Salisbury.[1]

The work fuses a frank "naturalism" made popular in the 1740s by William Hogarth with the more refined sensibilities of the English Rococo idiom as practiced by Francis Hayman. Beare's conflation of these two styles suggests that he may have spent time in London, and it is possible he trained at the St. Martin's Lane Academy —where he would have been exposed to both Hogarth and Hayman.

Over the course of the last fifty years, Beare's œuvre has slowly emerged from the shadows cast by these more celebrated contemporaries. The dearth of biographical evidence of his life has hampered both the assessment of his training and practice and, ultimately, the authentication of unsigned paintings. Most of his known paintings—including this one—are signed and dated, and most date from the period between 1743 and 1749. On May 22 of the latter year, the *Salisbury Journal* noted, "Last Week died near Andover, Hants, Mr Beare, lately an eminent Face Painter in this City."[2] JMA

1 Surry, 9 and 32.
2 Ibid., 4.

George Rogers with His Wife, Margaret, and His Sister, Margaret Rogers, about 1748–50

Oil on canvas, 41 x 39 in (104 x 99 cm)

Gift of Paul Mellon, 1981

Reference: Allen 1987, 102 (no. 24)

Hayman's major commission from the 1740s, the most productive decade of his career, was a series of decorative paintings for the supper boxes at Vauxhall Gardens, a pleasure garden and center of London nightlife that Jonathan Tyers, its proprietor, had made into a booming leisure enterprise. In addition to the work for Vauxhall, Tyers commissioned Hayman to paint several portraits of members of his family in various groupings, and the present work is one of two portraits of his elder daughter Margaret (1724–1786) with her husband George Rogers (1718–1792), an amateur landscape artist.

This outdoor portrait of the couple accompanied by another young woman was most likely done after the Rogers's marriage. (Another of Hayman's paintings in the Center's collection is probably the portrait commissioned by Tyers on that occasion.) The standing female figure was long thought to be Elizabeth Tyers, Margaret Tyers Rogers's younger sister, but now it is commonly accepted that she is, in fact, Margaret Rogers (1722–1806), George's younger sister. Widowed from her first husband, Margaret Rogers eventually married her sister-in-law's younger brother, Jonathan Tyers Jr., thereby further tightening the bond between the Tyers and Rogers families.

The format and setting of this lively family group confirm Hayman's ability to add verve to the conventions of conversation-piece portraits. Nearly all of Hayman's other portraits of Tyers's family conform to a fashionable stiffness, but here he tinkers with the composition so as to invert the traditional pyramid of sitters, placing the central figure lower than her surrounding companions. The gazes of George Rogers and his sister, looking admiringly at her brother's catch, quickly draw the viewer's eye to the outer edge of the composition, where the young man proudly thrusts the bird out for inspec-

tion while his wife confronts the viewer's eyes with her own. The artist's use of multiple focal points and an inverted pyramidal structure forces the viewer to move his or her eyes across the entire canvas and to interact visually with all the sitters in the portrait.

Hayman's creation of a dynamic group portrait is in no way a direct transcription of reality—however much it may appear so—and the energetic composition was evidently much altered from its original design. Two pentimenti show the extent of his changes to the canvas. At the right edge of the canvas, at the level of Margaret Rogers's head, a ghostly figure looms, barely visible: this would have been a sculpted cherub holding a cornucopia and seated on a rectangular stone pedestal, of the sort Hayman included in many of his portraits of the period. He has not erased all traces of the statue but has left the hem of the sister's dress still perching on the base of the stone column, the rest of which he eventually painted out. Another compositional change can be seen in the faint shadow of another leg just to the left of George Rogers's left calf: originally he stood in a more conventional and solid upright position, his left knee straightened. These alterations to the original composition, especially the transformation of George Rogers's stiff posture to a more animated one, give the work an immediacy of feeling and a lifelike appearance that set it apart from the rest of Hayman's more conventional portraits of the period. Almost humorous in tone, the contrast of the proud showmanship of George Rogers with the non-plussed expression of his wife—who continues to pet her dog calmly, apparently unimpressed by her husband's shooting prowess—makes this image a shrewd vision of how the Tyers-Rogers family, leaders of London's leisure activities, spent their time. JMA

15 THOMAS GAINSBOROUGH

The Gravenor Family, about 1754
Oil on canvas, 35½ x 35½ in (90.1 x 90.1 cm)
Gift of Paul Mellon, 1977

References: Cormack 1991, 52 (no. 11); Hayes 1975, 203 (no. 11)

Thomas Gainsborough's portrait of the Gravenor family dates from the years during which he lived and worked in Ipswich, near his native Sudbury in Suffolk. Not having found a sufficient clientele in Sudbury, Gainsborough and his family had moved to the larger town of Ipswich in 1752. The portrait depicts John Gravenor and his second wife, Ann (née Colman), with their two daughters Elizabeth and Ann, seated in a verdant landscape. Mr. Gravenor was a successful apothecary in Ipswich, and in 1754 he turned his hand to local politics. It is possible that he commissioned this portrait to celebrate his new role in public life.

Using dappled light to unify his composition, Gainsborough makes both the landscape and figures in *The Gravenor Family* vibrate with vitality, despite the relaxed poses of the sitters. The storm clouds looming in the background and the feather-like leaves that seem to rustle as our eyes move across the canvas combine to foretell a showery end to the Gravenors' outing, ostensibly spent plucking wildflowers from the flourishing wheatfields around Ipswich. By juxtaposing the darkening storm clouds in the background with the brightness of his sitters' faces, Gainsborough cleverly draws our eyes to their countenances, the focal points of any portrait, while he emphasizes the pervasive effects of the landscape in which they pose. The almost humorous, rubicund features of Mr. Gravenor contrast with those of his wife and daughters, pearl-like, and impart to him an air of healthy vigor. On the whole, the artist treats the features and dress of the Gravenors as he does those of the landscape around them—he eschews topographical and physiognomic detail for overall effect.

From early in his career Gainsborough received his greatest inspiration from the landscape, painting the countryside around Sudbury and later often copying the great seventeenth-century Dutch landscape masters, such as Aelbert Cuyp and Jacob van Ruisdael. At the same time he was always acutely aware of the realities of making one's living as a painter, eventually expressing his frustrations at the demands of his patrons who desired only to buy portraits: "a Man may do great things and starve in a Garret if he does not conquer his Passions and conform to…that branch which they will encourage and pay for."[1] Cleverly, if somewhat awkwardly at first, he fused his innate skills at representing landscape with his portraits of local gentry.

The Gravenor Family exemplifies Gainsborough's personal interpretation of the Rococo idiom as practiced by Francis Hayman and Hubert Gravelot, colleagues and mentors to the younger artist during his training in London in the 1740s. In fact, due in part to its stylistic affinity with some of Hayman's portraits of that period, *The Gravenor Family* was long thought to date from 1747–48. The sinuous if somewhat awkward forms of the figures, the nervous lines of their clothing, and the cool tones of the silks and satins recall Hayman's version of the "English Rococo." On the other hand, Gainsborough's palette and his particular method of modeling and shaping surfaces with flame-like brushstrokes—particularly noticeable in fabrics—give to his portraits of the 1740s and 1750s a shimmering quality that is quite distinctive; one modern critic aptly described the dress of the younger Gravenor daughter, seated in the foreground, as akin to a splendid piece of rococo silver or plaster-work decoration.[2] JMA

1 Woodall, 117.
2 Hayes 1975, 203.

16 GEORGE ROMNEY

A Conversation (The Artist's Brothers, Peter and James Romney), 1766
Oil on canvas, 43½ x 34½ in (110.5 x 87.5 cm)
Gift of Paul Mellon, 1981
First exhibited: Society of Artists, 1766 (no. 144)
Reference: Ward and Roberts, 1:29 and 2:135

One of Romney's earliest documented paintings, this portrait depicts his two younger brothers Peter and James. Peter Romney, himself a promising painter, had studied painting with George from 1759 until 1762, when the latter left their native Lancashire for London, and the portrait is presumably set in Peter's studio. Unlike his older brother, Peter never fulfilled his potential as an artist; he died in 1777, at the age of thirty-four, apparently from overindulgence in drink. James, the youngest of the three brothers, joined the East India Company and eventually rose to the rank of Lieutenant Colonel; he died in 1807.

Romney paints his brothers as gentlemen of learning and taste, although neither had any formal education — their learning having been furthered only by their father's love of books. In their portrait they discuss geometrical drawings on the easel in front of Peter and, in doing so, demonstrate the capacity to learn through intellectual discussions and demonstrations of scholarly theories as they pertain to art. Busts and statuettes casually scattered around the studio also suggest that Peter, like George, allied himself artistically with the emerging school of Neoclassical painters, who found beauty in the crisp, rational lines of geometrical forms.

By the time of the portrait George Romney had already developed a strong distaste for the sinuous and curving lines of Rococo design. He left England for the first time in 1764, traveling to Paris in order to study Continental art firsthand, and from there he wrote to Peter:

> *The degeneracy of taste that runs through every thing, is farther gone here than in London. The ridiculous and fantastical are the only points they seem to aim at... The vast collections I see every day, make me feel no inclination either for designing or writing at present.*[1]

His natural predilection for strong linear forms — as opposed to the "degenerate" forms of Rococo painting — can be detected in his portrait of his brothers: the clarity of composition and the lines of the figures, the cool colors of their clothes, and the spartan setting are harbingers of the Neoclassical style he would embrace wholeheartedly following his stay in Rome from 1773 to 1775. Although he aspired to gain fame as a painter of Historical subjects, his reputation was clearly made from his portraits. Painted at the outset of his career and richly suggestive of the ways in which his style would evolve, Romney's portrait of his brothers quietly evinces both his hopes for their futures and his own ambitions as a learned and serious artist.   JMA

1   Romney, 51.

17 JOSEPH WRIGHT, called WRIGHT OF DERBY
Academy by Lamplight, about 1768–69
Oil on canvas, 50 x 39⅜ in (127 x 101.2 cm)
Gift of Paul Mellon, 1973
First exhibited: Society of Artists, 1769 (no. 197)
References: Egerton 1990, 63–64 (no. 23); Nicolson, 1:234 (no. 189)

Joseph Wright's shadowy *Academy by Lamplight* was first exhibited at the Society of Artists in 1769, four years after his public debut at that institution's annual exhibition. From the outset of his career, Wright's name and reputation had been closely associated with the tenebrist style, one indebted to seventeenth-century artists influenced by Caravaggio and Rembrandt. From 1765 until the exhibition of this picture, he exhibited paintings featuring scenes spectacularly illuminated by the glow of candlelight. As early as 1767 a critic noted, "Mr Wright of Derby's Candlelights, have always been admired,"[1] and in 1768 another announced him "a very great and uncommon genius."[2]

Among his young academicians in this painting Wright shows us the different faces of the aspiring artist. While a few serious draftsmen carefully transcribe onto their paper the object before them, diligently perfecting their drawings, a genius (or one who thinks himself such), portfolio snapped shut and clutched to his breast, receives his inspiration from the touch of the sculpture and the light beaming on his forehead. In the shadows at the right, playful pupils — still too young to appreciate the delights of the craft — divert their attention from the statue and, with their inviting gazes, encourage the viewer to partake of the scene. At the left a besotted student has abandoned his drawing tools and fairly swoons at the beauty of the shadows cast by the sculpted nymph.

In this exploration of the awakening of artistic genius, Wright exploits the Pygmalion theme, a subject particularly popular at mid-century. The statue, warmed by the yellow candlelight, glows in the deep shadows as if she will soon rise and leave her plinth. The colorless "genius" averts his eyes from the sculpture in order to draw his inspiration from it, and seems himself stone-like, fixed in his thought, immobile in his gestural grandiloquence.

By contrast, the young, adoring artist stares intently — even longingly — at the beautiful maiden and is, like her, warmed by the glow of the hidden candle. These two are linked through their poses, echoing the curve of the arch above them. Intriguing though the narrative may be, the picture's subject remains nonetheless the transformative and enlivening power of light.

Wright's painting also illuminates our understanding of the instruction of young artists in the mid-eighteenth century. Students spent good portions of the early years of their training making copies of well-known and admired statues, usually plaster casts or copies of antique Roman or Greek statues. Here the sculpture at the center of the composition is a copy of the famed Hellenistic *Nymph with a Shell* (Louvre); a full-size copy of the *Gladiator* (one of the most famous sculptures to have survived from Antiquity, a smaller-scale cast of which had been the subject of the artist's first exhibited picture in 1765) can also be glimpsed in the shadows at the right. Art students frequently made drawings from sculptures by candlelight; in one gallery, for instance, "lamps were placed to form the happiest contrast of light and shade, and the improved effect of the marble amounted by this almost to animation…To a mind replete with classical imagery the illusion was perfect."[3] It was long speculated that Wright's painting depicted an actual spot in the sculpture gallery at Richmond House in Whitehall, opened by its owner the Duke of Richmond for the benefit of art students in 1758. Yet, Wright's image belongs not to a specific locale or incident but rather is an imagined scene. JMA

1   Egerton 1990, 52.
2   Ibid., 10.
3   Ibid., 63.

The Artist and His Family, about 1772

Oil on canvas, 20½ x 26¼ in (52 x 66.5 cm)

Gift of Paul Mellon, 1981

First exhibited: Royal Academy, 1777 (no. 367, "A small picture of a family")

References: von Erffa and Staley, 461–62 (no. 546); Prown 1986

The occasion for this family portrait was the birth of the artist's second son, also named Benjamin, in August 1772. Around the child and his mother, Betsy West, are grouped the chief members of the West family in England: the elder son, Raphael Lamar, aged six; the artist's half-brother Thomas West; his octagenarian father John West; and the artist himself on the far right, holding the painter's traditional attributes of palette and maulstick. The family history that brought them together at this time and place is a complicated and remarkable one.

John West was the son of English Quaker parents who emigrated with William Penn to Pennsylvania, leaving him in England to be raised by his mother's family, also Quakers, who lived in Warborough, between Oxford and Reading. At the age of twenty-six he too emigrated to Pennsylvania. His wife stayed behind because she was pregnant and shortly after his departure died giving birth to a son, Thomas. John remarried in Pennsylvania and with his second wife had ten further children, the tenth of whom was Benjamin, the artist. They lived largely in Chester County, where John kept taverns.

The young Benjamin West left America in 1760, spent three years in Rome, and decided to pursue his artistic career in London. Soon he arranged for his American fiancée, then Betsy Shewell, to come over from Philadelphia to join him; they were married in an Anglican ceremony at St. Martin-in-the-Fields. John West accompanied Betsy on the journey, returning to England for the first time in nearly fifty years. By now a widower for the second time, John was to stay in England for good, settling in his childhood home of Warborough. Thomas West, his long-lost son from his first marriage, lived in nearby Reading, where he made his living as a watchmaker; like John himself, he had been raised — and remained — a Quaker. Perhaps Benjamin West felt some pride in being the cause of their finally coming together, and certainly underlines their kinship and companionship in the portrait; not only in their Quaker dress but also in their postures and looks, they appear cast from the same severe mold. About the same time he also painted them together as companions of William Penn in his painting of *Penn's Treaty with the Indians* (Pennsylvania Academy of the Fine Arts).[1]

Next to his father and half-brother, West himself looks the very image of worldly sophistication, expensively dressed and wigged, his pose hinting at grace and accomplishment. Though still in his early thirties he was already at the height of his success; his painting of *The Death of General Wolfe* (National Gallery of Canada, Ottawa) had won acclaim at the Royal Academy in 1771, and in 1772 — the year of his second son's birth — he secured the lucrative royal appointment of Historical Painter to the King. He had a studio in Panton Square in the center of town and a villa near the Thames in Hammersmith — the latter may well have provided the setting for the portrait. On the left West's wife and children bear out the same idea of easy refinement. Like the man of the world he has become, the family of his own creation is clearly quite different from the family that created him: the stolid, blocky figures of the father and half-brother, with their straight-ahead staring expressions, suggest simple religious faith and simple lives; those of the artist, his wife, and children gently lean and incline, achieving harmony through balance and interplay rather than individual rectitude.

Though first and foremost a family portrait, *The Artist and his Family* opens out to some of the large issues West must have pondered as an American artist in England: the value of sophistication as against simplicity, success within the establishment as against devout nonconformism. It also recalls the traditional subject of the Ages of Man, even perhaps that of the Adoration of Christ. The work was published as an engraving in 1779 and went on to become one of West's best known and most admired compositions.   MW

1   For further biographical details, and information on the West family's religious background, see Prown 1986, 269–72.

19 FRANCIS WHEATLEY

The Browne Family, about 1773

Oil on canvas, 27¾ x 35 in (70.5 x 89 cm)

Gift of Paul Mellon, 1981

References: Egerton 1978, 139–41 (no. 133); Webster 1970, 125 (no. 27)

Wheatley shows George and Mary Browne and their children pursuing various fashionable leisure activities on the banks of a calm river or pond. Actively engaging the viewer with her stare, Mrs. Browne dominates the canvas. She cuts a self-assured figure, jauntily hitching up her crisp white apron to avoid soiling it with the muddy water lapping against the bank. She is at once sporty and fashionable; her fancy ribboned hat seems out of place in such a natural setting, yet it does serve to shade her eyes from the noonday sun. Her husband, also fashionably attired for their outing, relaxes with his family while he sketches quietly by the water.

One did not have to travel far into the countryside to angle, as fishing was most often called. From the 1650s onwards, angling was an increasingly popular leisure sport, and sales of how-to manuals and treatises thrived. Both men and women enjoyed the sport, and often artists, such as Francis Hayman, featured women anglers in their more decorative paintings. Although more complex methods of fishing, such as fly-fishing for trout, were commonly practiced, Mrs. Browne uses here a simple rod from which the line, probably of horsehair, dips into the water close to the bank. The older boy appears to be throwing something into the water — possibly food to help attract fish to his mother's line. The young girls, particularly the oldest, gesture as if to indicate that their mother will soon make a successful catch. In order to ensure the success of such outings, freshwater ponds, streams, and rivers were frequently stocked with carp, pike, and trout.

Picnicking, fishing, and drawing had become by the mid-eighteenth century suitable recreation for all classes of British society. Over the course of the century, improvements in transportation, such as faster, more affordable, and safer coaches, enabled Londoners to make frequent trips to country sites on the outskirts of the metropolis; for longer holidays many ventured to popular locations farther afield.

Wheatley's painting not only depicts a family engaged in pleasurable pastimes but also reflects current philosophies on child-rearing. In the 1760s Jean-Jacques Rousseau's *Emile*, a treatise on the proper education of the child, influenced the ways in which couples viewed and treated their children. Couching his philosophy in an engaging narrative, Rousseau counseled parents to participate actively in their children's upbringing and emphasized the positive effects that nature and outdoor activity had on children's mental and physical health. The Brownes, frolicking at water's edge and engaging in salubrious activities, stand as a model family of the Enlightenment.

Living with his family in Covent Garden, near where Wheatley had his studio in the years 1772–75, George Browne was Principal Clerk of the Westminster Fire Office, one of the oldest insurance companies in London. He and his wife had married and had their first child in 1764. This painting shows five of the Browne's eventual ten children; they are, from left to right: Amelia Wilhelmina (b. 1767); George Howe (b. 1764); Edward Walpole (b. 1766); Mary (b. 1769); and either Charlotte (b. 1770) or Harriet (b. 1772).   JMA

The Gore Family with George, 3rd Earl Cowper, about 1775
Oil on canvas, 31 x 38½ in (78 x 97.5 cm)
Gift of Paul Mellon, 1977

Reference: Webster 1976, 62–63 (no. 79)

In this lavish portrait George, 3rd Earl Cowper (1738–1783) at the center of the composition leans nonchalantly on the back of a chair and looks adoringly at his future wife, Hannah Anne Gore, at the left of the canvas. Surrounding the couple is the bride's family: her father Charles Gore plays the cello—his colored drawings of ships nearby (he was an amateur marine painter)—while her elder sister Emilie accompanies him on the square piano; her mother Mary Gore, book in hand, and her eldest sister Elizabeth are seated at the right. Painted in the months preceding the wedding, on June 2, 1775, the painting most likely was commissioned by Charles Gore to honor his daughter's marriage.

Ostensibly set in an open gallery in Cowper's villa giving onto the picturesque slopes of Fiesole in Italy, the intimate family portrait describes the members of the Gore family as well as their affection for each other. As a group they are at ease with each other in the home of their soon-to-be son-in-law. The bridal couple stands, coyly anticipating their union: Cowper looks at his betrothed from afar while she poses demurely, not participating in the convivial musical moment. Framing her head, an allegorical painting of a marriage *à l'antique* in a Temple of Hymen cleverly suggests her preoccupation with her imminent marriage; and it is possible that the specific allegory—in which Hercules is clubbing the unmasked Calumny—hints at the quashing of a former passion between the bridegroom, already in his late thirties, and an unsuitable Florentine lady. Opulent in its description of each detail of the dresses, musical instruments, and furniture, this conversation piece is more than a mere depiction of an intimate family afternoon. Zoffany has created a tribute not only to the young couple, her family, and her bridegroom, but also to their tastes and lifestyle.

Charles and Mary Gore were married in 1751, and her dowry, coupled with Gore's own inheritance, enabled them to live a life of leisure. Mrs. Gore's poor health led the family to seek mild climates. In 1773 they moved to Florence, and there, through their introductions to the Grand Ducal Court and the highest ranks of British society, they met George Nassau, 3rd Earl Cowper, a well-known member of that city's British expatriate society.

Cowper had first visited Florence in 1759 and thereafter played a large role in the Florentine artistic community. In particular, he was a great patron of contemporary British artists, musicians, and literati, whom he frequently championed to the Grand Duke of Tuscany, Pietro Leopoldo; indeed, this painting reflects his love for both music and art. During his courtship of and engagement to Hannah Gore, Cowper feted his fiancée with concerts, and in late 1774 he commissioned Zoffany to paint her portrait in the guise of a peasant-girl from Savoy. JMA

On Native Turf and Classic Ground

IN THE MID-EIGHTEENTH CENTURY the education of the young British nobleman was not considered complete until he had journeyed across Europe on a "Grand Tour." The high point of his tour would be Italy, and especially the great works of classical and Renaissance art. He would return home with an idea of culture formed on Italy, and this was reflected in the kind of art he chose to buy and commission. He may have bought a view by Canaletto while in Venice—it was the avid patronage of the British that led that artist to spend a period in Britain, where he painted London as a modern Rome, powerful and classical, the capital of the Enlightenment. But more significant still for the progress of British art, the Grand Tourists admired and collected Claude Lorrain, the seventeenth-century French painter whose idyllic scenes in the Roman campagna defined the idea of the classical in landscape: an Edenic or "ideal" version of nature, smooth and orderly, with nymphs and shepherds, temples and statues, bathed in golden light and seen from a high, godlike viewpoint.

The old academic notion that landscape was inferior to the painting of scriptural, mythic, allegorical, and historical subjects ("history painting") still held sway. On the other hand, some of the ideas that sustained that prejudice, especially the idea of nature as something base to be transcended, were breaking down: for the first time people began to believe in nature as a source of goodness, well-being, and high thoughts. The British landscapists looked for ways to dignify their art, to separate themselves at last from the mundane traditions of mapmaking and topography. They aspired to the classical, Claudean ideal, and Britain's own Claude, "the father of British landscape," emerged in the person of Richard Wilson. He studied in Italy, and through a deep understanding of Claude developed his own, British mode of classical landscape. His position was indeed parental: the alternative, more rustic, Dutch-inspired landscape dubbed "picturesque," represented at its best in the work of Gainsborough, defined itself against him; and the young Turner responded vitally and often to his legacy.   MW

21 RICHARD WILSON

Caernarvon Castle, about 1745

Oil on canvas, 25½ x 41¼ in (65 x 104.8 cm)

Gift of Paul Mellon, 1976

Reference: Constable, 173 (pl. 32a)

This and another closely similar version of the same view (private collection) may well have been Wilson's first essays in representing the scenery and antiquities of his native Wales. It was a field of subject matter that he was to explore throughout his career—indeed he painted several further views of Caernarvon Castle—and in which he was to be followed by countless other British landscapists, including the young Turner.

Caernarvon was the most imposing of the castles built by the English king Edward I to secure his occupation of Wales at the end of the thirteenth century. While still under construction it was the birthplace of the king's son, the future Edward II, who was the first English prince to be called Prince of Wales. Exactly how Wilson would have construed the historical significance of such a site is unclear, but for an artist who was Welsh it was surely one of particular resonance. The presence of the artist sketching in the foreground with a gentleman amateur at his side underlines the idea that this is also a place of serious interest from the artistic point of view.[1]

The view is from the south and shows the distinctive trio of turrets that rise above the Eagle Tower at the castle's western end. For the most part, however, Wilson has taken such liberties with the topographical facts of the place that it is barely recognizable. He has done away with the other towers along this side of the castle, cut down the Queen's Gate at its eastern end, and generally reduced a massive and forbidding fortress to a picturesque ruin, crumbling and overgrown. It is almost as though the work were a capriccio, showing the castle as it would appear after aging for another five centuries. The setting is fantastic too. In reality one sees the south side of the castle across the River Seiont, not across a pleasantly curving inlet of the sea. The town of Caernarvon, which surrounds the castle on the land side, has been almost completely omitted; and the hill on the right, Twt Hill, has been brought much closer than it actually is. The rude cottages to the right of the castle, which are the only indication of the town, seem placed to make what was a fairly commonplace point about ancient versus modern times: though in decay, the grandeur of the past makes the present seem mean and mundane.

Most of the landscapes Wilson painted before his stay in Italy follow models in earlier Dutch painting, but this example shows him moving toward the Italianate or classical pattern of his mature style. Although the handling of details is raw and rustic by the standards of his later compositions, the overall design recalls those French painters whose work was the touchstone of classical landscape, Claude Lorrain and Gaspard Dughet.   MW

1   For a discussion of the significance of the subject, in relation to the other version, see Solkin, 28–31, 148–49 (no. 7).

22 GIOVANNI ANTONIO CANAL, called CANALETTO
Westminster Bridge with the Lord Mayor's Procession on the Thames, 1747
Oil on canvas, 37¾ x 50¼ in (95.7 x 127.5 cm)
Gift of Paul Mellon, 1976

Reference: Constable and Links, 1:141 and 2:423 (no. 435)

In this view of the Thames Canaletto commemorates two civic events: the annual fluvial festivities honoring Lord Mayor's Day and the completion of Westminster Bridge. Canaletto's great popularity among his British patrons depended on his prodigious production of festive and atmospheric scenes of life in the piazzas and on the canals of Venice, and during his eight years in England, he would paint several views full of details of London life but redolent with Venetian allusions. The construction of Westminster Bridge was one of his most frequent London subjects, perhaps because several of his patrons sat on the committee governing its building.

Canaletto shows the Lord Mayor's Day procession from a bird's-eye view, looking south and directly facing the bridge. On the right the skyline of Westminster dominates; in the distance on the left is Lambeth Palace, London residence of the Archbishops of Canterbury. Hawksmoor's newly completed towers of the west front of Westminster Abbey peak above the cityscape to the right, and the Union Jack proudly flies above the tower of St. Margaret's, Westminster. To the left of the Abbey the sloping roof of Westminster Hall leads the eye to the double spires of St. Stephen's, then the seat of the House of Commons, and farther in the distance are the four spires of St. John-the-Evangelist in Smith Square.

Topographically faithful in its depiction of the London skyline, the painting is equally meticulous in its rendering of the mayoral procession. The City of London celebrated Lord Mayor's Day annually on October 29 (in 1752 the date was changed to November 9). On that day the Lord Mayor was sworn into office by the Barons of the Exchequer and presented to the king. The ceremony began in the City, from whence the Lord Mayor, attended by various livery and Aldermen, traveled upriver to Westminster in a lavish water procession of official and ceremonial barges. Canaletto paints the Lord Mayor's

barge broadside, displaying its eighteen oarsmen and various attendants. The other official vessels can be identified from a caption to a contemporary print of the painting: from left to right, the barges belong to the Skinners, the Goldsmiths, and the Fishmongers; navigating under the arches of the bridge are those of the Clockworkers, Vintners, and Taylors; directly behind the Lord Mayor's is that of the Mercers and, at the far right, that of the Drapers. Canaletto enlivens his festive view of the procession by dotting the river with sailing barges, some of which fire salutes, and by peopling the smaller boats, bridge, and windows with spectators eager to take part in the day's events.

Before Westminster Bridge was built, London Bridge was the only permanent structure crossing the Thames. The City Corporation, opposed to westward expansion of the city, and the Watermen of London, feeling their livelihood threatened, had lobbied vehemently to prevent its construction. Against their alarmist, self-interested objections, however, the Bridge Committee passed in 1736 an act to build Westminster Bridge; its foundation stone was dropped into the middle of the Thames in 1739.

Painted in 1747, the work was meant to coincide with the bridge's scheduled opening, but shortly before the inauguration one of the piers on the Westminster side began to settle dangerously, delaying the structure's completion until 1750. Canaletto, therefore, speculates on the bridge's final appearance: he ornaments each pier with an octagonal, half-domed alcove and decorates the central section with statues of the Thames and Isis. Only six pairs of these alcoves were actually built (one set at either end and one set at the central bay), and no such statues, although there may have been plans or drawings for them, ever adorned the bridge. JMA

23 GIOVANNI ANTONIO CANAL, called CANALETTO
Warwick Castle, about 1748–49
Oil on canvas, 28½ x 47½ in (72.5 x 120.5 cm)
Gift of Paul Mellon, 1994

References: Buttery, 23–30; Constable and Links, 1:142, note 1, and 2:429–30 (nos. 444 and 448)

Between 1748 and 1752 Canaletto completed five painted views and three drawings of Warwick Castle. In all his paintings of Warwick—as in those of the Thames and London—he impresses his own, particularly Venetian sensibility onto the sites of England yet also captures their unique, wholly English qualities.

Francis Greville, Lord Brooke (8th Baron Greville, later Earl of Warwick) and Canaletto most likely met through Sir Hugh Smithson (later Duke of Northumberland), who was married to Brooke's cousin and had been the painter's most active patron since his arrival in England two years previously. Eager to record the modern improvements he was making to his estate and aware of Canaletto's international reputation as a view-painter, Brooke commissioned him to paint the buildings and grounds of Warwick Castle sometime in 1748.

Warwick Castle had belonged to Brooke's family since 1604, when James I granted the property to Sir Fulke Greville the younger. Originally built in 1068 for William the Conqueror, the castle had undergone constant renovations until the fifteenth century, but the sixteenth century saw the decline of the complex, the buildings finally succumbing to years of neglect. The castle Brooke inherited in 1727 had been lavishly restored by his ancestor after 1604, but by then the complex was again in desperate need of repair, and Brooke, upon his return from his Grand Tour, set his hand to renovating it.

Canaletto's five paintings are at once spectacular views of the castle and tributes to Brooke's renovations. The Center's painting is the last in a series of three views painted in 1748 and 1749 that show the south front of the building as it would have been seen from Castle Park, across the River Avon. Although his other two paintings of this facade are similar in vantage point, here he expands the foreground and widens the vista to include Castle Meadow, a small island in the Avon, and farther to the right the town of Warwick, its medieval bridge, and the bell tower of St. Nicholas's Church. At the left of the castle is Ethelfleda's Mount, the only surviving remnant of William the Conqueror's fortifications. Famous for its spectacular view of the outlying countryside, the small park atop the mound attracted visitors from afar, and Canaletto portrays some of these ascending the "winding walk" and others admiring the prospect from the summit. Incidental details such as these—as well as the pair of boys at the lower right who surreptitiously climb over the fence—create a lively atmosphere in which the potentially foreboding castle becomes an animated locus of activity.

In contrast to Canaletto's second version of this view—presenting a speculative vision of how the finished facade and park would eventually look—the Center's painting renders the topography of the palace and land more or less as it was at the time the artist painted it. Earlier in 1748 Brooke had engaged the landscape architect Lancelot "Capability" Brown to refashion the grounds as a green tree-filled "natural" landscape both inside and outside the castle's periphery. Canaletto shows us these works in progress: at the base of Ethelfleda's Mount is a veritable construction site filled with workers, garden tools, and brown soil. The artist delights in the almost humorous juxtapositions of old and new inherent in the renovations, noting such details as the placement of the castle's finely detailed porch next to a ramshackle lean-to used to store equipment. Similarly, sash-windows in the upper story of the castle's west end, two imposing windows of the Cedar Room, and the west porch newly renovated in the Gothic style stand out as bright white beacons against the eroding stonework of the facade.

None of Canaletto's views of Warwick was executed on the spot; all were painted in his London studio. There he amplified in paint the sketches and studies of the castle he had made on his various visits to Warwick. JMA

Rome from the Villa Madama, 1753

Oil on canvas, 37⁹⁄₁₆ x 52⅛ in (95.5 x 132.4 cm)

Gift of Paul Mellon, 1977

References: Constable, 218–19 (pl. 107a); Solkin, 184–85 (no. 67)

Although Wilson lived in Rome for five years, only a handful of his many canvases showing the city and its environs are known to have been painted during that time. With its luminous late-afternoon sky, subtle gradations of tone, and deftly observed effects of light filtering through leaves, *Rome from the Villa Madama* is among the most beautiful. It shows the celebrated view from Monte Mario looking south and east. The Villa Madama itself, built to designs by Raphael for Giuliano de' Medici (Pope Clement VII), nestles among the trees in the middle ground to the right. On the left the curve of the River Tiber – made more pronounced by Wilson for the purpose – helps lead the eye toward the distant city, where the most readily identified landmark is the Castel Sant'Angelo to the right. In the far distance are the Alban Hills. Judging from the fact that Wilson later produced several replicas, the composition would seem to have been much admired.

The painting was designed to accord with the classical or "ideal" notion of landscape — represented in its canonical form by the work of the seventeenth-century painter Claude Lorrain — which Wilson was to make the cornerstone of his practice as an artist. Its whole disposition suggests balance and order: nature, rough and untidy, has been improved upon. The high vista is gracefully framed by trees to either side; the river winding into depth, the carefully stepped arrangement of tonal areas, and the delicately judged effects of atmospheric perspective give a sense of clear, stately movement from foreground to distance; and the various particulars and textures of nature are smoothed over in the interests of a broad general design. These qualities were understood as the parallel in landscape to the ideal of bodily beauty in the classical tradition of sculpture and figure painting. Writing of Claude Lorrain's landscape style, Wilson's contemporary Sir Joshua Reynolds observed that "its truth is founded upon the same principle as that by which the Historical Painter acquires perfect form."[1]

For the eighteenth-century classicist there was no more sacred site than Rome, and Wilson pays direct homage to Antiquity by placing a fragment of Roman sculpture prominently in his foreground, a female figure leaning against what may be an ancient sarcophagus. The implication is that Rome itself, for all its present beauty, stands as the remnant of a more glorious past. The "Claudean" landscape was essentially a landscape of nostalgia, a feeling conveyed not only by the symbolic presence of classical fragments and ruins, but also by the time of day: as here, the scene is generally set in the melancholy fading light of late afternoon and sunset.

Wilson was commissioned to paint the work by the young William Legge, 2nd Earl of Dartmouth, during the time the latter spent in Rome on his Grand Tour. Like many other English "milordi," Dartmouth came to Rome to complete his education in classical culture, and this led naturally to his becoming a patron of classical landscape painting. Typically, he sat to Batoni for his portrait; equally typically he engaged an artist-agent, Thomas Jenkins, to advise him on the acquisition of works of art for his collection, and it was probably through Jenkins that he met Wilson. Dartmouth and Wilson apparently went on a visit to Naples together in the spring of 1753, and after Dartmouth returned to England he gave Wilson further commissions: one was for a pendant to the present work, *Rome: St. Peter's and the Vatican from the Janiculum* (Tate Gallery); another was for a series of drawings of further celebrated views and classical sites around Rome, some of which are also in the collection of the Yale Center for British Art.   MW

1   Joshua Reynolds, Discourse IV, 70.

25 PAUL SANDBY

Hackwood Park, Hampshire, 1763–64
Oil on canvas, 40 3/16 x 50 1/4 in (102.1 x 127.6 cm)
Purchased through the Paul Mellon Fund, 1980
First exhibited: Society of Artists, 1764 (no. 101)
Reference: Yale Center for British Art 1985, 56–58 (no. 76)

Hackwood Park stands to the south of Basingstoke, and the view here is from the southeast. Built by the 1st Duke of Bolton in 1683–87, the house appears in the distance to the left, small but crisply rendered, with its statue of George I (a royal gift to the 3rd Duke, showing the king as a Roman emperor on horseback) clearly visible in front. The painting was commissioned by Charles, 5th Duke, who held the title from 1758 until his untimely death, by his own hand, in 1765. The Duke's architect, John Vardy, had been making improvements to the house, altering the south front in particular, and the view may well have been painted as a record and celebration of these; perhaps there were changes in the surrounding park and farmlands also. It was probably Vardy who suggested Paul Sandby for the commission. Around the same time Sandby painted a larger view of another of the Duke of Bolton's properties, Bolton Park in Yorkshire,[1] and the two canvases in all likelihood hung as decorations in the Duke's London house at 37 Grosvenor Square — where Vardy was also in charge of a scheme of improvements. Sandby worked mostly in watercolor and gouache, and this is one of just a handful of country-house views that he painted in oils; its light, relatively even tone and slightly chalky coloring suggest those other, more familiar techniques of his, although the scale is of course much larger.

The painting gives remarkably little idea of the best known feature of Hackwood Park, which is the large classical garden created around the house by the first three Dukes of Bolton. This was laid out on French lines, with a geometric pattern of avenues, canals, and basins, as well as classical pavilions designed by James Gibbs. Sandby has taken his view from such a distance that we see nothing of all this but the parterre to the south of the house and the evenly planted row of trees along an avenue leading away to the east. Clearly it pleased the 5th Duke to regard the setting of his house as rustic rather than formal, and his choice bears witness to a general shift of taste around this time, the beginnings of the "picturesque" movement. In this respect the work stands in striking contrast to Siberechts's view of Wollaton (no. 7), where the park is marked off from nature rather than integrated. The delight in the rough informality of the country carries over into the comic depiction of the farm workers and horses in the foreground, who are taking their midday rest during wheat harvesting. To the right a man and woman have fallen asleep and another woman is dangling something from her pitchfork, perhaps a blade of grass, to tickle the man's nose. Again, Sandby brings into play something of his practice as a watercolorist, allowing himself a levity not normally found in the "higher" art of oil painting.   MW

1   Sotheby's sale, London, July 9, 1986 (no. 83).

HACKWOOD PARK.   P. SANDBY.

26 RICHARD WILSON

Dinas Bran from Llangollen, 1770–71
Oil on canvas, 71 x 96⅜ in (180.4 x 244.7 cm)
Gift of Paul Mellon, 1976
First exhibited: Royal Academy, 1771 (no. 222)
References: Constable, 175–76 (pl. 36a); Solkin, 130–32 (no. 133)

Dinas Bran is an ancient fortress that occupies the top of a steeply conical hill of slate in the valley of the river Dee in Wales, on the estate of the Myddelton family of nearby Chirk Castle. The origins of the name Dinas Bran are obscure, but it has commonly been anglicized as "Crow Castle." The present view is looking up the valley from the east, showing the hill higher than it actually is, looming majestically over the small town of Llangollen with its fourteenth-century bridge. Wilson carefully places some trees in the right foreground as a pictorial counterweight to the hill and composes his scene generally to suggest a world of easy balance and harmony, both within nature and between nature and man. The landscape is not just a pleasure to the eye, but productive: sheep graze in the middle distance; some fishermen draw in a net on the river; a family breaks off firewood from a dead tree. In the foreground the figure of the man swinging an axe introduces an heroic note, perhaps even a hint of the medieval combats we might romantically imagine to have taken place at Dinas Bran.

The work is the complementary pair to a view along the valley from the other direction, looking down from a hilltop, with the distinctive form of Dinas Bran in the far distance (also at the Yale Center for British Art). Both were commissioned from Wilson by a fellow Welshman, the young Sir Watkin Williams-Wynn, Bart., one of the richest men in Britain. Sir Watkin made his Grand Tour in 1768–69 and probably gave Wilson the commission just after coming of age in 1769. He would also employ Joshua Reynolds to paint family portraits and Paul Sandby to accompany him on a sketching tour of north Wales, and indeed was one of the most generous British patrons and collectors of the 1770s and 1780s. The countryside shown in the Wilsons was part of his homeland, and the more distant view of Dinas Bran is taken from a point on his family estate of Wynnstay. The pair was later recorded as hanging at Sir Watkin's London residence, 20 St. James's Square, which was built for him by Robert Adam in 1771–74, and in all likelihood this was the purpose for which they were painted; they served as proud reminders for Sir Watkin when he was in town, as well as for his visitors, of his place in the country and his Welsh origins. He was to make Welshness a key part of his persona and cherished the idea—which may or may not have had any real genealogical basis—that he was descended from Rhodri Mawr, a king of Wales in the ninth century. He was also involved in societies for the revival and promotion of Celtic traditions. The wild, rugged appearance of Dinas Bran perfectly suited current ideas of the Celtic spirit. All important, it dated from before the English subjugation of Wales in the later thirteenth century. There seems little doubt that, for patron and painter alike, it stood not merely as a local landmark, but as a symbol of national identity.   MW

27 JOSEPH WRIGHT, called WRIGHT OF DERBY
Blacksmith's Shop, 1771
Oil on canvas, 50½ x 42 in (128.3 x 104 cm)
Gift of Paul Mellon, 1981
First exhibited: Society of Artists, 1771 (no. 201)
References: Egerton 1990, 99–100 (no. 47); Nicolson, 1:237 (no. 199)

In an account book dating probably to the late 1760s, Wright of Derby recorded the following idea for a "Night Piece":

Two Men forming a Bar of Iron into a horse shoe – from whence the light must proceed. An Idle fellow may stand by the Anvil, in a time-killing posture, his hands in his bosom, or yawning with his hands stretched upwards – a little twisting of the Body. Horse Shoes hanging upon Ye walls, and other necessary things, faintly seen being remote from the light – Out of this Room, shall be seen another, in Wch a farier may be shoeing a horse by the light of a Candle. The horse must be Sadled and a Traveler standing by The Servant may appear with his horse in his hand – on Wch may be a portmanteau – This will be an indication of an Accident having happen'd, & shew some reason for shoeing the horse by Candle Light – The Moon may appear and illumine some part of the horse if necessary.[1]

In the *Blacksmith's Shop* he has translated these ideas into pictorial form; in fact, between 1771 and 1773, he painted three variations on this theme as well as two of the related but slightly more modern subject of workers in iron forges. Of the three paintings representing blacksmiths' shops, the Center's version most closely adheres to his original idea.

Bought by Lord Melbourne for £150 while still "on the easel" in the painter's studio, the painting is a dramatic nocturnal vision of a smithy, located in a ramshackle building whose thatched roof has fallen into disrepair, gaping open to the moonlit sky. Curiously, the building in which the three smiths work is not a simple stone edifice but what appears to be a converted religious building, most likely an abandoned church or perhaps a monastery. Throughout the countryside it was common in the eighteenth century to see such disused structures adapted into workspaces, and Wright seems to take a delight in such country pragmatism: the vestiges of a grandly appointed building, with fluted columns, arched doorways, and stone floors provide a startling setting for the hardworking blacksmiths and their apprentices. Although highly suggestive of a "real" place, painted with careful attention to detail (especially in the tools strewn about the floor or the horseshoes hanging from pins nailed into the brick wall), his smithy is imaginary. Within this intense atmosphere the smiths focus tightly on their workaday tasks, seemingly unperturbed by the late hour; theirs is a labor of dignity and force, almost heroic in its ardor.

The painting is full of religious overtones, most explicit in the angelic stone figure carved in the spandrel above the arch. The composition readily prompts comparison with nocturnal representations of the Nativity, in which figures similarly huddle together around a central object from which emanates a brilliant light, but through his substitution of the glowing Christ-child with a white-hot iron bar that the smiths hammer into a horseshoe, Wright has transformed an Adoration into an adoration of human strength and skill.

This overtly spiritual (but in no way sentimental) depiction of the ancient craft of smithery seems at odds with Wright's by-then famous paintings of more scientifically progressive subjects. In the context of his five paintings of smiths and forges, the *Blacksmith's Shop* is best understood as the exploration of the spectacle of the traditional occupation as compared to its more modern form. Rendering each method equally spectacular and heroic, Wright does not choose one above the other. Perhaps this painting—along with his other images that focus on the transformative, almost magical powers of light—can be seen as a pictorial analogy for his own labors as a painter, a testament to his own role as a visual craftsman. JMA

1 Egerton 1990, 98.

28 THOMAS GAINSBOROUGH

Landscape with Cattle and Figures, about 1773
Oil on canvas, 47¼ x 57¼ in (120 x 145.4 cm)
Gift of Paul Mellon, 1981

References: Cormack 1991, 114 (no. 42); Hayes 1982, 2:452–53 (no. 108); Waterhouse 1958, 112 (no. 890)

---

*I'm sick of Portraits and wish very much to take my Viol
da Gamba and walk off to some sweet Village when I
can paint Landskips and enjoy the fag End of Life in
quietness and ease.*

Thomas Gainsborough to William Jackson[1]

Although forced to support himself by portrait-painting, Gainsborough preferred landscape painting. He sold few of his pure landscapes, and those he did sell brought him little income. At the artist's death his obituarist Bate-Dudley remarked:

*His mind was most in its element while engaged in
landscape. These subjects he painted with a faithful
adherence to nature; and it is to be noticed they are more
in approach to the landscapes of Rubens, than to those of
any other master. At the same time we must remark, his
trees, foreground, and figures, have more force and spirit;
and we add, the brilliancy of Claude, and the simplicity
of Ruysdael, appear combined in Mr. Gainsborough's
romantic scenes.[2]*

The present picture is one of Gainsborough's most obvious tributes to the seventeenth-century master of the classical landscape, Claude Lorrain; like Claude, Gainsborough uses the lightly colored trees on one side of the canvas to lead the viewer's eye through the picture, away from the foreground and out to the far distance where the atmosphere is at its most glowingly pink and yellow. The feathery trees rise from the slope, serving to push our eye to the distant, central horizon, hazy with yellow and blue clouds that color the mountainous vista beyond. From the luminous distance our eye slowly grazes back across the canvas, tracing the opposite trail from the cattle and sheep; we wander from afar, back over the bridge in the middle distance, across the languorous, sunlit field where a shepherd tends his flock. Once in the foreground, shaded from the glowing autumnal sunlight, our eyes follow the stream back out again to the verdant pastures, above which towers a ruined castle, embedded in the landscape like a man-made rock.

A chalk study for this composition (present whereabouts unknown) differs from the painting in the placement of the cows and figures in the foreground, reminding us that these seemingly "natural" views were carefully constructed compositions. Like the earlier masters he emulated, Gainsborough methodically thought out his landscapes, making sketches outdoors and working out the final composition in his studio, often using props (including sand, cork, reflecting glass for ponds, and even broccoli for the trees) to recreate compositions in model form.

Gainsborough clearly allied his paintings with those of his illustrious predecessors, but his works record his own visions of the landscape and are at once his most personal and most academic productions. Whatever its inspiration, nature or art or both, this work, with its feathery touch, golden tone, and quaint yet majestic depiction of the land and its occupants, exemplifies Gainsborough's conception of the ideal landscape, one that Reynolds, almost begrudgingly, termed poetical.[3]
JMA

1   Woodall, 115.
2   Brenneman, 42.
3   Joshua Reynolds, Discourse XIV, 253.

29 JOSEPH WRIGHT, called WRIGHT OF DERBY
Matlock Tor by Moonlight, probably 1777–80
Oil on canvas, 24⅞ x 30 in (63 x 76 cm)
Gift of Paul Mellon, 1976

Reference: Nicolson, 1:88, 90–91, 264 (no. 308)

*I find myself continually stealing off, and getting to
Landscapes.*

Joseph Wright, 31 December 1792[1]

This painting is one of Wright's earliest pictorial explorations of the Derbyshire landscape. Before his two-year sojourn in Italy, the artist had shown little interest in landscape painting other than as a backdrop to his portraits and subject pictures. The majestic beauty of Rome and Naples, however, seems to have aroused his sensibilities to the potential of landscape as a pictorial subject in itself.

Most of his first landscapes were painted after his return to England in 1775 but were based on the sketches he had made in Italy. These showed either fantastic views of spectacular fireworks taking place in the night sky above famous Roman monuments on the Tiber, or dramatic representations of nighttime eruptions of the then-active volcano Mount Vesuvius, outside Naples. *Matlock Tor by Moonlight* marks a return to Wright's native Derbyshire, but his focus in this night landscape remains the stirring power of light on his subject.

His exploration of the effect of a full moon on Matlock Tor (known locally as such to differentiate it from Matlock High Tor) and the River Derwent lends to the picture an eerie, almost overwhelming atmosphere, one in which the mountain and river seem to awaken from a heavy slumber. He describes the heavy vegetation on the Tor with thick impasto dotted onto smooth, translucent areas of paint; the surfaces of the mountain seem to sparkle and come alive in the shadowy moonlight. Similarly, the gently rolling water of the Derwent, whose lapping waves have created the mammoth mountain beside it, seems to gain strength in the cold rays of the bright moon. Although heightening the awesome qualities of his landscape by including a small horse and rider who wonder and cower before the moon, clouds, and mountain, Wright paints an image in which the overall atmosphere is not one of foreboding evil but of cool, powerful silence.

Painted early in his career as a landscapist, this picture, along with a nearly identical version (Detroit Institute of Arts), stands at a transitional point in Wright's work. In these two versions of the same subject, he remains largely faithful to his own painterly idiom—relying on dramatic chiaroscuro effects to enliven his subjects, and painting with a sharpness of touch and tonal contrast that implies direct, almost scientific observation of the scene. Yet in the present painting Wright has toned down the spectacle. The quiet atmosphere hints at his imminent shift from the awe-inspiring, powerful mode of the Sublime so evident in his volcanic views of Italy to the lighter, brighter colors and lyrical tonalities of the Picturesque that he would use in his later English landscapes.   JMA

1   Egerton 1990, 11.

Harlech Castle, from Twgwyn Ferry, Summer's Evening Twilight, 1798–99
Oil on canvas, 34¼ x 47 in (87 x 119.5 cm)
Gift of Paul Mellon, 1977
First exhibited: Royal Academy, 1799 (no. 192)
Reference: Butlin and Joll, 6–7 (no. 9)

The thirteenth-century Harlech Castle, shown in the distance on the left, was one of the coastal strongholds built by the English king Edward I to secure his conquest of North Wales. Turner visited the castle during a sketching tour of Wales in the summer of 1798 and painted the present canvas in his London studio from drawings made on the spot. One of these he worked up in watercolor, possibly as a preparation for the painting, possibly to provide an idea of its final appearance for the patron who commissioned it, the Hon. Edward Spencer Cowper, later 5th Earl Cowper.

The painting is a study of twilight, in which the artist seems to be darkening his scene to the limit, testing how far he might go in suppressing color and detail. The process reduces much of the landscape to interlocking wedge shapes differentiated by tone and brings attention to the relatively bright light of the sunset and the gleam on the waters of the estuary, both of which are observed with an effortless acuity. Some of the most telling forms in the composition are silhouettes, with the four-square castle played off against more complicated clusters of buildings, ships and rigging, and a skeletal hull under repair in a shipyard. Turner underlined the twilight theme in both his title for the painting and the literary extract that he had printed in the catalogue when the work was first exhibited at the Royal Academy in 1799:

Now came still evening on, and twilight grey,
Had in her sober livery all things clad.
— Hesperus that led
The starry host rode brightest 'till the moon
Rising in clouded majesty unveiled her peerless light.

The lines are a freely adapted quotation from Milton's *Paradise Lost* (Book IV, lines 598–99 and 605-8), from the poet's description of night falling on the evening of Satan's first attempt, through a dream, to lead Eve into temptation. The first two lines are apt enough, but since the painting shows neither Hesperus, the evening star, nor the moon, it is unclear what the other three add.

The abstracting effect on the landscape of fading light was a preoccupation of both Claude Lorrain and Richard Wilson, the predecessors to whom Turner was looking most intensely at this early stage in his career as a painter. One reviewer of the Royal Academy exhibition, writing in the *True Briton*, recognized this highly respectable artistic lineage but feared that the young man's taste for dusk and abstraction would lead him to sacrifice his great gift for observing nature:

This Landscape, though it combines the style of CLAUDE *and of our excellent* WILSON, *yet wears an aspect of originality, that shows the painter looks at Nature with his own eyes. We advise* MR. TURNER, *however, with all our admiration of his works, not to indulge a fear of being too accurately minute, lest he should get into the habit of* indistinctness *and* confusion.[1]

The sombreness of *Harlech Castle* is more than just a matter of artistic style and tradition, however. The overall gloom and melancholy about the scene fits the historical associations of the castle, which was a symbol of the oppression and suffering of the Welsh people. The forlorn-looking group of mothers and children on the rocky promontory in the foreground, presumably waiting for the ferry, might almost represent the Welsh and Wales in microcosm. Certainly there is an end-of-the-world feeling that reflects the general image of Wales at this time as a raw, tough place, far removed from the comforts and subtleties of civilized life.   MW

1   Butlin and Joll, 7.

31 J. M. W. TURNER

Lake Avernus: Aeneas and the Cumaean Sibyl, 1814–15
Oil on canvas, 28¼ x 38¼ in (72 x 97 cm)
Gift of Paul Mellon, 1977

Reference: Butlin and Joll, 135–36 (no. 226)

The story of Aeneas and the Sibyl is from the sixth book of Virgil's *Aeneid.* The Trojan hero and his men have landed on the Italian coast at Cumae, near Naples, which is famous as a shrine to the god Apollo. Here Aeneas consults the Sibyl, Deiphobe, who serves as the god's priestess and prophetic mouthpiece. He knows that within the sacred precincts there is an entrance to the underworld, and begs the Sibyl to take him down to the nether regions to see the shade of his dead father, Anchises. The Sibyl tells him of a tree in a neighboring grove that bears a golden bough; if he breaks this off and takes it as an offering to the queen of the underworld, Proserpine, it will protect him from the perils of the journey. She leads him to a cave near Lake Avernus, named from the Greek for "birdless" since its hellish vapors supposedly killed any birds flying overhead. He makes sacrificial offerings to Proserpine and Pluto; then he and the Sibyl make their descent into the underworld, carrying the golden bough. In the Elysian Fields Aeneas meets the shade of his father, who shows him the souls of his descendants as yet unborn, the line of kings, consuls, and emperors who will rule the future Rome. As the story of a hero who braves the unknown, leaving Apollo's realm of light and sun to follow his destiny in that of Stygian gloom, this was the kind of classical legend that appealed most powerfully to the Romantic imagination.

Turner shows the Sibyl holding aloft the golden bough, gesturing toward the lake, and calling upon Aeneas to follow her: "Now, Trojan, take the way thy fates afford; / Assume thy courage, and unsheathe thy sword" (from the translation by Dryden, which Turner probably used). A couple of his men and a priest are making a burnt offering, presumably part of the sacrifices to Proserpine and Pluto. In the shadows to the right, a foretaste of the darkness of the underworld, the relief carved on a piece of fallen masonry represents the parallel story of the twelfth labor of Hercules, in which the hero descends into the underworld to bring back the monstrous three-headed guard-dog Cerberus. The view over the lake is from the north side looking south. The ruins on the edge of the lake to the left were believed in Turner's time to be an ancient temple of Apollo, but are in fact Roman baths. The large building in the distance on the right is the Castle of Baiae; and the island visible on the horizon is Capri. The fall of light indicates late afternoon or early evening: Aeneas prepares to enter the darkness of the underworld just as darkness encroaches on the world above.

As the second version of a picture of more or less the same size, painted in about 1798, this is a rare instance of Turner's repeating himself.[1] He had never seen Lake Avernus (he was to make his first visit to Italy in 1819–20) and based the first version on a topographical drawing by Sir Richard Colt Hoare of Stourhead, Wiltshire. Hoare was a lover of Italy and the Antique, and as a child had watched his grandfather Henry Hoare create the magnificent classical gardens at Stourhead, with their lake and temples—including one dedicated to Apollo. As well as providing the drawing, Hoare may actually have commissioned the first version of *Lake Avernus,* probably to hang as a pendant to a view of Lake Nemi by Richard Wilson that was already at Stourhead: the canvases are close in size; they deal with related subjects—Lake Nemi was associated with Apollo's sister Diana—and the Turner was obviously intended as an imitation of Wilson's style.[2] The exact chain of events is a matter for speculation, but we know that Hoare did commission this, the second version, and that it did hang as a pendant to the Wilson at Stourhead. Perhaps there was an exchange in which Turner took back the first version—which would explain why it was in his studio at his death and became part of the Turner Bequest (Tate Gallery). Certainly the second version represents the artist more impressively than the first; with its brighter palette and wonderfully subtle effects of aerial perspective, it typifies his artistic development around the middle of his career. MW

1 See Butlin and Joll, 24–25 (no. 34).
2 For the Wilson, see Solkin, 192–93 (no. 77).

The British Persona

PORTRAITURE LIES at the heart of British art. The roots of its particular success lay in the sixteenth century, when a rising tide of humanism combined with the forces of religious reform. Beginning with the ardent iconoclasm of the Protestant Reformation, artists in England had largely to forego the traditional religious, mythological, and allegorical subjects that were so central to painting in Roman Catholic Europe; these all smacked of idolatry or popery. The most accomplished artists specialized in portraiture and were well rewarded.

From the standards set by artists such as Holbein and Hilliard in their hieratic, decorative, and often propagandistic portraits of Henry VIII and Elizabeth I, the genre evolved over the next century — primarily through the examples set by van Dyck and Lely — into something more fluid, colorful, and lively. Eighteenth-century sitters saw themselves portrayed in finery fit for kings, their bodies larger than life. Flattered by overt or implicit comparison to gods, muses, military heroes, and intellectual geniuses, they gathered at the annual exhibitions of the Royal Academy (from 1769 onward) to see their portraits on display, their identities only slightly disguised by titles such as "Portrait of a Lady." Participants in and spectators of a sort of parlor game of national dimension, artists and sitters colluded in their transformation of edenic Britain into a modern-day Olympus, at the summit of which were displayed their beauty, creativity, and wealth.

Joshua Reynolds, more than any other, led the campaign to raise portraiture and its reputation from that of a "mill-horse business," lucrative yet intensely confining, to an important Grand Style. In his lectures to the Royal Academy he articulated his belief that portraits should strive not to expose "all the minute breaks and peculiarities" but to "ennoble the character of a countenance" and create likeness "more in taking the general air, than in observing the exact similiture of every feature."[1] Whereas Reynolds preferred to avoid the details of modern dress and to present his sitters in roles and costumes, Thomas Gainsborough sought to capture them in their more fashionable outfits and natural settings. Nonetheless, he too bathed his sitters in a glowing, flattering light; they emerge from the canvas with a glamor that transcends ordinary human appearances.

Despite our urge to discern the sitters' true personalities in these likenesses, they are only as true as masks; what we see is a persona, designed for public consumption. Glorious and shimmering visions of their era, the sitters happily toy with our perceptions of them and their characters. Like Mrs. Abington, who so coyly confuses her audience by posing for her portrait not as herself but "in character," the men and women in these portraits appear only partially as they were—yet fully as they wished to be. JMA

1 Joshua Reynolds, Discourse IV, 72 and 59.

James Caulfield, 4th Viscount Charlemont (later 1st Earl of Charlemont), 1753–56

Oil on canvas, 38½ x 29 in (97.7 x 73.6 cm)

Gift of Paul Mellon, 1974

Reference: Clark and Bowron, 39 and 265 (no. 190)

If Lord Cholmondeley goes to Rome, pray tell him
I wish he would bring me a head of himself by
Pompeio Battoni.

Horace Walpole to Horace Mann, 1771 [1]

As Horace Walpole's comment suggests, Pompeo Batoni was the portraitist of choice for young British men on the Grand Tour in the second half of the eighteenth century. In the 1730s and 1740s he had made his name primarily as a painter of historical and religious subjects, but his portraits catapulted him into the ranks of the most famous European artists of his time.

James Caulfield, born in Dublin in 1728, became the 4th Viscount Charlemont at the death of his father in 1734. He left his home in Ireland in 1746 for his Grand Tour, a voyage on the European continent that mainly consisted of a lengthy stay in Italy and had become by mid-century a mandatory element of a British gentleman's education. Charlemont's Grand Tour was extensive: from 1746 until his return in 1754, he traveled throughout Italy visiting, among other places, Naples, Florence, and Turin; outside Italy he explored the major archeological sites of classical Antiquity in Greece, the Levant, and Egypt. His main base throughout his Grand Tour was, of course, Rome, where he was an integral part of British social and artistic circles. This portrait was apparently commissioned sometime in the early 1750s. By 1754 he had returned to Dublin and, in October of that year, he began a distinguished career as a politician, soon making a name for himself as one of the leading champions for Ireland's peaceful emancipation from England. He was made 1st Earl of Charlemont in 1763.

Batoni's progress on the portrait is documented in letters to Charlemont from his agent John Parker:

26 July 1754: Pompeo has not finished nor can I get the portrait out of his hands; he is paid half of the great one.
24 December 1755: Pompeo…had promised me to get [the portraits] *done by such a day and failed me…*
I have so tormented him since, as there is little to doe to them, so hope in a few days to send them, together with the rest of your Lordship's pictures.
28 February 1756: I have just got your Lordship's two portraits from Pompeo, I shall forward them with the rest of the pictures. [2]

Batoni frequently painted variously-sized versions of his portraits, which young Tourists often gave away as spectacular mementos of their travels, and it is likely that the "great one" Parker refers to was a full-length, more elaborate version of the present work.

One of Batoni's first specifically "Grand Tour" portraits, this is also the earliest known composition in which he included a view of the Roman Colosseum—seen here through a window in the upper right corner of the canvas. After this painting Batoni's formula for Grand Tour portraits became increasingly static: most often dressed in their finest "Italian" clothes, Tourists were surrounded by overwhelming vistas of the recognizable sites of the Roman landscape, by famous antiquities, and, occasionally, by some of the works of art (either antique or modern) that they had purchased. Although Charlemont did not bring home the Colosseum, he was an avid collector of ancient and modern works of art; through his patronage he greatly contributed to the understanding of Antiquity and, by extension, to the development of art and architecture in mid- to late-eighteenth-century England and Ireland. JMA

1 Clark and Bowron, 42.
2 Ibid., 265.

33 ALLAN RAMSAY

Lady in a Pink Silk Dress, about 1762
Oil on canvas, 30 x 25⅜6 in (76.2 x 64 cm)
Gift of Paul Mellon, 1981

References: Smart SNPG 1992, 152 (no. 106); Smart YUP 1992, 237

Mr Reynolds and Mr Ramsay can scarce be rival, their manners are so different. The former is bold and has a kind of tempestuous colouring…the latter is all delicacy. Mr Reynolds seldom succeeds in women, Mr Ramsay is formed to paint them.

Horace Walpole, 1759[1]

Allan Ramsay's portrait of a young woman leaning pensively on a parapet and looking wistfully out at the viewer is one of his most striking. Combining a delicacy of costume and pose with a realistic treatment of the sitter's features, Ramsay imparts to her an arrestingly bold yet quiet beauty. In capturing the very idiosyncrasies of the young woman's face, he conveys the immediacy of her quiet charm—her square jaw, her cleft chin, and especially her thin lips, the upper of which droops down at its center as if to indicate a slight overbite. Her large eyes openly entice and beguile; they are, as a Frenchman once said of English women's eyes, "not so sparkling as melting."[2]

Ramsay's exploitation of the evocative powers of his sitters' facial particularities is at the heart of his immense success as a portraitist. Like his close friend and colleague William Hogarth, he sought to use the individual physiognomies of his subjects to evince character. Unlike that of Hogarth, however, his realism was heavily tempered by his affinities for the soft, delicate lines, surfaces and tones of the French Rococo. Artists like François Boucher, in his portraits of Madame de Pompadour, or Jean-Marc Nattier, in his of Louis XV's daughters, used the delicate, fine, and luxurious fabrics and textures of their sitters' clothing and hair adornments to evoke the sensuality of the women they were painting. Similarly, Ramsay revels in the transformation of paint into lace, silk, and flowers; every precious detail of the young woman's clothing reflects her beauty. Not only showing his French sensibilities, this portrait also hints at the artist's growing awareness of and impending rivalry with Joshua Reynolds, who in 1759 had used this same pose in his portrait of Miss Kitty Fisher (National Trust, Petworth).

Despite its references to other contemporary works, this image remains intensely personal. Some have suggested that the sitter is the painter's daughter Amelia, who was born in 1755; if so, the painting would presumably date from about 1772. The young woman's dress and hairstyle are very much in accordance with the fashions of the early 1760s, however, and the portrait closely resembles in style and format other of Ramsay's female portraits of that earlier date   JMA

1   Shawe-Taylor, 104.
2   Ribeiro, 56 .

34 THOMAS GAINSBOROUGH

Mary Little, later Lady Carr, about 1763
Oil on canvas, 50 x 40 in (127 x 101.6 cm)
Bequest of Mrs. Henry Payne Bingham, 1987

References: Cormack 1991, 76 (no. 23); Waterhouse 1958, 58 (no. 120)

This painting may have been commissioned to celebrate the marriage of Mary Little to Robert Carr, who became a baronet in 1777 on the death of his brother. Mrs. Carr, as she would have been called previous to that year, displays her well-adjusted and adorned figure to advantage, and her portrait clearly takes as its inspiration images of seventeenth-century English beauties by van Dyck and Lely. Like his predecessors, Gainsborough flatters the proportions and beauty of Mrs. Carr by setting off her features with the various fabrics and textures of her attire.

Her translucent white hands and face are indeed complemented by her dress and its accessories: her black-lace ribbon necklace, the transparent lace-edged kerchief over her breast, the elaborate tiers of lace cuffs and bows, and the radiantly textured pink silk. Gainsborough (whose sisters were milliners and whose father was a weaver) favored this type of pink silk, a glossy taffeta called lute-string or lustring, since it created flattering comparisons between the colors of the sitter's dress and the rosy tints of her complexion. The artist gives life and depth to Mrs. Carr's flesh — particularly in her left hand, modeled with flecks of greens, whites, and pinks — and draws a pictorial analogy between her skin and the leaves and petals of the spring bouquet she holds at her breast.

Unlike Reynolds — who painted his sitters unadorned by the trappings of contemporary clothing so as to emphasize the timeless qualities of their characters —

Gainsborough revels in the depiction of Mary Carr's stylish dress, a sort that was popular in England during the 1760s. A *sacque* (or *robe à la française*), her gown has voluminous pleated panels of fabric attached at the shoulder blades that fall down in a train over the back of her skirt. Her bodice is decorated with three-tiered lace ruffles and bows, and some of the flowers at her breast may even be held there in a small vase inserted into her bodice. Her twin pearl bracelets match the larger pearls woven into her unpowdered hair and in her pompon, a decorative hair ornament that moved and shimmered whenever the wearer moved her head. These details of her costume add what Gainsborough called the "variety of lively touches and surprizing Effects to make the Heart dance…[the] Lustre and finishing [that] bring it up to individual Life."[1] Here, the artist's virtuoso rendering of the sumptuous fabrics of her dress are all the more appropriate since Mary Little's future husband was a prosperous mercer.

This painting belongs stylistically to a group of female portraits Gainsborough painted in Bath during the early 1760s. As such, it evinces the transformation in his work that occurred upon his move in 1759 to that city, where, on the whole, his clients were wealthier and lived more luxuriously than his patrons from Ipswich.
JMA

1 Woodall, 97.

96

Mrs. Abington as Miss Prue in Love for Love *by William Congreve*, 1771
Oil on canvas, 30¼ x 25⅛ in (76.8 x 63.7 cm)
Gift of Paul Mellon, 1977
First exhibited: Royal Academy, 1771 (no. 161)
References: Graves and Cronin, 1:4; Penny, 246–47 (no. 78); Waterhouse 1941, 61

When this portrait was shown as *Portrait of a Lady* at the third annual exhibition of the Royal Academy in 1771, Horace Walpole noted that it was "easy and very like."[1] Walpole's comment, which he accompanied with the epithet "Actress," proves that he immediately recognized the painting as a portrait of his friend, the comic actress Mrs. Abington. Indeed, since Mrs. Abington was one of London's most famous actresses, it seems unlikely that the identity of the anonymous "Lady" went unrecognized by many, if any, of the visitors to the Royal Academy that year.

Mrs. Abington was born Frances—or Fanny—Barton in 1737. Called "Nosegay Fan," she began her career as a flower girl and street singer but continually strove to better herself, learning to speak and read French and Italian. Making her stage debut in London in 1755 at the Haymarket, she became a year later a member of the Drury Lane company, then under the direction of David Garrick. In 1759 she married her music-master, James Abington, from whom she was to separate in 1763, paying him an annuity to keep his distance from her and her career. She left London in the mid-1760s for Ireland, where she hoped to rise to greater fame. Her five-year Irish sojourn did indeed prove successful, and when she returned to Drury Lane it was at the direct and pressing behest of Garrick himself.

She first performed the role of Miss Prue from Congreve's Restoration comedy *Love for Love* in December 1769 and again at least five times before the end of the season in 1770. Although a relatively small role, her performance as the ingénue delighted her audiences and cemented her comeback to the London stage.

In choosing to paint Mrs. Abington as Miss Prue, Reynolds pays tribute both to her success in that particular role and, more generally, to her abilities as an actress. Although belonging to the more intimate, small-format female portraits popular in the early 1760s, this painting contrasts with those more "personal" images by confusing the identity of his sitter: the artist depicts not simply Mrs. Abington but Mrs. Abington in her role of the naïve and awkward country girl Miss Prue. The portrait straddles the line between what was commonly called an "historical picture," one whose associations extended beyond the sitter's physical likeness, and a straightforward portrait. Immensely recognizable as a likeness of the actress, the image comes alive with references to her role: is this the scene where the lusty Tattle seduces the silly country maiden, or is it that in which she meets Ben Legend, the seaman to whom she is to be betrothed? Certainly, the conflation of sitter and character allows Reynolds to enliven his canvas by showing Mrs. Abington as leaning on the back of a Chippendale chair—a pose appropriate only for the uncouth Miss Prue. This ambiguity of identity adds vigor to the portrait—and ultimately to Mrs. Abington's likeness—and would have delighted visitors to the Royal Academy exhibitions who reveled in such pictorial games.

Reynolds painted this image of Mrs. Abington over the course of at least ten sittings in the spring of 1771. An entry in his sitters book of that year indicates that on March 1 the "Ruffles of the Picture" were supplied; it seems likely that, because of his close friendship with Mrs. Abington, Reynolds painted much of the dress and setting himself, contrary to his normal studio practice in which he would leave these lesser parts of portraits to be completed by his assistants. JMA

1 Graves, 6: 271.

William Johnstone-Pulteney, later 5th Baronet, about 1772

Oil on canvas, 93½ x 59 in (237.5 x 149.8 cm)

Gift of Paul Mellon, 1981

First exhibited: possibly Royal Academy, 1772 (no. 96)

References: Cormack 1991, 110 (no. 40); Waterhouse 1958, 86 (no. 565)

Mr. Pulteney, as he was commonly known in Bath, appears to have sat for this portrait a number of times; in an undated letter, probably of 1772, Gainsborough wrote to inform his client of his progress on the work:

> *I think we could still finish a little higher, to great advantage, if it would not be intruding too much upon your good nature to bestow one more little sitting of about half an hour…I am fired with the thoughts of Mrs. Pulteney is giving me leave to send you to the Royal Exhibition, and of making a good Portrait of you.*[1]

It is possible, as this letter suggests, that Gainsborough exhibited the picture at the 1772 Royal Academy as "Portrait of a Gentleman."

Although deeply rooted within the tradition of English full-length portraiture—Gainsborouth looked to van Dyck for inspiration—this portrait is clearly of its own age. Gainsborough was acutely aware of the potential excesses he considered inherent in contemporary conventions of the full-length, and he exclaimed to his friend the actor David Garrick:

> *There is certainly a false taste & an impudent style prevailing which if Vandyke was living would put him out of countenance; and I think even his work would appear so opposed to such a glare. Nature is modest and the artist should be so in his addresses to Her.*[2]

Gainsborough paints Pulteney with none of the "false taste &…impudent style" that he feared in portraits of its kind, and it is, above all, the sitter's dignity and modesty that he captures. As Malcolm Cormack has pointed out, the painting conveys visually the qualities described in Pulteney's obituary of 1805:

> *Under a forbidding exterior and still more neglected or almost threadbare dress which he usually wore, he manifested a strong sense, a masculine understanding, and very independent as well as very upright principles of action.*[3]

Born in 1729 in Westerhall, Dumfries (Scotland), William Johnstone was the third son of Sir James John-

stone, 4th Baronet; he became 5th Baronet in 1794. As a young man he moved in Scottish intellectual circles, and among his friends were Adam Smith and David Hume. Without an inheritance to speak of, he pursued a career as an advocate at the Scottish bar. In 1760 he married Frances Pulteney, heiress to the Pulteney estates through her relationship to the Earls of Bath; in 1767, when she succeeded to her lands and wealth, he added the Pulteney name to his own. Though living mainly in Bath from this time onwards, he sat as Member of Parliament for Cromartyshire from 1768 to 1774 and for Shrewsbury from 1775 to 1805.

As a man of "upright principles of action," Pulteney ardently supported the American colonies in their bid against taxation without representation; nonetheless, he steadfastly promoted continuing union with the colonies and eventually met with Benjamin Franklin in Paris in 1778 in a futile attempt to find a peaceful solution to the conflict. His interest in the colonies' fate stemmed from his ownership of over a million acres of land between Lake Ontario and the Pennsylvania border.

Vocal and active not only in politics, Pulteney financed projects of artistic and scientific merit in Bath and beyond. In 1790, for instance, he helped to fund the first Chair of Agriculture at Edinburgh University. Closer to home, he continuously, though not always successfully, funded major projects of urban development. At the same time this portrait was being painted, in fact, he was deeply involved with the planning and building of Pulteney Bridge, one of Bath's most significant landmarks and a monument to the Neoclassical vision of its architects, Robert and James Adam.   JMA

1   Woodall, 127.
2   Ibid., 63.
3   Cormack 1991, 110.

37 JOSHUA REYNOLDS

Miss Mary Hickey, mainly 1773

Oil on canvas, 30³/₁₆ x 25¹/₁₆ in (76.8 x 63.7 cm)

Gift of Paul Mellon, 1976

References: Graves and Cronin, 2:465; Waterhouse 1941, 63

Miss Hickey first sat to Reynolds on February 28, 1769, around the time he was working on a portrait of her father, Joseph Hickey, friend and legal advisor to the philosopher Edmund Burke. Only in 1773, however, did the artist seriously undertake painting this image, and she sat again five times in August of that year.

Despite its completion in or around 1773, her portrait belongs to the group of bust-length images of women Reynolds painted throughout the 1760s, and as such it stands in contrast to his grander, so-called historical or Grand Manner portraits in which sitters were shown in dress and attitudes removed from their everyday lives. He had experimented with such relaxed attitudes in his portraits from the outset of his career, especially when painting his friends and colleagues, such as Kitty Fisher or Catherine Moore, wife of the architect William Chambers. His likeness of Mary Hickey captures her individuality largely through its intimate format, her relaxed pose, and her frontal, yet non-confrontational gaze. Her manner, as she comfortably leans on a carved pedestal, is at once casual and art-historical, bringing to mind Renaissance and Baroque portraits by artists such as Titian or Frans Hals as well as examples by more contemporary Continental painters like François Boucher.

The intimacy of the portrait is heightened by Reynolds's use of light and shadow to accentuate his sitter's features; the dabs of light on the tip of her nose and lower lip, for instance, draw the viewer's eyes quickly to her smooth white cheek and rosy lips. Reynolds increases the power of Hickey's coy glance by shading her eyes with the brim of her white satin hat, a technique that again has clear art-historical precedents, including, especially, Rembrandt's 1633 portrait of his wife, Saskia

(Dresden). But like Hickey's pose, her supremely fashionable hat—similar to that which Mrs. Browne wears in Wheatley's portrait of the Browne family (no. 19)—contributes to the painting's aura of immediacy. A writer in the *Gentleman's Magazine* in 1776 noted the alluring—if somewhat comical—aspect of such headgear:

Hats that only shew the chin
And the mouth's bewitching grin.[1]

Indeed, all of the trimmings and accessories of her outfit serve to intensify the overall painterly effect of the picture and, by extension, her beauty.

Painting as much an essay in texture as a portrait, Reynolds revels in the vigorous and nervous lines and folds of the black silk of her hooded cloak and the sinuous curves of her clasped fingers within their gray gloves. He uses the sensuality of the painted fabrics to augment the vibrancy of the white flesh against which they rest. Especially evocative are the delicate black silk string sweeping sensuously against her chest and dangling a small gold ring at her breast and the hint of white lace sleeve peeping out from under her cloak where her glove begins. As opposed to his historical portraits, this image has an emphatic presence that commands a direct response from the viewer. Nonetheless, it does project an air of atmospheric remoteness, a quality inherent in many of Reynolds's portraits, one his pupil and biographer James Northcote described as "a vagueness that gives them a visionary and romantic character, and makes them seem like dreams or vivid recollections of persons we have seen."[2]   JMA

1 Cunnington and Cunnington, 355.
2 Shawe-Taylor, 108.

Charles Stanhope, 3rd Earl of Harrington, 1782
Oil on canvas, 93 x 56½ in (236.2 x 143.5 cm)
Gift of Paul Mellon, 1977
First exhibited: Royal Academy 1783 (no. 193)
References: Allen 1986; Graves and Cronin, 2:437–38; Waterhouse 1941, 74

This was the only full-length portrait Reynolds exhibited at the Royal Academy in 1783, a year in which his contribution to the annual exhibition was affected both in size and reception by his having suffered a paralytic stroke in November 1782. Although his recovery was rapid, critics were quick to find evidence of his declining health in his work. This painting, for instance, underwent close scrutiny from visitors to the exhibition, despite the fact that much had been completed well before his stroke, the sittings having taken place in the summer of 1782. It elicited fervent and diverse reactions. One critic proclaimed in the *London Courant*:

> [The] *portrait, No. 193, of Lord Harrington (as we hear) is the worst production we have seen of Sir Joshua's; the head is a frightful dirty daubing; the figure is badly drawn — on the whole it looks like a devil hunted, escaping from the infernal regions, which appear too hot to hold him.*

An ardent supporter retorted:

> [I] *was both surprised and shocked at a paragraph in the "London Courant" on Friday — a criticism on one of the finest productions of Sir Joshua Reynolds! who has long shone the brightest luminary of the heaven-born of painting…and must the greatest ornament of the present Exhibition, the portrait of Lord Harrington, be fixed on as a proper object on which to vent all his "proud spite and burning envy"?*

Another critic praised the portrait as:

> *a noble, striking, and capital whole length of Lord Harrington in armour, in which the dignity of the hero is agreeably softened by the elegance of the gentleman. The attitude is bold, animated, and natural.*

The same writer did remark, nonetheless, on the presence of "a sort of brown tinge [that] pervades the armour, which gives an unfinished appearance to the whole."[1]

Charles Stanhope, the eldest son of the rakish William, 2nd Earl of Harrington, returned to England in the spring of 1782 from America, where he had served under General John Burgoyne in the American Revolutionary War. Although he had been deeply involved in the embarrassment of the decisive British defeat at the Battle of Saratoga, Harrington was exonerated of any guilt in the action; in fact, on his return to England he was promoted to colonel and an aide-de-camp to the king. It is likely that he commissioned this portrait to commemorate both his rise in military rank and his succession to the earldom, an event that had taken place while he had been in America.

The presence of the black slave may allude to the sitter's military service in Jamaica (where, before his return to England, he had formed a regiment intended to protect the island from an expected attack from the French); but it is first and foremost a direct tribute to seventeenth-century conventions of full-length portraiture, particularly those of van Dyck, who often included black servants in his portraits. Reynolds's debt to van Dyck in this portrait is manifest and multifold: the striding posture of Harrington, his powerful and aspiring gaze, and the battle raging in the hazy background all find their sources among van Dyck's portraits of Caroline military figures; like many of these men, Harrington does not wear his contemporary uniform but antiquated armor that romantically likens him to a legendary hero.
JMA

1 Graves and Cronin, 2:437.

39 JOHN SINGLETON COPLEY

Richard Heber, 1782
Oil on canvas, 65¼ x 51³⁄₁₆ in (165.7 x 130 cm)
Purchased through the Paul Mellon Fund, 1979

References: Neff, 126 (no. 13); Prown 1966, 294–95, 422

With his long hair and loose shirt, and holding his jacket nonchalantly over his arm, the eight-year-old Richard Heber shows the signs of that "naturalness" that was such a desideratum of British portraiture toward the end of the eighteenth century. The paraphernalia of cricket underlines the idea that this is a boy who enjoys healthy sport and the outdoors. Looking fearlessly toward the bowler's end, leaning on his bat and holding the ball—which means that play cannot start until he chooses—he strikes a pose that combines ease with control.

The portrait was commissioned by the boy's father, the Reverend Reginald Heber, Rector of Malpas in Cheshire, a well-to-do, intellectually-minded clergyman who had been a Fellow of Brasenose College, Oxford. Richard's mother, Mary Baylie, had died shortly after his birth. At about the time the portrait was painted, in the summer of 1782, the father remarried; it is tempting to speculate that the two events were in some way connected, although exactly how remains elusive. Despite the references to cricket in the portrait, there is no record of any athletic tendency on the part of the sitter, and the ruling passion of his life was to be the distinctly indoor pursuit of book collecting. Even at the age of eight, when he posed for the portrait, he had not only books but enough of a collector's mentality to have compiled a catalogue of them. He was to be one of the leading bibliophiles of his generation, dubbed by his friend Walter Scott "Heber the magnificent, whose library and cellar are so superior to all others in the world."[1] From his father he inherited estates in Shropshire and Yorkshire. He represented Oxford University in Parliament from 1821 to 1826 and in 1824 was one of the founders of the Athenæum Club. His search for rare volumes, especially editions of English poetry and drama

of the sixteenth and seventeenth centuries, led him to travel widely at home and abroad. In addition to his country properties he owned houses in London, Oxford, Paris, Brussels, Antwerp, and Ghent. When he died, unmarried, in 1833, these were found to contain a total of some 150,000 volumes. Heber is credited with the saying: "No gentleman can be without three copies of a book: one for show, one for use, and one for borrowers."[2]

From the cricketing point of view, perhaps the most intriguing feature of the portrait is the wicket with its bail dislodged, which is difficult to explain or interpret. Surely the artist would not have wished to imply that Heber has been bowled out. Perhaps the previous batsman has been bowled, and he is the next man in, although he would be unlikely to be holding his jacket if that were the case. In the end, the portrait hardly stands up to such a literal, narrative reading and was probably never intended to show a particular moment in a game. As the implausible setting of woods and stream makes clear, the boy's cricketing is notional rather than actual. The cricketing objects are included more as emblems, like the attributes of a saint in an altarpiece, and the wicket may be shown with its bail down only to signal its function in a general sense. It may even be down for purely compositional reasons: in other words, because the artist felt that a diagonal would work better than a horizontal at this point in his design. It is just possible, however, that it is biographical, the image of a motherless childhood: dependent on his father as a single parent, the boy is like a dislodged bail leaning on a single stump.   MW

1 *Dictionary of National Biography*, 9:357.
2 Ibid., 358.

40 THOMAS LAWRENCE

Lord Granville Leveson-Gower, later 1st Earl Granville, begun 1804

Oil on canvas, 94 x 57 in (238.8 x 144.8 cm)

Gift of Paul Mellon, 1981

References: Garlick, 224 (no. 488); Levey, 44–45 (no. 20)

This portrait, painted by Lawrence during a time of personal and professional crisis, embodies his ability to channel his almost fevered sensibility into his art. His voluptuous handling of the paint on the canvas, combined with the virtuosity in his treatment of the various fabrics (fur, silk, linen) and the accessories of the setting, become themselves representative of his sitter's status, importance, and character; as with van Dyck's portraits of Caroline royalty and nobility two centuries earlier, the richness of the paint surface is used to express and to symbolize the aristocracy of the person portrayed. Lawrence's affinities with van Dyck extend both to his composition (which features a column that stabilizes and aggrandizes the subject, as well as a red velvet curtain pulled back to reveal a dramatic broad landscape) and to his use of the particularities of contemporary dress to evoke the sitter's immediate presence. Leveson-Gower's red silk watch-fob, peeking out from below his waistcoat, along with his gold pinkie ring, are intimate and personal reminders of his individuality — these are the "minute breaks and peculiarities" Reynolds sought to wipe from his own portraits in order to give them "the acquired dignity taken from general nature."[1] Although adhering to the traditions of full-length portraits from van Dyck to Reynolds, the painting of Leveson-Gower is firmly of the Romantic Era: the overall aloof expression and attitude of the sitter (whose pose openly recalls that of the *Marble Faun,* an ancient Roman copy of an earlier Greek sculpture) combine with the melodramatic light effects that play around his figure to convey a sense of inner darkness worthy of a Byronic hero.

Born in Bristol in 1773, Lord Granville Leveson-Gower was the third and youngest son of the 1st Marquess of Stafford. His familial and aristocratic connections enabled him to move in political circles from an early age, and in 1800 he was appointed a Lord of the Treasury. In 1804 he became a member of the Privy Council, and in July of that year he was made Ambassador Extraordinary to St. Petersburg. It is likely that this appointment prompted the commission of this portrait.

Lawrence had the work well under way and perhaps almost finished by November of that year. Lady Bessborough, the sitter's longtime mistress and mother of his illegitimate daughter, wrote to him that month: "Lawrence told me (perhaps by way of flattery) that your Picture had given him more pleasure than any he ever painted."[2] It was still not ready by May 1805, however, and the sitter's mother wrote her son expressing great consternation at the delay:

> I have not got your Picture. Lawrence has not touch'd it since you left England; he pays no Attention to my repeated Messages. He is accused of constantly keeping all the Pictures that are pay'd for, and of sending those unpay'd Home to receive the Money when they are finish'd. That is a sad illiberal way of going on.[3]

Indeed, the portrait was still in Lawrence's studio in Greek Street as late as 1806, by which time the painter's banker Thomas Coutts had compiled an inventory of his studio that lists this portrait alongside the sum of £147 (140 guineas) — the same figure that appears with other paintings of similar size still in Lawrence's possession. It is not clear whether this was the sum already paid to Lawrence, the sum owed on the picture, or (as is most probable) the total price to be paid. In any case, a year after making her irritated comments about Lawrence's lax and unprofessional business practices, Lady Stafford had clearly not received the painting. And, from notes in the painter Joseph Farington's diary of 1809 indicating that he had recently seen Leveson-Gower at the painter's studio, one may speculate that even by that late date the work was not yet finished.   JMA

1   Joshua Reynolds, Discourse IV, 72.
2   Leveson-Gower, 1:494.
3   Ibid., 2:66.

Sport and the Noble Beast

LIKE THE CONVERSATION PIECE, the sporting picture has been a British specialty. Among the aristocracy and gentry of the eighteenth century the ownership of fine horses was a mark of status second only to the ownership of land. The sports of horse racing, hunting, and shooting were considered healthy and dignified pursuits for the gentleman, and the breeding of horses seemed especially apt as the occupation of those who were themselves supposedly the product of good breeding. For a ruling class the masterful horsemanship on which they prided themselves carried the right associations too. It was natural that the gentleman should have himself painted as the sporting gentleman, and immortalize his most prized four-legged possessions in portraits of their own. The portraiture of animals could take on a character and nobility equal to that of humans, a reflection of the Protestant Briton's openness to the idea of animals having souls.

This was a boom period for sports, fostered on the one hand by the increasing wealth and leisure time of the upper classes, and on the other by the growing belief in nature and the outdoor life as ennobling influences. The early part of the eighteenth century brought important innovations in horse-breeding techniques, which made for more powerful thoroughbreds and more thrilling races. It was also the great age of foxhunting, which developed as a microcosm of British society: it allowed anyone to take part, provided they could afford to subscribe to one of the various hunts around the country, yet maintained strict rules of decorum and class distinction.

The towering figure in British sporting art is George Stubbs, who raised the painting of animals—the lion and zebra as well as the horse and hound—to a higher plane of expression. His achievement stands alongside Wilson's in landscape and Reynolds's in portraiture, part of a remarkable coming of age of the supposedly lesser branches of painting. It was in these and not the "high" art of history painting that British artists made their greatest contributions.   MW

41 JOHN WOOTTON

The Duke of Rutland's Bonny Black, probably 1715
Oil on canvas, 30 x 48½ in (76.2 x 123.2 cm)
Gift of Paul Mellon, 1981

Reference: Egerton 1978, 11–12 (no. 12)

Wootton was one of the first artists to paint scenes from the Newmarket races, and in this portrait of Bonny Black, a prize-winning mare, he captures the lively spirit of the race in its early eighteenth-century form: in the distance a horse runs the course on the heath; to the right a group of gentlemen cluster around a mounted jockey (likely himself a gentleman racer); and before the viewer Bonny Black's majestic figure looms large as her jockey proudly leads her to the rubbing-down house.

Racing had gained popularity as an exciting sport, pastime, even a business, over the course of the seventeenth century. In large part because of its flat, open landscape, Newmarket Heath had risen to prominence as one of the best hunting and racing grounds in the country. Charles II's love of the thrill of horse racing turned what was formerly a sleepy town into a mecca for aficionados, and by Wootton's time it was the proving ground for any thoroughbred in search of fame. Bonny Black's reputation was made on the Heath, and in an inscription in a second version of this painting (Wimpole Hall, Cambridgeshire) Wootton carefully recorded her successes there:

> *at four years old and a half She won ye Prince's gold cup att Newmarket against Mares of Six years old and a half. After that she won two Gold Cups against Mares of her own Age.*[1]

No doubt these wins prompted her owner, the Duke of Rutland, to have her portrait painted.

The artist first painted Bonny Black, most likely in life-size, in 1711; that year the accounts of Belvoir Castle, the Duke of Rutland's seat, indicate that he was paid £40 for a portrait of the mare. The present painting postdates this larger portrait and corresponds in date with the version at Wimpole Hall, which was painted in 1715 for the artist's great patron Edward, Lord Harley. It is an example of the ostensibly "realistic" race scenes, gaining in popularity, that were painted as documentary records of the victorious horses — prized and beloved — at the sites of their successes. Wootton's composition shows his subject to advantage; he frames his image tightly around the deep black thoroughbred, unsaddled, unbridled, and nearly entirely in profile. The majesty of the animal comes across in its graceful step, its velvety smooth sheen, and its grand yet sleek figure. Wootton gives to Bonny Black an almost human presence: her amusingly animated expression engages the viewer, while the boisterous jockey, unaware of any others save his mare, leads her away with the aid of only a light stable rubber. The artist's attention to the mare's body, coat, and movements highlights the impeccable pedigree that lay at the root of her racing prowess. The rise in the popularity of horse racing was concomitant with a growing preoccupation with the art (and science) of breeding. Fine thoroughbreds such as Bonny Black were expensive investments and prize possessions, and their portraits commemorated not only their own successful careers but also the wealth and racing acumen of their owners.   JMA

1   Egerton 1978, 11.

42 GEORGE STUBBS

Zebra, 1762–63
Oil on canvas, 40½ x 50¼ in (103 x 127.5 cm)
Gift of Paul Mellon, 1981
First exhibited: Society of Artists, 1763 (no. 121)
References: Egerton 1984, 112 (no. 77); MacClintock

The *Zebra* is possibly the first, and arguably the most beautiful, of the documentary studies of exotic species that Stubbs painted alongside his better known sporting pictures and fantastic scenes of horses attacked by lions. Typically, he brought to the subject the detailed anatomical knowledge he had gained through his dissections of horses, as well as habits of painstaking inquiry, observation, and drawing from nature. The result is an image of objectivity and precision, recording special characteristics of the animal such as the particular backward lean of the ears, the dewlap on the underside of the neck, and the "gridiron" pattern of stripes on the back immediately above the tail. By comparison, the efforts of contemporary engravers to represent it appear absurdly crude and conventional, showing merely a horse or donkey with stripes added.

This was the first zebra to be seen in Britain. From Stubbs's painting it can be identified as a Cape Mountain Zebra, the smallest of the three distinct zebra types. It was brought from the Cape of Good Hope (South Africa) by Sir Thomas Adams, captain of HMS Terpsichore, for presentation to Queen Charlotte, who was a keen collector of unusual animals. In Noah's-ark fashion, Adams took on board a male and a female, but only this, the female, survived the voyage, arriving in Britain in the summer of 1762. The "painted African ass" (as it was sometimes called) was installed at Buckingham House, the royal residence recently bought by the queen and her husband George III, and became the object of much public interest. "This animal," the *London Magazine* of July 31, 1762, reported, "from her majesty's good natured indulgence, has been seen by numbers of people, and is now feeding in a paddock near her majesty's house." As a biographer of the Queen later noted:

The Queen's she-ass…was pestered with visits, and had all her hours employed from morning to night in satisfying the curiosity of the public. She had a centinel and guard placed at the door of her stable…The crowds that resorted to the Asinine palace were exceeding great.[1]

The zebra was the talk of the town, even the subject of a bawdy song entitled "The Queen's Ass." Later it was joined at Buckingham House by an elephant and eventually moved to the menagerie at the Tower of London. It died on April 3, 1773, after which its skin was preserved, stuffed, and displayed with other animal curiosities in a touring exhibition.

By portraying the royal zebra against an obviously British rather than African landscape, presumably representing the park at Buckingham House, Stubbs underlines the idea of the scene as directly observed rather than imagined. Here is the animal just as it appeared to him and the rest of its British audience—incongruous almost to a comic degree, with its stripes acting as the opposite of camouflage. Surprisingly, he seems to have painted the work without a commission, whether from Queen Charlotte, George III, or any other interested party, and it remained in his possession throughout his life, appearing in his studio sale in 1807. Perhaps he always intended to keep the work with him, to serve as a kind of advertisement, recognizing such an entirely foreign, "virgin" subject as the ideal showpiece for his abilities as a naturalist-painter. MW

1 MacClintock, 4.

43 GEORGE STUBBS

Turf, with Jockey Up, at Newmarket, about 1765
Oil on canvas, 39 x 49 in (99.1 x 124.5 cm)
Gift of Paul Mellon, 1981

References: Egerton 1978, 78-79 (no. 76A); Egerton 1984, 87 (no. 57)

The painting of commissioned racehorse portraits, following in the tradition established by Wootton earlier in the eighteenth century, was central to Stubbs's practice as an artist from about 1760 onwards. The present work was painted for one of his most important early patrons, the young Frederick St. John, 2nd Viscount Bolingbroke. (The 1st Viscount, the prominent statesman and political thinker, was his uncle.) Bolingbroke was a member and for a time Steward of the prestigious Jockey Club, and owned a number of the most successful horses of the time, including the famous Gimcrack. He employed Stubbs to paint several of them. Turf, the subject of the present work, was a bay colt foaled in 1760 by Match'em out of the Duke of Ancaster's Starling mare. He raced mostly at Newmarket, and the high point of his career was beating King Herod in a match for a thousand guineas over the Beacon Course on April 4, 1766. He was retired as a result of lameness in 1767. The identity of the delightfully nonchalant-looking jockey is unknown; he wears Bolingbroke's colors of a black jacket and cap with buff breeches.

The brick building to the right is a rubbing-down house, a shed in which the stable lads would wipe off the horses' sweat with straw or cloths after they had exercised or raced. There were four rubbing-down houses at Newmarket, and the present one seems to have been reserved for horses belonging to royal owners and members of the Jockey Club like Lord Bolingbroke. Stubbs painted a pair of oil sketches of different views at Newmarket in which it features prominently (Tate Gallery and Paul Mellon, Upperville, Virginia), the only known works by him without animal or human figures, and used them repeatedly as the basis for backgrounds to his racehorse paintings. The Mellon sketch clearly served for *Turf* and for a portrait of Gimcrack when he belonged to his previous owner, William Wildman (Fitzwilliam Museum, Cambridge), and the Tate sketch for a portrait of Gimcrack done for Bolingbroke after he had bought him (private collection).

Turf shows not only Stubbs's detached, meticulous approach to recording the particulars of a horse's stance, coloring, and musculature, but also his impeccable feeling for design. The simple, rather bare landscape, the low horizon, and the large, blocky shapes of the rubbing-down house are carefully contrived as foils to the subtly undulating forms of the horse's body, which stand out like relief sculpture against a flat background. The side view was traditional in horse portraiture, but at this moment when the Neoclassical movement was taking shape in European art, it assumed special significance: the profile was the viewpoint most associated with Antiquity—with ancient relief sculpture, and especially with the portraits of emperors and other illustrious personages on coins and medals—and with the simplicity and clarity that were essential to the eighteenth-century idea of classicism. To offset the static look of the profile, Stubbs gently implies motion, showing Turf's tail overlapping the wall of the rubbing-down house and open ground before him as though he were moving from indoors to out. Another refinement is the placement of the white post at the left edge of the canvas, which checks the tendency of the composition to run off at that side. The result is a design that appears so scrupulously judged that to change any element would be to disrupt the whole.   MW

GEORGE STUBBS
The Shooting Series

44 *Two Gentlemen Going a Shooting, with a View of Creswell Crags, Taken on the Spot*, about 1767
    Oil on canvas, 40 x 50¹⁄₁₆ in (101.6 x 127.2 cm)

45 *Two Gentlemen Going a Shooting*, 1768
    Oil on canvas, 39¹⁵⁄₁₆ x 50¹⁄₁₆ in (101.5 x 127.2 cm)

46 *Two Gentlemen Shooting*, about 1769
    Oil on canvas, 39 x 49 in (99 x 124.5 cm)

47 *A Repose after Shooting*, 1770
    Oil on canvas, 40¼ x 50½ in (102.2 x 128.3 cm)

Gift of Paul Mellon, 1976. In memory of his friend James Cox Brady, Yale College, Class of 1929
First exhibited (respectively): Society of Artists, 1767 (no. 157); 1768 (no. 167); 1769 (no. 177); 1770 (no. 134)

References: Deuchar, 114–21; Egerton 1978, 81–83 (no. 79); Egerton 1984, 108–11 (nos. 73–76); Egerton 1986

With the title of the first painting in this series of episodes from a day's sport, Stubbs indicates that the setting is supposed to be at Creswell Crags, which are steep limestone formations on the border between Derbyshire and Nottinghamshire. The Crags contain caves in which were found the remains of prehistoric animals, as well as tools and weapons that were some of the oldest signs of human life in Britain. With their primeval and savage associations, they clearly appealed to Stubbs's imagination, and he used them as the setting for some of his paintings of horses attacked by lions. In the Shooting Series, where he shows them prominently in the first scene and in the distance in the fourth, they serve to suggest the idea of the hunt as an age-old human endeavor: in their shooting expedition his eighteenth-century sporting gentlemen follow literally in the footsteps of early man. At this time the Crags and the land around them were part of the estate of the Duke of Portland. Stubbs was painting an equestrian portrait of Portland in about 1766–67, and it may have been then that he sketched them for his first shooting scene; as his title reminds us, the view was "Taken on the Spot."

Although the portrait of Portland and the first shooting scene were hung together at the Society of Artists exhibition of 1767, Portland seems not to have commissioned this or any other work in the series. In 1787 the whole series was sold at Christie's by the executors of William Wildman, and it is possible that Wildman commissioned it, or purchased it directly, from the artist. Wildman was a meat salesman who made a fortune as the middleman between some of the great estates and Smithfield Market in London. He was also a lover of sport, the owner of racehorses, a friend of Stubbs, and one of his best patrons. Judging from Stubbs's painting of him and his sons with the racehorse Eclipse (Baltimore Museum of Art), the man in the darker coat in the Shooting Series may be intended as a likeness of him too. Certainly the features of both men have a portrait-like quality.

Between 1769 and 1771 the Shooting Series was published as a set of prints, engraved by William Woollett and published by Thomas Bradford. The prints are captioned with descriptions of the scenes in verse, and—though by no means literary masterpieces—these throw light on the way in which the paintings were enjoyed and understood in their own time. They present the series as dealing not just with four typical moments from a shooting expedition, but also with four times of day. With its beautiful effects of mist softening the forms of the landscape, dew sparkling on the grass and leaves, and a rosy glow in the sky, the first scene shows a time shortly after dawn—in "the grey-ey'd Morn's uncertain Light." More sharply defined than the rest of the composition, the two gentlemen load their guns, watched by their "well taught Dogs." In the second scene it is later in the morning—"The Dew's exhal'd from off the spangled Spray" and "Bright Sol's all chearing Beams illumine the Day"—as the sportsmen walk by a cottage in search

of good shooting. The third scene, set probably in the afternoon, recounts the shooting of a bird: the pointers indicate its position in the undergrowth; it "springs to find some safe resort"; one man half-raises his gun; the other fires, with dark clouds looming behind like the puff of gunsmoke magnified; "Like Lightning flys the Shot"; and the bird falls from the air. In the final scene darkness begins to fall, and "Calm Eve's approach here bids the slaughter cease." One sportsman rests as the other adds another hare to the hare, cock-pheasant, snipe, and other game that are the day's spoils. Leaving the open air that has been so important for their shooting, the men end the day in the natural shelter of the woods.

The absence of any servants or attendants suggests that Stubbs's gentlemen—whether William Wildman and friend or not—are probably not wealthy landowners shooting over their own property, and the lines accompanying the first scene confirm that they are on a day's outing from the city: "Lo! the keen Sportsmen rise from Beds of Down, / And quit th'Environs of the Smoaky Town." The fact that the cottage in the second scene appears to be derelict underlines the idea of their getting away from it all: far from the city crowds, they have the countryside all to themselves. On a darker note it also calls to mind the rural depopulation lamented by Oliver Goldsmith in his almost exactly contemporary poem *The Deserted Village* (published 1770). Goldsmith would have considered such city sportsmen, probably well-to-do merchants of some kind—as William Wildman was—to be part of "trade's unfeeling train," who "Usurp the land and dispossess the swain." But clearly Stubbs had no such critical point in mind and presents both the sportsmen and their sport in a wholly positive light. As Stephen Deuchar has pointed out, his protagonists are in fact flouting the Game Laws of the time, which reserved the right to hunt game to landowners. The laws were a controversial issue, and there was much debate about whether the bounties of the countryside should be restricted in this way or open to all as a natural right. It is even possible that Stubbs intended his Shooting Series as a statement in favor of the latter point of view, showing the "unqualified" sportsman not as a form of poacher, but as a gentleman enjoying wholesome leisure. MW

48 GEORGE STUBBS

Horse Frightened by a Lion, probably early 1790s

Oil on canvas, 27¾ x 41 in (70.5 x 104 cm)

Gift of Paul Mellon, 1977

Reference: Egerton 1978, 74 (no. 73)

Stubbs painted a number of variations on the theme of a horse being attacked by a lion. Given that animal painting was regarded by connoisseurs and theorists as one of the lowest branches of art, he was quite deliberately testing its limits, showing animals in the kind of serious, dramatic encounter normally reserved for scenes from human history, the Bible, and myth. His horse-and-lion paintings evoke a world of savagery and danger, in which an animal so familiar to mankind as to seem part of civilization falls victim to the merciless law of the jungle. Always the horse's facial expression is anthropomorphic, like the equine translation of a head of "Terror" in one of the textbooks of physiognomy that were so popular at this time. In its extreme emotional and physical state the beautiful creature becomes "sublime" (a key term in later eighteenth-century artistic thinking), intended gently to touch the viewer's atavistic senses of fear, danger, and awe.

Some of his horse-and-lion paintings show the lion's approach, others the actual attack, with the lion sinking its teeth into the horse's back. He treated each episode against a variety of different backgrounds and with horses of different colors. Here the horse seems suddenly to have stopped, throwing its mane and tail forward, on seeing the lion emerge menacingly from the shadows of a cave. The artist's early biographer records that he studied the pose by having someone frighten an actual horse by pushing a brush along the ground toward it.[1]

A much earlier version of the present composition, probably its prototype, was the subject of a poem by Horace Walpole. Clearly Walpole was moved largely by the horse's near-human expression, and suggests that even David Garrick, the great actor of the age, might learn something from it:

I feel his feelings: how he stands transfix'd!
How all the passions in his mien are mix'd!
How apprehension, horror, hatred, fear,
In one expression, are concenter'd there!
In terms pathetic we peruse his pain,
And read his pang through each transparent vein.
Through that stretch'd nostril see each feeling fly,
And Garrick's self might study close that eye...[2]

Walpole saw the earlier version at the Society of Artists exhibition of 1763. It can be identified as one showing the lion and horse more or less as they appear in the present version, but with a different landscape setting, based on Creswell Crags (see nos. 44–47); the work is now in a private collection.[3] In 1777 Stubbs published his own engraving from this, showing the design in reverse, and in 1780 he used the engraving as the basis for a plaster mold from which ceramic bas-reliefs were cast by Wedgwood.[4] Like many of Stubbs's compositions, the *Horse Frightened by a Lion* was designed in a relief-like form in the first place, and so lent itself naturally to casting in actual relief. Clearly he considered it successful, and the present painted version is datable on stylistic grounds to the early 1790s, some thirty years after the prototype.   MW

1 Egerton 1984, 90.
2 Walpole, 111–12.
3 Egerton 1984, 94 (no. 62).
4 See Egerton 1978, 73–74 (no. 72).

49 BENJAMIN MARSHALL

George, Marquess of Huntly (later 5th Duke of Gordon) on Tiny, about 1806–7
Oil on canvas, 41½ x 50 in (101.5 x 127 cm)
Gift of Paul Mellon, 1981

References: Egerton 1978, 198–99 (no. 210); Aubrey Noakes, 43 (no. 125)

Marshall shows the Marquess of Huntly and his horse preparing for the day's hunt. The hounds are poised and ready for the coming chase, their tails wagging and their bodies tense and excited. At the right two grooms lead away the extra horses (provided to relieve animals that became tired or hurt during the hunt). Placed at the top of a pyramidal composition, Huntly sits easily astride, nonchalantly acknowledging us with his glance; his upright posture contrasts sharply with those of the huntsmen at the left who slouch atop their mounts. Similarly, his long-legged, well-proportioned body provides an aristocratic foil to that of his squat valet, who has to reach above his head in order to grasp the bridle of the horse — whose name Tiny ironically refers to his enormous height of seventeen hands. Like his rider, Huntly's majestic mount seems to pose for his audience. His beautifully toned muscles and powerful, healthy veins glisten in the gray light.

The scene fairly bursts with energy. Marshall delineates each figure, animal, and even the muddied rocks on the ground, with taut and tensile lines, hinting at the power and energy of the chase to come. The flat open fields stretching across the middle distance and horizon, possibly the heaths surrounding Newmarket, are peppered with fences and hedgerows to provide swift riders and deft hounds with exciting jumping possibilities. Over these fields Huntly's horses and hounds, carefully and methodically bred for speed and endurance, will fly in pursuit of the quick and wily fox.

In its portrayal of Huntly's aristocratic demeanor and the power and beauty of his animals, Marshall's portrait could hardly be more flattering. It was most likely painted in 1806 or 1807, years when Huntly sat as Member of Parliament for Eye (Suffolk). He was a successful soldier and known particularly for his leadership between 1795 and 1799 of the Gordon Highlanders, a regiment that he raised on the estate of his ancestral home in Scotland, Gordon Castle. He succeeded his father as Duke of Gordon in 1827. He and his wife had no children, and with his death in 1836 the dukedom became extinct.

Marshall's love of horses extended beyond his paintings of them; under the pseudonym "Observator" he wrote a racing column in the *Sporting Magazine*, a journal by and for sportsmen. In 1812 he moved from London to Newmarket and there continued to thrive as a painter of horses and their riders. When questioned as to why he would chose Newmarket over the cosmopolitan and bustling London, Marshall is said to have replied, "the second animal in creation is a fine horse; and at Newmarket I can study him in the greatest grandeur, beauty and variety."[1] JMA

1 Aubrey Noakes, 17.

50 JAMES WARD

The Day's Sport, 1826
Oil on canvas, 39½ x 51¼ in (101 x 131.2 cm)
Gift of Paul Mellon, 1977
First exhibited: Royal Academy, 1827 (no. 204)
References: Egerton 1978, 218–19 (no. 234); Grundy, 53 (no. 809)

The title of this somewhat mysterious painting, which is the artist's own, seems deliberately to give little away. At the center of the composition a gamekeeper is shown loading a dead hare into a pannier on a mule. Behind him to the left another keeper walks up the hill holding a dead mallard, presumably just retrieved by the dog that follows him. Since they are identically dressed, there is a sense of sequential movement about these two figures, almost as if they represented the same man carrying out different parts of his job. The third man in the scene, seated in the left foreground with a retriever and spaniel at his feet, is less readily identified. He is dressed like the others, which might suggest that he too is a gamekeeper. Yet the fact of his resting while the others work implies that he is their master, an idea borne out by a contemporary description of the painting in the *Sporting Magazine* as "A Gentleman and his keepers loading a mule with the spoils of the day: a Snow Piece."[1]

Despite the observed, portraitlike character of the seated man and the keeper with the hare, it is unlikely that they are intended to be recognizable individuals. In a portrait it would be most unusual for a gentleman to be subordinated visually to a servant. Furthermore, the artist sold the work at auction a couple of years after it was painted, which strongly suggests that it was uncommissioned. He seems to have had something more general than portraiture in mind, and indeed something more ambitious than one would expect from a picture called *The Day's Sport*. Clearly this is no sociable shooting party of the kind painted so often and so fondly by sporting artists. In fact, with no more than one gentleman in attendance, and the second keeper carrying a gun,

it seems probable that the day's outing has been less for sport than for provisions. The killing has been abundant, including not only the hare and duck, but various other birds that are laid out across the foreground: snipe, partridge, pheasant, and a swan. It is sunset in the autumn, the dying times of the day and year, and the light pall of snow is spotted with blood. The subject is redolent of death. Yet, thanks largely to Ward's robust and animated manner of painting, the general mood of the piece is far from deathly. There is the same sense of nature's bounty that comes across so powerfully in the landscapes of his great artistic hero, Rubens; the far distant view to the left, the bold inclusion of the sun, even the shooting theme, recall the famous *Autumn Landscape with a View of Het Steen* (National Gallery, London), then in the collection of Sir George Beaumont. Although the old tree in the middle ground has lost most of its leaves and shows a dead stump where a large branch has been cut, the branches that survive seem to writhe, almost van Gogh-like, with growth and energy.

The lighter-haired of the village children to the right looks on with a melancholy expression, as though feeling sympathy for the animals, lamenting the massacre of fellow innocents; the dark-haired child seems affected less, perhaps regarding the massacre more in the light of a feast in the making. It is only the keeper with the hare, going about his business with the solemnity of some ancient seasonal rite, whose features hint at some understanding of the day's sport in its larger significance—as a microcosm of life and death in the cycle of nature.   MW

1   Egerton 1978, 218.

51 JOHN FERNELEY SR.

Thomas Wilkinson, M.F.H., with the Hurworth Foxhounds, 1846

Oil on canvas, 58 x 95 in (147.3 x 240.5 cm)

Gift of Paul Mellon, 1981

Reference: Egerton 1978, 249–50 (no. 270)

Ferneley's portrait of Thomas Wilkinson, Master of Foxhounds (M.F.H.), evokes the end to a good day's hunt. Still astride his bay hunter named The Squire, Wilkinson presides over his pack, the Hurworth Hounds, and converses with the dismounted amateur huntsman, Frank Coates. He gestures nonchalantly toward the patch of growth at the base of a tree that has apparently been the "covert" where a fox has been trapped, killed, and eaten by the hounds. The pack, exhausted after their fast-paced chase, lounge at the feet of the three hunters and their riders, while in the background other riders—some dismounted—approach over the verdant, rolling moorland to join their companions.

Like Marshall in his equestrian portrait of the Marquess of Huntly (no. 49), Ferneley has placed his most important sitter at the apex of a wide pyramidal composition. Also like Marshall, with whom he studied, Ferneley is careful to convey the differences in social status among the huntsmen, which are made clear largely through his orchestration of the various elements of the composition. He has separated the canvas into two halves: on the right are the two huntsmen, distinguished as such by their upright, dignified posture and splendid mounts; on the left the working hunt servants, the Hoppers, father and son. The elder Tom Hopper, wearing a hat but no coat, stands in the near distance as he waits with two hounds and a smaller hunt terrier, Tip. Tom Hopper the younger is part of the central group and has laid down his whip in order to leash one of the hounds. Cleverly, Ferneley has chosen a pose for the young servant that mimics a bow to his employer, the M.F.H.

The Hurworth Hounds was a reputable private pack, founded in the late eighteenth century by three brothers, Thomas, Lozalure, and Matthew Wilkinson. Originally harriers (dogs trained to hunt hare), the pack became foxhunters at the beginning of the nineteenth century, hunting in Yorkshire and Durham. The Thomas Wilkinson in the present painting was the nephew of the Hurworth's founders. Born Thomas Raper, he adopted the surname of Wilkinson when the mastership passed to him following the death of his uncle Matthew in 1840. JMA

Point-to-Point Meeting, probably 1920
Oil on canvas, 20 x 24⅛ in (50.8 x 61.3 cm)
Gift of Paul Mellon, 1996

A point-to-point is a short horse race of about three and a half miles, most often run by hunters associated with a particular pack of foxhounds. In the spring of 1920 Munnings painted a number of pictures of the point-to-point meeting of the Belvoir hunt on Barrowby Hill in Lincolnshire, and the present sketch is likely from that campaign of work. Through both its design and execution it captures the lively atmosphere of the preparations before the race, when riders, grooms, spectators, and hangers-on mingle in anticipation of the event.

By his own account Munnings had little desire to be simply a painter: his ruling passion was the beauty and nobility of horses and their riders. Some of the thrill he felt at the sight of horses in motion comes through in his memory of an early visit to the races, while he was still working as a commercial draftsman:

I saw the thoroughbred horses and jockeys in bright silk colours, going off down the course. The peaceful School of Art, the smelly artists' room at Page Brothers faded away and I began to live![1]

This painting represents the kind of uncommissioned sketch he most enjoyed painting, its fresh, animated surface suggesting the pleasure and freedom he felt as an observer of such events. His reputation as a painter of equestrian subjects was launched in 1918, when he painted a large-scale portrait of a Canadian military commander, Major-General the Rt. Hon. J. E. B. Seely, on horseback (Canadian War Museum, Ottawa). In the wake of his efforts as a war artist, Munnings was rapidly inundated with requests for similar portraits, and as a result he began to move in the highest circles of society. The son of a Suffolk miller, he cherished his newfound social standing and its accompanying lifestyle but despised the means by which he had to support himself. Nevertheless, he seldom refused such commissions, saying, "you can't throw good money away."[2]

Like any sporting artist, Munnings looked to Stubbs for inspiration and considered Stubbs's *The Anatomy of the Horse* one of the shaping forces in his own artistic career. But the *Point-to-Point Meeting* also attests to the extent to which he was aware of the artistic climate in which he lived. His use of bright color to create highlights and shadows—most evident in the haunches of the horse in profile—shows his stylistic affinities with the proponents of British Impressionism, and particularly with the flashy, virtuoso brand of that style practiced by John Singer Sargent, whom he called "the last bright flame of a glorious world for the artist."[3] Despite his vehement opposition to anything "modern," moreover, Munnings painted figures and forms that are strangely abstract, often described only by broad, flat brushstrokes and dabs of thick paint. JMA

1 Booth, 4
2 Ibid., 9.
3 Baillio, 9.

The Romantic Vision

THE PERIOD FROM THE French Revolutionary and Napoleonic wars (1793–1815) until the middle of the nineteenth century was the heyday of British Romanticism. During the wars Britain was cut off from the rest of Europe, and British art, for reasons both nationalistic and practical, became less bound up with the Continental, Grand-Tour sensibility that had been so dominant in the eighteenth century. Romantic artists and writers developed the revolutionary belief that art should be a matter of personal feeling rather than aspiration toward a universal ideal of beauty—that it should be charged with the artist's own loves and loathings, hopes and fears, and inspire the same emotions in the viewer. Living in disturbing times—through war, then through the beginnings of the immense social upheaval set in motion by the Industrial Revolution—the Romantics rejected the man-centered world-picture created by eighteenth-century rationalism; indeed they rejected the very idea that a world-picture was possible. Of great importance for the art of landscape painting, they thought of nature not as one thing, separate from humanity, but as a flux moving around and through us, knowable only by individual feeling and faith.

The heroes of British Romantic art, arguably the greatest artists Britain has produced, were Constable and Turner; they were almost exact contemporaries. Constable painted the places that meant the most to him, above all the area of East Anglia where he grew up. This was his Garden of Eden, and his whole project as an artist could be described as regaining the lost paradise of childhood impressions, an aim in which he came close to the poet Wordsworth. Turner was more the Byronic wanderer, moving restlessly through the world in search of sights sympathetic to his moods. For him nature was a thing of terrible beauty, akin to fate, and man a doomed creature, heroic and absurd by turns. In personality and style these two could hardly have been more different. What they shared was the Romantic understanding of art's purpose. "Painting," Constable once wrote, "is but another word for feeling." MW

53 JOHN CONSTABLE

Stratford Mill, 1819–20

Oil on canvas, 51½ x 72½ in. (131 x 184 cm)

Purchased through the Paul Mellon Fund, 1983

References: Cormack 1986; Parris and Fleming-Williams, 200–1 (no. 99); Graham Reynolds 1984, 45 (no. 20.2)

Constable considered his highest achievement as an artist to be the series of exhibition pictures on a large scale, about six feet across, that he showed at the annual Royal Academy exhibitions from 1819 onward. Unlike his great contemporary Turner, he was slow and meticulous in his working processes, and prepared for each of these grand compositions by painting a full-scale oil sketch. The present work is the sketch for the second in the series, which he showed as his main picture at the exhibition of 1820 (National Gallery, London).

Stratford Mill, which appears at the far left of the composition, was a watermill that powered a paper factory on the river Stour in East Anglia. The view is looking downriver, roughly to the south, with the Langham Hills in the distance on the right; judging from the light, it is about noon on a late summer's day. This was Constable's native countryside. He knew the Stour valley intimately and found most of his landscape subjects there, choosing views that represented not just the beauty of the area, but an Edenic relationship between the land, mankind, and God. He delighted in nature for its own sake, here noting such facts of natural history as the slanted growth of trees in the prevailing wind and, with the dead trunk in the foreground, the way a river could kill trees by washing through their roots. But his particular interest lay in nature as tended and turned to good use by man, and *Stratford Mill* illustrates almost as in a diagram the uses of the Stour: it is a source of power for the mill; a working thoroughfare for the barge, which is waiting to pass a lock outside the picture to the right; and, as shown by the children fishing and the horse drinking (to the right of the mill), the provider of food and fresh water.

Unlike the nearby Flatford and Dedham mills, which Constable also painted (see no. 54), Stratford Mill was not a family property. Nevertheless it was full of boyhood associations for him, and there is little doubt that the children fishing represent some form of nostalgic autobiographical recollection. Like the great Romantic poet Wordsworth, he thought of childhood as a state closer to nature and to God, and his Stour valley landscapes are his attempts to see the place as a boy again, his vision pristine, intense, and sparkling.

As he worked out the composition of the painting in his studio in London, Constable drew on earlier material: the left half clearly derives from an oil sketch made on the spot in 1811, and some of the woodwork and water-lilies near the lower right corner are from drawings in a sketchbook of 1813. He tried out his idea for the composition as a whole in a small sketch, then painted the present full-scale sketch as a run-through before embarking on the more finished, exhibitable version.[1] The work is rough and experimental. It shows the artist changing and elaborating on the smaller compositional sketch in a number of ways, notably by replacing the reclining figure of an angler with the dead tree trunk. It also shows him trying and rejecting ideas as he went along: an obvious pentimento reveals that the fishing rod of the standing boy in the red waistcoat was originally much higher, for instance. His main aims in the work were probably to establish the number and positions of the figures, and to see how the broad masses of light and dark would work together across the composition. In the end he concluded that there should be fewer figures and in the final version omitted both the standing boy and the girl near the mill on the left. Constable did not usually sign his full-scale sketches, considering them to be private studio work and not for public consumption; the signature on the present work is almost certainly false.

Constable exhibited the finished picture as simply *Landscape*; it has been known as *Stratford Mill* for convenience, as has the present sketch. Both works have also been given the additional title of *The Young Waltonians*, a reference to Izaak Walton's famous book on angling. This caught on after being used for a mezzotint of the finished picture published some years after the artist's death.   MW

1 See Parris and Fleming-Williams, 198–201 (nos. 97–99).

134

Dedham Lock, about 1819–20

Oil on canvas laid on board, 13¼ x 19⅝ in (33.7 x 49.8 cm)

Gift of Paul Mellon, 1981

Reference: Graham Reynolds 1984, 65 (no. 20.92)

Painted in a busy variety of different kinds of brush-stroke, often with areas of rich impasto, Constable's small oil sketches played a key part in his working process. He made many of them outdoors on the spot, at the favorite sites in the Stour Valley that were the mainstay of his subject matter throughout his career; his studies of clouds were also done in the open air (see no. 55). Such quick, private visual notes would serve him in the studio as points of departure, aides-mémoires, and raw material for the larger, more finished pictures that he would show at the London exhibitions. In the course of synthesizing and adapting, he would make further oil sketches to strike the right balance of compositional elements and lights and darks, sometimes completing his preparations with a sketch on the same scale—as large as six feet across—as the projected exhibition piece (no. 53 is an example). The present work is one of the smaller-scale studio sketches, a step toward a larger, more finished work that appears never to have been realized.

It shows the view looking south from Dedham Lock toward Dedham itself, with the skyline dominated by the tower of the village church. The vessel with a sail to the left is a barge waiting inside the lock for the water to rise to the level of the river beyond. The view is similar in form and content to another painted by Constable repeatedly between 1817 and 1820, looking in more or less the same direction but from the other end of the lock, i. e. from a point some distance back and to the left. The composition also centers on the church tower rising above the lock; the main difference is that in the position occupied by the row of trees on the left is a building instead, Dedham Mill. There are four relatively large versions of this other Dedham view, including one that is unfinished; two of the finished versions, both datable to 1820, show a barge in the lower left corner like the one here.[1] The present view, without the mill, is seen in only three works, all of which are sketches; the others, both smaller, are at the Tate Gallery and also at the Yale

Center for British Art.[2] The three may represent an idea for a full-scale Dedham view that was superseded by the one with the mill, which would suggest a date of about 1817 or earlier. In style, however, they seem to belong with other sketches datable to about 1819–20; the present work, for instance, relates to the small compositional sketch for *Stratford Mill* (see no. 53). Constable may have painted them for the same purpose as the latter, as a preparatory work for an exhibition picture on his largest scale, a never-realized "six-footer."

As the scene of boyhood memories, Dedham was full of sentimental associations for Constable, and the mill featured in the other, similar view was part of his own family's business. But in his paintings of this and other places along the Stour, he sought to suggest ideas of more than personal importance. He painted the locks that made the river navigable in large part for their symbolic connotations: they represented the man-made at its best, a positive and productive intervention in nature. Dedham Church was also a favorite motif. At 130 feet in height, it was actually one of the valley's most prominent landmarks. But its position at the heart of so many of Constable's compositions is more a matter of theology than topography. He was devoutly religious and saw the beauty and well-being of his home countryside as inseparable from the idea of a presiding, beneficent God.

As Graham Reynolds has noted, the first known owner of the sketch was Albert Hecht, the early collector of works by the French Impressionists. The Impressionist painters probably would have seen it at Hecht's and no doubt appreciated its remarkably free, spontaneous-looking touch. MW

1 Parris and Fleming-Williams, 186–91 (nos. 93–96); Graham Reynolds 1984, 47–49 (nos. 20.10–20.13).
2 Graham Reynolds 1984, 64–65 (nos. 20.90 and 20.91).

55 JOHN CONSTABLE

Study of a Cloudy Sky, 1820s

Oil on paper laid on millboard, 10⅜ x 13 in (26.5 x 33 cm)

Gift of Paul Mellon, 1981

Reference: Graham Reynolds 1984, 113 (no. 22.63)

For Constable the sky was more vital to a landscape than the land itself; and he observed and recorded cloud formations, weather conditions, and the light effects to which they gave rise more avidly than any painter before him. The present work is one of the many small oil sketches of clouds he made, outdoors in the open air, to keep himself in practice for the larger skies that he would improvise in the studio when he came to paint his grand exhibition pictures. He was sometimes criticized for affording the skies too dominant a role in these but maintained that it was better to err in that direction than to treat them as mere backdrops as—almost incredibly —people advised him to do. As he wrote in a letter to his friend John Fisher:

> *That Landscape painter who does not make his skies a very material part of his composition— neglects to avail himself of one of his greatest aids…It will be difficult to name a class of Landscape, in which the sky is not the "key note," the standard of "Scale," and the chief "Organ of sentiment."*[1]

In other words, he thought of the sky as the emotional, mood-setting element of the landscape: just as the history painter or portraitist must master human physiognomy and expression, the landscapist must master the face of the heavens. It was the most changeable element, which meant that—if painted convincingly—it could transmit the sense of life and freshness that was so important to his vision of the English countryside; in a way it was the key to the whole Romantic idea of nature as ceaselessly in flux. The Constable sky was synonymous with clouds, and as such it was also distinctively British: the emphatically overcast sky, with rain or the promise of rain to come, was one of the ways in which he distanced himself from the balmy Mediterranean type of landscape that many still considered the ideal of natural beauty.

Clearly Constable thought of his cloud studies as akin to entries in a diary or log, and would often annotate them with the date, time, wind direction, and so on. He once remarked that in nature "no two days are alike, nor even two hours."[2] Growing up in farming and windmilling country, he had developed a keen eye for the weather and its changes as a boy. His cloud studies were a way of maintaining this, his means of ensuring that all his pictures would make sense from the weather point of view. He was interested in the science of meteorology, and his reading on this subject and his cloud studies came from the same impetus, the desire to see and paint nature not as an "innocent eye" but with knowledge and understanding.

When not inscribed by the artist himself, Constable's cloud studies are difficult to date, and this is a case in point. He did most of his "skying," as he called it, on the high natural observatory of Hampstead Heath in 1821–22, producing about a hundred works. But he painted others in later years and different places, and the strip of landscape at the bottom of the present example recalls particularly those he made while staying with John Fisher in Salisbury in 1829. It was among the works that passed to the artist's son Lionel, who in 1876—to mark the centenary of Constable's birth— presented it to one of his father's most successful Victorian followers, George Vicat Cole.   MW

1   Beckett, 76–77.
2   Leslie, 118.

56 RICHARD PARKES BONINGTON
Fishmarket, probably 1824
Oil on canvas, 32⅜ x 48¼ in (82 x 122.5 cm)
Gift of Paul Mellon, 1981
First exhibited: probably Salon, Paris, 1824 (no. 191)
References: Noon 1986; Noon 1991, 116–18 (no. 29)

The *Fishmarket* is among Bonington's largest and most ambitious paintings in oil, and perhaps his greatest success in bringing to oil painting the subtle observation of light and atmosphere that he had mastered as a landscape watercolorist. The gradually warming light of dawn appears suspended in the atmosphere, veiling buildings with its golden glow, soaking through the sails of the nearer fishing boats, dissolving the distant ones into the sky. Against this scene of natural glory, the buyers and sellers of fish carry on their distinctly unglorious business crowded together in shadow. The artist sees what they do not, finding beauty in the morning sky, the reflections on wet sand, the slithering catch of skate and eels; he takes a delight in luminosity and gleaming freshness for their own sakes, almost as abstract qualities separate from the mundane realities they are associated with. As Bonington's friend Eugène Delacroix remarked, he possessed a quickness of the eye and lightness of touch that made his work "a type of diamond which flatters and ravishes the eye, independently of any subject and any imitation."[1]

Bonington lived in France for most of his short life, and his favorite source of subject matter at this early point in his career was the landscape, architecture, and people of northern France. The *Fishmarket* represents a scene in that region and probably dates from the year 1824, during the ten months that the artist spent living and working in Dunkerque; he later described this as "the happiest year of my life."[2] The work has generally been described as showing the fishmarket in Boulogne, about forty miles southwest of Dunkerque. There is no record of its being described as such in the artist's lifetime, however, and the idea seems to have appeared for the first time in print as late as 1857, when the work belonged to the great Turner collector H. A. J. Munro of Novar. The fact that the coast at Boulogne faces due west is surely incompatible with a view of the sun rising over the sea, and Bonington's intention may in fact have been to show a type of scene—perhaps composed of observations in different places—rather than a view of a particular place. He made chalk drawings of fisherfolk while staying in Dunkerque and probably used some of these as the basis for figures in the *Fishmarket*. The three figures of women carrying baskets on their backs, one of them near the water's edge on the right and the others to the left of the main group, might well have been based on drawings of the same model in the same pose seen from different angles.

In all likelihood the *Fishmarket* was the painting Bonington exhibited as *Marine. Fishermen Unloading Their Catch* at the Paris Salon that opened on August 25, 1824. This was not only his debut as an exhibiting oil painter (he showed four oils, three of them marine subjects, along with a watercolor and a lithograph), but also a landmark exhibition for the showing of British art in France. The Boningtons were part of a British contingent that included two portraits by Thomas Lawrence and three landscapes by John Constable, including *The Haywain* (National Gallery, London). These were the talk of the exhibition; both Bonington and Constable were awarded gold medals, and Lawrence was made a Chevalier de la Légion d'Honneur. Aged only twenty-one, Bonington became almost a cult figure among French artists and connoisseurs of a certain Romantic and Anglophile frame of mind, who found in his work a naturalness and freedom they felt had been stifled in their own national school. To the academic old guard, on the other hand, it represented a dangerous taste for mere realism and "low" subjects, a threat to the classical ideal. "I avow that a sad sky, or a surging sea, or briney fishermen disputing in the middle of a pile of fish have little attraction for me," wrote the critic Etienne Delécluze in his review of the 1824 Salon. "The truth of the imitation actually enhances my aversion, and I inadvertently step aside to where I am able to view the radiant landscapes of Greece and Italy."[3]
MW

1 Noon 1991, 12.
2 Ibid., 10
3 Ibid., 116

57 JOHN CONSTABLE

Ploughing Scene in Suffolk, about 1824–25
Oil on canvas, 16¾ x 30 in (42.5 x 76 cm)
Gift of Paul Mellon, 1977

Reference: Graham Reynolds 1984, 152 (no. 24.81)

This is the second version of a painting of 1813–14 (collection of Mr. and Mrs. David Thomson).[1] Constable sold the original to the wine merchant and collector John Allnutt shortly after it was painted, the first instance—as he later recalled—of his selling a work to a stranger rather than through family connections and friends. Allnutt came to dislike the sky—the prominence of Constable's cloudy skies was a sticking point for many of his contemporaries—and employed another artist, John Linnell, to overpaint it. Later he regretted this and eventually approached Constable to restore the work, asking him also to reduce its height to make it a pair to an Augustus Wall Callcott landscape that he had just acquired.[2] Instead of doing so, Constable took back the original and painted a new version to the required dimensions, the present work; it is about three and a half inches shorter than the original. Still grateful to Allnutt for his patronage early in his career when he sorely needed such encouragement, he made no charge. The version follows the original faithfully, with the addition of a hawk and other birds in the sky toward the right, and an overall warming of the color scheme, possibly to accord with the Callcott.

The view is from just outside the park of Old Hall in the artist's native village of East Bergholt, looking across his beloved Stour Valley, with the churches of Langham and Stratford visible in the distance to the left and right respectively. When published as a mezzotint, the original version was given the title of *A Summerland*; this was a field that was ploughed and harrowed in the summer, then allowed to lie fallow for a period as part of a crop rotation system. Typically, Constable shows the working of the countryside as well as its beauties: the emblem-like image of the ploughman at the lower center of the composition suggests the idea of the whole rural order emanating from agricultural labor. When the original version was first exhibited, he had a couple of lines from Robert Bloomfield's poem *The Farmer's Boy* printed in the catalogue: "But, unassisted through each toilsome day, / With smiling brow the Plowman cleaves his way." Ploughing "unassisted," that is, without a ploughboy, and harnessing the horses abreast rather than in a line were methods distinctive to Suffolk and the Stour Valley and regarded locally as instances of the agricultural efficiency that made the region so productive and prosperous.[3]   MW

1   Parris and Fleming-Williams, 151–53 (no. 71); Graham Reynolds 1996, 189–90 (no. 14.1).
2   *Open Landscape: Sheep Grazing* (exhibited 1812; York City Art Gallery); see Brown, 75–76 (no. 13).
3   For further discussion of the painting from the local and agricultural points of view, see Rosenthal, 19 and 71–82.

Corso Sant'Anastasia, Verona, 1828
Oil on millboard, 23⅝ x 17⅜ in (60 x 44.2 cm)
Gift of Paul Mellon, 1981

Reference: Noon 1991, 292–93 (no. 155)

Bonington visited Italy in 1826, and some of the master-pieces of his last years are views of Venice and Verona. This exquisite and dazzling Veronese street scene shows the Corso Sant'Anastasia looking toward the Piazza dell'Erbe, the city's main market square. In the middle distance to the right is the projecting facade of the Casa Maffei, the palace of the eighteenth-century historian and man of letters Count Scipio Maffei. For travelers of the Romantic age, the chief importance of Verona lay in its resonant literary associations. It was here that Dante lived in exile during the power struggle between the Black and White Guelph factions in Florence, as de-scribed in his *Paradiso*, and lovers of English literature knew the city well—at least by name—as the setting of plays by Shakespeare. In his guidebook *Voyages historiques et littéraires en Italie, pendant les années 1826, 1827, et 1828* (1831), the French writer Antoine Valery remarked:

> *Shakespeare and Dante seem to meet at Verona, the one*
> *through his works, the other through his misfortunes,*
> *and the imagination delights here in bringing together*
> *these two great geniuses, so tremendous, so creative and*
> *perhaps the most astonishing of modern literature.*[1]

Though showing the people on the balconies dressed in the fashion of the day, Bonington gives pride of place to a religious procession that would have looked much the same in the time of Dante or Shakespeare; and he could surely count upon the sight of Veronese balconies and friars to conjure up memories of *Romeo and Juliet*. The spectacle is redolent of the past in general, of the faded glory that was almost every British or French visitor's leading impression of Italy, and of the fascination with which modern Europeans regarded the picturesque and mysterious aspects of Roman Catholicism. Some of the people on the balconies are undoubtedly tourists, looking down as though from one period of human history upon another.

Leaving his home in Paris on April 4, 1826, Bonington came to Italy with his aristocratic friend and patron Charles Rivet. They reached Verona on April 18 and stayed there for a few days before moving on to their principal destination, Venice, where they spent about a month. In Verona Bonington made one or more draw-ings of the view along the Corso Sant'Anastasia and possibly the watercolor version of the subject now at the Victoria and Albert Museum, London; the watercolor, which he gave to his fellow watercolorist Thomas Shotter Boys, was to become one of his most celebrated works, especially among other artists. The present painting is the second of two oil versions of the same view that followed; he never revisited Italy, and almost certainly based them on the earlier watercolor, in both cases varying the figures and certain architectural details. The first oil, which is smaller, dates from 1827 (private collection). The second was probably painted in the summer of 1828, by which time the artist was living in London. It is the only version to include the religious procession, which Bonington seems to have adapted from a large exhibition picture of a Venetian subject that he had painted in the preceding year, *The Ducal Palace with a Religious Procession* (Tate Gallery). *Corso Sant'Anastasia, Verona* may well have been his last painting before the onset of his fatal illness; it was still in his studio at the time of his death on September 23, 1828, appeared in the sale of his remaining works at Sotheby's in 1829, and was bought by the Marquess of Stafford.   MW

1   Noon 1991, 251.

59 JOHN CONSTABLE

Hadleigh Castle, The Mouth of the Thames— Morning after a Stormy Night, 1829
Oil on canvas, 48 x 64¾ in (122 x 164.5 cm)
Gift of Paul Mellon, 1977
First exhibited: Royal Academy, 1829 (no. 322)
References: Cormack 1980; Hawes; Graham Reynolds 1984, 199–200 (no. 29.1)

The ruins of the thirteenth-century Hadleigh Castle stand on the northern shore of the Thames estuary, overlooking the stretch of water known as the Nore, where the river meets the open sea. Constable shows the view looking southeast from the castle, with the tower of St. Clement's, Leigh-on-Sea further along the near shore, the shoreline and hills of Kent in the distance opposite, and the town of Sheerness on the far right. He first visited this spot in 1814 and wrote admiringly of the view in a letter to his fiancée Maria Bicknell: "At Hadleigh there is a ruin of a castle which from its situation is really a fine place—it commands a view of the Kent hills the nore and the north foreland & looking many miles to sea." In the same letter he mentions a walk on the beach at nearby Southend-on-Sea, remarking that he was "always delighted with the melancholy grandeur of a sea shore."[1] He made a rough drawing of the scene at Hadleigh in a sketchbook, and this was to serve as the basis for the present large exhibition picture, painted some fifteen years later—one of the series of "six-footers" that the artist considered his most important contributions to the art of landscape painting.

When Constable first showed the painting at the Royal Academy exhibition of 1829, he had the following lines from James Thomson's poem *The Seasons* printed in the catalogue:

> *The desert joys*
> *Wildly, through all his melancholy bounds*
> *Rude ruins glitter; and the briny deep,*
> *Seen from some pointed promontory's top,*
> *Far to the dim horizon's utmost verge*
> *Restless, reflects a floating gleam.*

The association of ruins with desolation and melancholy was by this time a commonplace of art and literature. In the Romantic imagination ruins were awe-inspiring, or "sublime," because they suggested the shortness of human life as against the passage of the ages and showed the ravages visited by time upon even the sturdiest works of mankind; they were a memento mori, a symbol of universal decay. Through his choice of viewpoint in *Hadleigh Castle*, Constable sets his ruins against a scene full of the grandeur and power of nature: the flow of the mighty river toward the infinite "briny deep," the drama of morning sunlight bursting through clouds. As the painting's subtitle tells us, there has been a storm in the night, and the craggy remains of the castle appear as though lashed by wind and rain, perhaps even struck by lightning.

Beyond its general significance as an image of transience, there is little doubt that Constable thought of *Hadleigh Castle* as autobiographical. His beloved Maria, whom he married after a long engagement in 1816, died of consumption in November 1828. He was left desolate and depressed, a ruin of a man—he used this metaphor himself—for the rest of his life. "Hourly do I feel the loss of my departed Angel," he wrote in December 1828. "I shall never feel again as I have felt. The face of the world is totally changed to me."[2] He began *Hadleigh Castle* in January or February 1829; and it seems likely, given his deep grief and abiding Christian faith, that he would have thought of this view from ruins to distant open sea as a view, in spiritual terms, from grief toward consolation. The sunbursts and "floating gleam" on the horizon suggest the light of heaven and the bereaved's hope of reunion in the afterlife, while the Nore, between river and sea, serves as an image of the passage from earthly to eternal realms.   MW

1 Graham Reynolds 1984, 199.
2 Hawes, 456.

Staffa, Fingal's Cave, 1831–32

Oil on canvas, 36 x 48 in (91.5 x 122 cm)

Gift of Paul Mellon, 1978

First exhibited: Royal Academy, 1832 (no. 453)

Reference: Butlin and Joll, 198–99 (no. 347)

Staffa is a small uninhabited island in the Hebrides, off the west coast of Scotland. The place is famous for its many caves and for its strange, columnlike formations of purple-gray basalt. By Turner's time it was already a much visited tourist attraction. The most spectacular of the caves, discovered by chance by Joseph Banks in 1772, was dubbed Fingal's Cave after a central character in the poems of Ossian. Published in 1762–63, these were supposedly the writings of a third-century bard of that name, a kind of Celtic Homer, but were in fact a modern pastiche of northern myths and legends composed by James Macpherson. The Ossianic poems were wildly popular, and the main fuel for Romantic ideas of Scotland until superseded by the poems and novels of Walter Scott. In them Fingal is the warrior king of Morven, a righter of wrongs and defender of the oppressed. He is the son of a giant, a hero of superhuman proportions, almost a force of nature, for whom an awe-inspiring cave on an island lashed by the sea would seem a fitting habitation. To the Romantic imagination, the cave also had a mysterious and spiritual aura, like the temple of some primeval Ossianic religion, a natural cathedral. Scott took up this kind of imagery, likening the noise of the sea to resounding organ music, in his poem *The Lord of the Isles*. Here was a place, he wrote,

> *Where Nature herself, it seemed, would raise*
> *A Minster to her Maker's praise!*
> *Not for a meaner use ascend*
> *Her columns, or her arches bend;*
> *Nor of a theme less solemn tells*
> *That mighty surge that ebbs and swells.*
> *And still, between each awful pause*
> *From the high vault an answer draws.*

Turner had Scott's poem in mind when he painted *Staffa*, and quoted the last four lines of the passage above in the catalogue when he showed the work at the Royal Academy exhibition of 1832. Although Scott was describing the inside of the cave and Turner's view is from a distance, the general idea of waves echoing among rocks and elements responding to one another suits the paint-

ing well: storm clouds arch over the island as though imitating its outline; the cliffs take on an orange-pink tinge from the light of the setting sun. Against all this sublime natural drama, the man-made element in the scene, the paddle-steamer, appears dwarfed—suggesting the familiar Romantic idea of mankind at the mercy of fate. It steams away from the island, and the smoke from its funnel trails down toward a darker area of the cliffs that may be the entrance to the cave, as though it had come from inside. Indeed the composition slightly echoes that of a much larger and more ambitious recent work of Turner's, *Ulysses Deriding Polyphemus—Homer's Odyssey* (exhibited 1829; National Gallery, London), in which the Greek hero's ship has emerged from the cave of the monstrous one-eyed Cyclops. Perhaps Turner thought of his steamer in *Staffa* as the plucky hero of the piece, like a modern Ulysses, challenging the mighty powers of nature and—this time at least—managing to evade them.

The painting resulted from Turner's travels in Scotland in the summer of 1831. After visiting Scott at his home, Abbotsford, he proceeded north, reaching Staffa probably in early September. From Tobermory on the larger island of Mull, he took the *Maid of Morven*, a tourist paddle-steamer much like the one in his painting. He later recalled: "After scrambling over the rocks on the lee side of the island, some got into Fingal's Cave, others would not. It is not very pleasant or safe when the waves roll right in." By the time everyone was back on board, the weather had deteriorated and the decision was taken not to proceed beyond Staffa to Iona as planned. "To allay the displeased," he continued,

> *the Captain promised to steam thrice round the island in the last trip. The sun getting towards the horizon, burst through the rain-cloud, angry, and for wind; and so it proved, for we were driven for shelter into Loch Ulver, and did not get back to Tobermory before midnight.*[1]

MW

1 Butlin and Joll, 198.

61 JOHN MARTIN

The Deluge, 1834

Oil on canvas, 66¼ x 101¾ in (168.5 x 258.6 cm)

Gift of Paul Mellon, 1978

First exhibited: Salon, Paris, 1835 (no. 1523)

Reference: Feaver, 92–97

As a painter fascinated with cataclysms, in which humanity appears as the plaything of terrible, "sublime" natural forces, Martin was almost inevitably drawn to the biblical story of the Deluge. According to the Book of Genesis, mankind showed such wickedness in the generations after Adam that God repented of the whole of Creation and sent down a huge flood, destroying almost every living thing on earth. The only people spared were the old and righteous Noah and his family, whom God warned of the impending disaster and instructed to build an ark, taking on board with them a male and female of every animal species. The flood rose throughout forty days and forty nights of rain, until even the tops of the highest mountains were covered, and lasted in all about a year. When the land was finally dry again, Noah made a sacrifice to God, who told him and his family to go forth, procreate and "replenish the earth" (Genesis 9:1). He undertook never again to visit such destruction upon the world, and set a rainbow in the sky as a sign of his new covenant with Creation.

In *The Deluge* Martin attempts to capture the divine violence at the moment of its greatest destructiveness, when "all the fountains of the great deep [were] broken up, and the windows of heaven were opened" (Genesis 7:11). What he lacked in technical skill he made up for with his genius for conception and spectacle, and his master stroke in this work is to show the great mountains crashing down upon humanity in a tidal wave of stone; this is a universal storm, erupting not merely through air and water, but through earth as well. Perhaps Martin associated the flood of Genesis, coming at the beginning of the Bible, with the apocalyptic events described in the Book of Revelation at its end. Some of the figures hint at damned souls from a Last Judgment. Certainly it is the horror of the scene, and the futility of mankind's struggle against fate, that have caught the artist's imagination. Noah's ark, the symbol of hope and redemption, is barely visible, resting on one of the highest rocky ledges, near the ominous conjunction of sun, moon, and blood-red comet.

This appears to have been Martin's second Deluge picture. He exhibited an earlier treatment of the subject at the British Institution in 1826; although the actual work is lost, we know its appearance from a reproductive print published in 1828. He first showed the present version at the Paris Salon in 1835, where it was much admired by the French and won him a gold medal. In 1837 he exhibited the work again, this time at the Royal Academy in London; in the exhibition catalogue the title was accompanied by quotations from Genesis and from Byron's dark poetic drama on the Deluge, *Heaven and Earth*. In 1839 Prince Albert, the husband of Queen Victoria, paid a visit to Martin's studio, saw *The Deluge* (it was as yet unsold) and suggested that he should paint further works on the same theme to create a narrative cycle. Martin took up the idea and conceived a kind of triptych, with *The Deluge* as centerpiece and slightly smaller "wings" showing scenes before and after the cataclysm. He painted his new subjects and exhibited them at the Royal Academy in 1840. In the first, *The Eve of the Deluge* (Royal Collection), Noah and his family appear grouped around the ancient Methuselah, who recognizes the coming together of the sun, moon, and comet as the fulfillment of prophecies made by his father Enoch. The final work in the sequence, *The Assuaging of the Waters* (Fine Arts Museums of San Francisco), shows the mountains reappearing as the flood subsides, with the dove sent out by Noah to discover whether the earth is again habitable flying back with the hopeful sign of an olive branch in its beak. These were bought from Martin respectively by Prince Albert and the Duchess of Sutherland, the Queen's Mistress of the Robes, and *The Deluge* was bought from him in about 1845 by his most important patron, Charles Scarisbrick, a wealthy landowner, developer, and collector from Lancashire. The three paintings remained in different collections and, curiously, appear never to have been exhibited together in the artist's lifetime.   MW

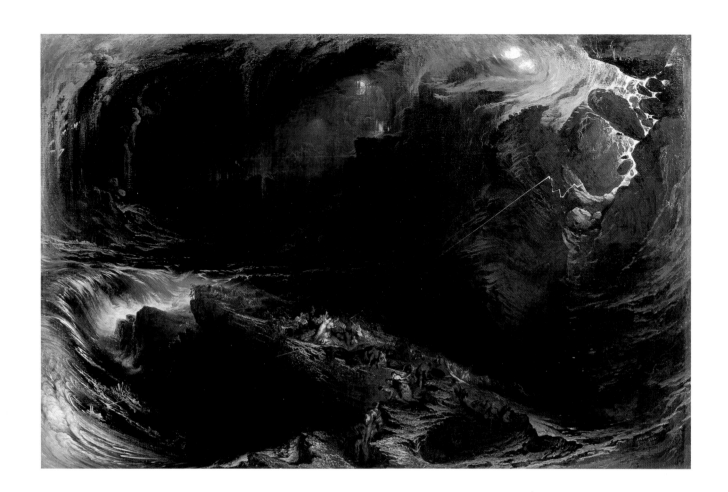

62 J. M. W. TURNER

Inverary Pier, Loch Fyne: Morning, about 1845
Oil on canvas, 36 x 48 in (91.5 x 122 cm)
Gift of Paul Mellon, 1977

References: Butlin and Joll, 304 (no. 519); Shanes

In the twentieth century, paintings such as this from Turner's later career—in which sky, water, and land emerge as glowing, vaporous presences, and colors are brushed, scraped, and dripped across the canvas in an experimental fashion—have commonly been admired as precursors of abstract art. It is true that by this stage Turner had moved far away from the idea of landscape as the record of a given place, looking always for elemental dramas of light against dark, warm coloring against cool—dissolving forms to suggest a world of transience, even painting dreams and visions. On the other hand, he never publicly exhibited a painting as naked of detail as this, and would almost certainly have regarded it as unfinished. In fact, it is typical of the canvases with basic rough-hewn compositions that he would keep in his studio, sometimes for years, before sending them in for an exhibition and working them up to a higher degree of finish at the last minute, in the "varnishing days" immediately before the exhibition opened. One contemporary wrote of these raw beginnings of pictures as being "divided into large masses of blue, where the water or sky was to come, and the other portions laid out in broad orange yellow, falling into delicate brown where the trees and landscapes were to be placed."[1] Another described one as "a mere dab of several colours, and 'without form and void,' like chaos before creation."[2]

The work is from a distinct group of nine such paintings, close in size, coloring, and degree of finish, all of which are based on compositions from the artist's much earlier series of prints, the *Liber Studiorum*; probably the best known painting of the group is *Norham Castle* (Tate Gallery). Turner's *Liber Studiorum* consisted of seventy-one mezzotint plates, engraved after drawings made by him specially for the project, and was published in parts between 1807 and 1819. The plate of Inverary Pier, which was published in 1811, clearly shows the same disposition of mountains and hillsides around the loch and enables us to identify the vague rectilinear form to the left in the painting as the pier. Inverary stands on the western shore of Loch Fyne in the Scottish Highlands, and the view is looking east toward the head of the loch and, of course, the morning sun. In transposing from print to painting, Turner edited out not only smaller details, but also some figures and boats at the pier, losing a key vertical accent provided by a boat's mast at the center of the composition. Perhaps he would have used the area of scraped-in red in the lower left as the groundwork for elements of this kind if he had finished the painting for exhibition.[3]   MW

1   Butlin and Joll, 298.
2   Ibid., 209.
3   The fact that the present painting shows Inverary Pier and derives from the earlier print of that subject was first pointed out by the Turner scholar Eric Shanes. Previously it had been misidentified as a view of Monte Rosa and Lake Maggiore in Italy.

From Truth to Beauty

BRITAIN WAS THE CRADLE of the Industrial Revolution and during the reign of Queen Victoria—from 1837 to 1901—the most advanced and powerful country in the world. Dominated by the "self-made men" of manufacture and trade, it was the first modern industrial society, empirical, forward-looking, and at the same time plagued by problems and doubts.

In Victorian painting we see a playing-out of some of the ideas and attitudes, the tensions and debates that marked the age. The Pre-Raphaelite Brotherhood was formed in 1848, during the heyday of Victorian optimism and materialism. With their painstaking attention to fact and detail, the "P.R.B." and their friends tried to forge a style to match the times. Unlike almost any other artists since the Renaissance, they claimed, they would deal honestly and heartily in the Truth. With the gradual deflation of national morale from the 1860s onward, more and more artists shunned this kind of engagement with the realities of life in favor of escape, offering a better world of their own creation. This was the tendency known as the Aesthetic Movement, which held the only essential concern of art to be Beauty.

When Whistler painted the Thames veiled in mist and darkness in his "nocturnes," it was a calculated anti-Pre-Raphaelite decision. The business of the artist, he argued, was not to gather facts like a scientist—as William Bell Scott did in his view of Ailsa Craig, for instance—but to create beautiful harmonies of form and color. The same idea of art for art's sake underlies Leighton's portrait of Mrs. Guthrie. Clausen's *Schoolgirls,* on the other hand, shows a younger artist moving out of Aestheticism under the sway of avant-garde painting in France, a sign of things to come in British art of the twentieth century.   MW

63 JOHN EVERETT MILLAIS

L'Enfant du Régiment, 1854–55

Oil on prepared paper, laid on canvas, mounted on board, 18⅛ x 24½ in (46 x 62.2 cm)

Purchased through the Paul Mellon Fund, 1980

First exhibited: Royal Academy, 1856 (no. 553)

References: Bennett 1967, 40 (no. 52); Tate Gallery, 136 (no. 70)

Millais derived the subject of this painting from Donizetti's opera *La Fille du régiment*. The heroine of the opera is Marie, offspring of a secret liaison between the Marquise de Berkenfield and an officer in the French army. Since her father's death in battle the child has been brought up by the regiment of grenadiers to which he belonged. The action of the opera takes place in 1805, during the Napoleonic Wars, and Marie is no longer a child but a young woman. Millais's painting would therefore show an imagined incident from her early life. The scene may have been suggested by the lines sung by her and the regimental sergeant, Sulpice, as they reminisce about her unusual upbringing: "Et j'avais, fille militaire, pour berceau votre fourniment / Où tu dormais paisiblement…au doux bruit du tambour battant! (And I, a military girl, had your soldier's kit as my cradle / Where you slept peacefully…to the sweet sound of the beating drum!)." The opera was performed in London at Her Majesty's every season from 1847 to 1851, except for 1849, and also while Millais's painting was on show at the Royal Academy in 1856. Millais was an avid operagoer, and had already based two major paintings on operatic plots: the highly successful *A Huguenot* (1851–52; Makins Collection) and *The Proscribed Royalist, 1651* (1852–53; private collection).

The setting was painted in Winchelsea Parish Church, Sussex, in the autumn of 1854; the exterior of the same church can be seen on the horizon in Millais's *The Blind Girl* (Birmingham City Art Gallery), the background of which he also painted in Winchelsea in 1854. He shows the injured girl sleeping on the fourteenth-century tomb of Gervaise Alard, first Warden of the Cinque Ports, which is painted with a typically Pre-Raphaelite attention to details and particulars. Millais had first visited Winchelsea a couple of years earlier, writing enthusiastically to his friend Harriet Collins: "I shall never rest quiet till I am painting there. We went over the church which is celebrated for its early monuments of Knights Templars, such glorious old tombs."[1] In 1854 he was there from about August 24 to November 22, in company with his friend, assistant, and pupil, Michael Halliday. He probably painted the setting of *L'Enfant du Régiment* after that of *The Blind Girl*, in October-November, leaving the center of the composition blank for the addition of the figure. This he painted about a year later, after moving to Perth in Scotland.

One of the leading principles of the Pre-Raphaelite Brotherhood was to paint everything and everyone faithfully from life as an individual likeness. Their figures are never imaginary or "ideal," but exact portraits of carefully chosen models. In this case the model for the child was Isabella Nicol, a Perth girl who also posed for the younger companion in *The Blind Girl*. The coat draped over her is identifiable as part of the uniform worn by grenadiers of the French infantry of the line between 1795 and 1808. Whether Millais intended the fighting in which he shows the regiment involved to be taking place during the French revolutionary wars or under Napoleon is unknown, and he may have had no exact historical moment in mind.   MW

1   Millais Papers, Pierpont Morgan Library, New York.

The Irish Girl, 1860

Oil on canvas, laid on board, 11¼ x 10⅞ in. (28.5 x 27.3 cm)

Purchased through the Paul Mellon Fund, 1989

First exhibited: Liverpool Academy, 1860 (no. 241)

Reference: Bennett 1964, 24 (no. 38)

From the later 1850s onward there was a fashion among more advanced British artists, led by the Pre-Raphaelite painters John Everett Millais and Dante Gabriel Rossetti, for painting simple, small-scale studies or "cabinet pictures" of the heads of women and children. Though Pre-Raphaelite in their attention to detail and to the particulars of the model's features and skin tones, these were essentially decorative in conception—the head is generally set against a flat background, and the colors of clothing and props carefully harmonized—with no clear narrative, moral, or documentary purpose. As such, they played an important part in the beginnings of the Aesthetic Movement.

The model for *The Irish Girl*, Ford Madox Brown's most beautiful contribution to the genre, was an orange-seller whom he found while scouting for models for an altogether different kind of painting, his grand, didactic magnum opus, *Work* (begun 1852, completed 1856–63; Manchester City Art Gallery). Among the many figures in this modern allegory of labor in its various forms, inspired by the gospel of work laid down by the social critic Thomas Carlyle, are some Irish vagrants. These were a common sight in England, especially since the Irish Famine of the 1840s, and in the moral scheme of Brown's painting symbolize the evil of unemployment, resulting from idleness and bad management on the part of the more privileged members of society. Presumably Brown considered using the girl shown here for a young vagrant but dropped the idea and painted her alone instead. In *The Irish Girl* she appears neither as a vagrant nor as an orange-seller, but as another of the lowliest kinds of street vendor, a flower girl.

The work was painted as a pendant to a slightly larger study showing a boy of about the same age, also in full face: *The English Boy* (1860; Manchester City Art Gallery). The model for this was the artist's own son Oliver, then five years old. The natural way to hang the two works together would be with the girl to the left, which would create the impression that she was looking sideways at the boy. He, by contrast, stares straight out at the viewer. Whereas she is clearly poor, he is identified by his dress as comfortably-off, a child of the middle class. Whereas she holds a cornflower, his "attribute" is a whipping top: she is associated with nature, he with the man-made; she is at work while he is at play. Brown enjoyed setting up such contrasts and *Work* is full of them—as for instance, in the confrontation between a rough mongrel and a refined-looking whippet in the foreground.

Both pictures were painted at Brown's home in Kentish Town, north London, as he painstakingly brought *Work* toward completion. They were bought from him by the patron who, four years earlier, had undertaken to buy *Work*, Thomas Plint of Leeds. A young stockbroker, evangelical churchman, and philanthropist, Plint had built up a spectacular Pre-Raphaelite collection. For *Work* he had pledged 400 guineas; for *The Irish Girl* he paid forty.

The Liverpool Academy, where the painting was first exhibited in 1860, was a favorite forum of the Pre-Raphaelites and associates of the group including Brown. By showing their works there and occasionally winning the annual prizes—Brown had won two—they could attract the wealthy northern collectors who accounted for such an important part of their patronage. In 1861 Brown showed *The Irish Girl* again, this time at the Hogarth Club in London. The Hogarth was a short-lived, private exhibiting society founded by Brown, his friend Rossetti, and other avant-garde artists who found themselves at odds with the Royal Academy. They chose the name in honor of William Hogarth, "the stalwart founder of Modern English art." Brown deeply admired Hogarth and, as the vivid combination of realism, satire, and moralizing in *Work* demonstrates, his approach to the depiction of modern life was founded on Hogarthian principles. Perhaps even his idea of contrasting the Irish girl and the English boy came from Hogarth's opposition of types such as the apprentices in his *Industry and Idleness* series. MW

65 WILLIAM BELL SCOTT

Ailsa Craig, 1860
Oil on canvas, 12⅞ x 19¼ in (33 x 48.6 cm)
Gift of Paul Mellon, 1976

Ailsa Craig is an island off the southwest coast of Scotland, at the entrance to the Firth of Clyde; though only about a mile across, it is steep, almost conical in shape, and rises to over a thousand feet. The view here is looking west and north from the mainland, with the Isle of Arran on the horizon to the right and Kintyre to the left. Scott painted it while staying at Penkill Castle, a few miles inland from Girvan, in July 1860. There he was the guest of Alice Boyd, whom he had met in the previous year, and with whom he was to have an intimate friendship for the rest of his life. From this time on he would regularly spend his summers at Penkill, where he painted pictures and murals, wrote poems, and entertained artistic and literary friends such as Dante Gabriel Rossetti. He died there in 1890 and was buried in the local church.

Scott had moved in Pre-Raphaelite circles since the earliest days of the movement, and *Ailsa Craig* is a thorough and wholehearted essay in Pre-Raphaelite landscape painting, a tribute particularly to William Holman Hunt's densely symbolic early landscape *Our English Coasts, 1852 (Strayed Sheep)* (1852; Tate Gallery). In their approach to landscape the Pre-Raphaelites tried to rid their minds of all preconceptions about natural beauty, especially theories of the "ideal" and the "picturesque" handed down from the eighteenth century. For them the purpose of art was neither to order nature so as to please the eye; nor to invest it with human feelings; nor to capture its fleeting effects in an "impression." They tried instead to document its appearance, to provide the viewer with as much information about the given place as possible. Typically, Scott chose a time of day for his scene, late afternoon, at which the best light fell on his foreground. He painted everything on the spot, from direct observation, in crisp, all-over detail, and with little or no concession to the limitations of human eyesight. The work is an assemblage of facts to be examined like specimens in a glass display case, and every bright, ringing detail is in focus at the same time.

The Pre-Raphaelites aspired to make art more like science, and Scott's foreground shows a characteristic keenness to identify botanical species. He gives us no generic, fill-in vegetation, but plant portraits: yellow irises, thistles, and so on. He chose a place to paint whose geology shows through clearly, and provides everything we might wish to know on this subject too, resisting all temptation to improve on nature's own designs. As a result, there is a sense of the bending, moulding, wearing down, and crumbling of rock—the operation of great forces over great periods of time. We find ourselves wondering how and in what far-distant epoch Ailsa Craig was formed. The sheep tracks following the contours of the land resemble undulating strata; the scattered boulders and pebbles at the beach remind us of the eroding power of the sea. Geology was a key issue for the Victorians, fascinated as they were by its latest findings, troubled as they were by the threat these posed to traditional religious beliefs. In another great Pre-Raphaelite coastal landscape, William Dyce's *Pegwell Bay* (1858–60; Tate Gallery), a comet sighted over some fossil-rich cliffs represents the vastnesses of space and time that modern science was opening up; in *Our English Coasts, 1852 (Strayed Sheep)*, Hunt shows sheep near a cliff edge to represent the Christian flock in peril; and in *Ailsa Craig*, his *Scottish* coast—a landscape of fact and geology crossed by sheep—Scott may well have intended resonances of a similar kind.   MW

160

66 FREDERIC LEIGHTON

Mrs. James Guthrie, about 1864–65

Oil on canvas, 82$^{15}\!/_{16}$ x 54½ in (210.7 x 138.5 cm)

Gift of Paul Mellon, 1978

First exhibited: Royal Academy, 1866 (no. 7)

References: Ormond and Ormond, 155 (no. 107); Royal Academy, 138–39 (no. 33)

Ellinor Guthrie was born in 1838 in Perth, Australia, the daughter of James and Ellen Stirling. Her father, a naval officer of Scottish background, had led the party of British colonists who settled Perth and Fremantle in 1829 and was Western Australia's first governor. When Ellinor was still an infant, her father left the governorship to return to active service in the navy, eventually becoming an admiral. She and her ten brothers and sisters were brought up at the family home in Guildford, England, and a succession of naval stations in the Mediterranean and Far East. In 1856, aged eighteen, she married James Alexander Guthrie, a successful Scottish merchant banker of the firm of Chalmers and Guthrie; they lived in London, in the fashionable and affluent Portland Place, and between 1857 and 1869 had nine children. Sittings for the present portrait took place after Mrs. Guthrie had recovered from the birth of their fifth daughter in October 1864.

The Guthries probably commissioned the portrait, although Leighton may possibly have painted it as an expression of friendship; he seldom accepted portrait commissions and felt uncomfortable painting sitters who were not also friends. Certainly he was drawn to Mrs. Guthrie's Mediterranean-looking features and after the portrait used her as the model for the central figure of a priestess in his large friezelike painting of *The Syracusan Bride* (1865–66; private collection).

The work typifies the movement in advanced British painting of the 1860s away from the intensely factual and didactic manner of the Pre-Raphaelites toward an art of unashamedly decorative and sensual appeal. Under the Aesthetic Movement, as it came to be called, the artist regarded his first duty as the creation of beauty—often through the representation of people and things beautiful in themselves, always by means of the most exquisitely refined technique. Mrs. Guthrie is shown surrounded by objects of decorative art that seem to pay homage to her beauty. In the flowers and vases the colors appear as a separating-out of those subtly blended in her complexion. The ornate chair and the large Baroque painting in the background, which were probably in Leighton's studio, suggest the idea that she is not only beautiful herself but the inhabitant of a world—albeit a hothouse world—full of beauty and culture. The inclusion of the painting also serves to associate Leighton's brilliantly animated brushwork, displayed especially in the treatment of the dress, with the painterly tradition of the Old Masters.

Mrs. Guthrie's husband died young in 1873, when she was only thirty-five, leaving her a large fortune. Later she married as her second husband Guthrie's cousin, Forster Fitzgerald Arbuthnot; he was a translator and publisher of Oriental literature who collaborated with Richard Burton on the first English edition of the *Kama Sutra*. She died in 1911, aged seventy-three. MW

67 JAMES McNEILL WHISTLER

Nocturne in Blue and Silver, between 1872 and 1878
Oil on canvas, 17½ x 24 in (44.4 x 61 cm)
Purchased through the Paul Mellon Fund, 1994
First exhibited: probably Grosvenor Gallery, 1878 (no. 53)
Reference: Young et al., 89–90 (no. 151)

The series of paintings Whistler called his "nocturnes" resulted from evening expeditions on the river Thames near his home in Chelsea. Rowed out by the Greaves brothers, young men from a nearby boatyard who worked as his assistants, he would study a prospective subject intently but without making any sketches or notes. The painting that resulted, a view through the veil of memory as well as those of darkness and mist, would come the following day in the studio. Whistler's aim in this was anti-topographical: he wished people to enjoy his painting not as the image of a given place, but as a refined arrangement of forms and colors, free of all anecdotal content.

As a leading figure in the Aesthetic Movement, Whistler worked very much in the spirit of Walter Pater's famous dictum, first published in 1873, that "all art constantly aspires towards the condition of music."[1] He borrowed the title of "nocturne" from the famous piano pieces by Chopin and hoped that it would lead his viewers to appreciate his night scenes on the abstract rather than the representational level. As he declared in his "Ten O'Clock" lecture (1885):

Nature contains the elements, in colour and form, of all pictures, as the keyboard contains the notes of all music. But the artist is born to pick, and choose, and group with science, these elements, that the result may be beautiful— as the musician gathers his notes, and forms his chords, until he brings forth from chaos glorious harmony.[2]

Bringing forth his glorious harmony from as squalid, unaesthetic a chaos as that of the industrial riverfront near his home was typical of his taste for mischief and the unexpected. Then again, he would argue, part of the task of the artist was to see poetry and beauty where others might be blind to them:

When...the poor buildings lose themselves in the dim sky, and the tall chimneys become campanili, and the warehouses are palaces in the night, and the whole city hangs in the heavens, and fairy-land is before us— then the wayfarer hastens home; the working man and the

cultured one, the wise man and the one of pleasure, cease to understand, as they have ceased to see, and Nature, who, for once, has sung in tune, sings her exquisite song to the artist alone.[3]

Here the basic "notes" from which he composed his painting were the buildings and lights on the Battersea side of the Thames, opposite Chelsea, looking upriver: on the left appears the large illuminated clock tower known as "Morgan's Folly," which stood by Morgan's Crucible Works; behind this are some factory chimneys and in the foreground a river barge.

When painting his nocturnes Whistler had the Greaves brothers prepare quantities of various tones of the keynote color, generally blue, thinning the paint to such a washy "sauce" that the canvas would sometimes have to be laid flat on the floor to prevent it from running off. Usually he made a number of attempts at the image, simply wiping the failures off the canvas until he arrived at what he wanted. The thinness of the paint lends the nocturnes an air of cool virtuosity—there is no gestural or finicky brushwork to betray labor, changes of mind, or anything but the purest aesthetic feelings on the part of the artist. Here, typically, the fairly rough weave of the canvas shows through across the entire surface. Like the pervasive blue, this helps bind each element to the whole. It also reproduces the slight vibration of night vision.

The stylized butterfly near the lower edge is a signature derived from the artist's monogram (an "M" above a "W" with a "J" through the middle); he probably added this at some time in the 1880s. He associated the butterfly with beauty, delicacy, and the lack of any useful function in life, the essential qualities of the artist. The design mimics the stamps on Japanese woodblock prints.   MW

1 Pater 1910, 135.
2 Whistler 1890, 142–43.
3 Ibid., 144.

68 EDWARD LEAR

Kangchenjunga from Darjeeling, 1879

Oil on canvas, 48 x 71¼ in (122.9 x 182.4 cm)

Gift of Donald C. Gallup, 1997

Reference: Vivien Noakes, 155–56 (under no. 63)

This imposing canvas, one of three versions of the subject, was the result of Lear's visit to India and Ceylon in 1873–75, the last and longest expedition of his career as a travel artist. He went, with some reluctance, at the invitation and expense of his patron Lord Northbrook, the Liberal statesman who had been appointed Indian Viceroy. On his arrival in November 1873 he was immediately enraptured and for the next fifteen months traveled all over the subcontinent, making rough sketches and notes to be used as the basis for more finished work on his return home. He reached Darjeeling, on the southern edge of the Himalayan Mountains, in January 1874, stayed for several days at Doyle's Hotel, and studied the spectacular views of Kangchenjunga—one of the highest peaks—along the well-known scenic route of the Birch Hill Road. After a couple of days he felt overwhelmed, wondering if he could ever make what he saw work as the subject of a painting. "Kinchinjunga is not, as it seems to me, – a sympathetic mountain"; he wrote in his journal for January 18,

> *it is so far off – so very God like & stupendous, – & all that great world of dark opal vallies full of misty, hardly to be imagined forms, – besides the all but impossibility of expressing the whole as a scene, – make up a rather distracting and repelling whole.*[1]

By the end of the following day, however, he was more hopeful: he had made a number of drawings and "jottings" and determined that the mountain looked its best in the early morning. In his journal he noted that

> *the "light and shade" is too broken at sunset, & the absence of the beautiful broad morning effect is not atoned for by the finer color of later hours. Kinchinjunga at sunrise is a glory not to be forgotten: Kinchinjunga PM is apt to become a wonderful hash of Turneresque color & mist & space, but with little claim to forming a picture of grand effect.*[2]

As further aides-mémoires he bought a number of scenic photographs at the hotel before leaving.

Lear returned from India to his home in San Remo on the Italian Riviera early in 1875. Before the trip he had been commissioned to paint an Indian landscape by another of his patrons, Henry Austin Bruce, at the time Home Secretary. It was for Bruce, who in the meantime had been created Baron Aberdare, that he painted the first version of *Kangchenjunga*, between 1875 and 1877; it now belongs to Cynon Valley Borough Council.[3] The second, which he despatched from San Remo at the same time as the first, was commissioned by Louisa, Lady Ashburton and is now in a private collection. The present work, dated 1879, is the third and final version, painted for the man who had encouraged Lear to visit India in the first place, Lord Northbrook.

A member of the Baring family, which had been prominent in the worlds of finance and politics for generations, Northbrook commanded a large fortune. He also had longstanding family connections with India. He enjoyed a successful term as Viceroy and, in recognition of his good work, was almost immediately elevated from baron to earl. In 1879 his friend Lear desperately needed money for a new house at San Remo, and Northbrook gave him an interest-free loan of £2,000. It seems likely that the painting of the present work was related in some way to this: perhaps Northbrook commissioned it as a further means of helping Lear; perhaps Lear presented it to his patron in gratitude.

As he intended after his encounters with the actual place, Lear sets his scene in the morning. He shuns the "Turneresque" mistiness of afternoon in favor of a clear, fresh light that affords definition to every massive ridge and peak. The awe-inspiring "grand effect" that was his highest aim as an artist is achieved in two directions: the mountains piling up to fantastic heights above, and the V-shaped avenue of trees plunging as though into an abyss below. In the left foreground some tea-pickers in local dress gather near a Buddhist shrine, included perhaps to point up the aspiring, spiritual feeling associated with great mountains.   MW

1   Vivien Noakes, 155.
2   Ibid., 155–56.
3   Ibid., no. 63.

69 GEORGE CLAUSEN

Schoolgirls, 1880

Oil on canvas, 20½ x 30⅜ in (52 x 77.2 cm)

Gift of Paul Mellon, 1985

First exhibited: Hanover Gallery, London, Winter 1880 (no. 44)

Some pupils from a ladies' academy, the fashionably dressed daughters of well-to-do parents, are taking a midday walk in the street, lined up in a "crocodile" with the eldest at the head. Near them are female types clearly positioned by the artist to set off, by means of contrast, the blessings of youth, good looks, class, and education that the girls are fortunate enough to enjoy: a comically plain, bespectacled stick-figure of a schoolmistress brings up the rear; to the left an elderly milkmaid looks on, carrying her churns by that very emblem of the working class, a yoke across her shoulders; to the right a young flowergirl, the lowliest of street vendors, practically a beggar, offers the girls a posy. The presence of the milkmaid and the flowergirl, with their ruddy, outdoor complexions and the rural associations of their jobs, also suggests the idea of country as against town. The girls seem unaware of the milkmaid, but toward the poor flowergirl—who is trying to attract their attention—show a range of responses from charity and pity to patent indifference: one girl holds her hand down to drop a coin; the girl on the far left turns her head with a becomingly melting expression; some, notably the one in front, look fixedly ahead.

The location of the scene is neither country nor town exactly, but suburban north London. The girls are walking down Haverstock Hill in the southern part of Hampstead, a distinctively modern, middle-class environment. The artist was renting one of the Mall Studios on nearby Tasker Road at the time, so the setting of his picture was almost on his doorstep. In all likelihood he painted the setting largely on the spot and the figures largely in the studio, making pencil studies for both in the sketchbooks that he always kept as part of his working process.

The most immediate precedent in Britain for this kind of modern-life scene, combining feminine beauty, fashion, and an understated element of social commentary, lay in the paintings of James Tissot, who had lived in London and enjoyed increasing success since 1871. Still young and casting around for a style to develop as his own, Clausen seems to have been looking particularly to Tissot at this point in his career. The slightly titillating way in which the girl dressed in light blue looks out of the picture, as if making eye contact with an assumed male viewer, is a typically Tissot-like touch; the line of girls behind her might represent the stages of girlhood, progressing from the mere children at the back to young women ripe for exchanges of looks with admirers. Like Venus in a Judgment of Paris, she is flanked by others not quite as pretty as she, and our encounter with her is given immediacy by the cutting-off of her figure by the bottom edge of the canvas, a device the artist may well, again, have borrowed from Tissot. The distinctive technique in which the work is painted, with its suggestions of the "raw" brushwork and color of avant-garde painting on the Continent, owes something to both Tissot and to the conservative form of Impressionism developed by Jules Bastien-Lepage, a key influence on many young British artists around this time.

Such foreign influences were a touchy issue, and it is typical that even those who admired *Schoolgirls* when it was first exhibited found the combination of everyday, modern subject and relatively adventurous technique difficult to take. "The first feeling about this picture is an angry one—that the artist should make all his damsels' features so blunt and indefinite in outline, and their complexions of such purply tinge," wrote the critic of *The Times* (November 20, 1880);

> but if we get over these drawbacks, and that, perhaps, of the subject itself—for schoolgirls in close column with lampposts behind, and a longish vista of pavement can hardly be said to lend themselves to pictorial treatment …what a fresh and charming little picture it is!"

The girl in light blue was a favorite model of Clausen's, and she also appears in his follow-up picture of 1881, a larger scene of people on the same street entitled *A Spring Morning, Haverstock Hill* (Bury Art Gallery). After this he moved to the country and abandoned street scenes in favor of agricultural subjects, some presenting rural life with the bleakness of Thomas Hardy's novels. MW

The Moderns

THE MODERN MOVEMENT came to British art through a variety of channels. Walter Sickert returned from France to England in 1905. Through his friendship with Edgar Degas, Sickert brought a renewed and darker version of late Impressionism to British painting. The painting of modern life meant for Sickert, and the group that quickly sprang up around him, the urban scene. The Camden Town School took its sobriquet from the drab, lower-middle-class area north of London's more fashionable zone. The leaders of the School—Harold Gilman, Spencer Gore, Charles Ginner, and Sickert himself— were quick to translate the new freedom offered by French painting into a specific English locale and moved British painting away from the pastoral sentimentalities of late Victorian art.

Barely five miles away from Camden Town in another slightly grander but still shabby area of London, Bloomsbury, another set of artists and writers were forming their own revolt against the standards of Victorian art and morality. Their leaders were the critics Roger Fry and Clive Bell and the artists Duncan Grant and Vanessa Bell. The two Post-Impressionist exhibitions organized by Roger Fry at the Grafton Gallery in 1910 and 1912 were a *succès de scandale* and struck the most decisive blow for the modern movement in England, introducing both the work of the principal Post-Impressionists— Cézanne, van Gogh, and Gauguin—and the newer directions of the School of Paris as established by Picasso and Matisse. After these exhibitions the modern movement had the Royal Academy, the conservative establishment of British art, on the run. Modernism became the accepted and expected mode of the twentieth-century British artist.

The effect of World War One on all aspects of British life and culture cannot be underestimated. In painting it spawned the brilliant but short-lived movement of Vorticism, led by Wyndham Lewis and numbering among its collaborators C. R. W. Nevinson and Edward Wadsworth. The new conditions of the twentieth century demanded a new language for artists, albeit the admixture of Cubism and Futurism of which Vorticism was largely the compound. It would also eventually work itself through to the surprising and widespread phenomenon of British Surrealism in the 1930s and early 1940s.

Although Vorticism produced some remarkable and original works, it was too short-lived to have an influence on European art generally. British art until the 1930s frequently seemed to echo sharper and more original innovations elsewhere. In the 1930s Henry Moore and Barbara Hepworth in sculpture and Ben Nicholson in painting produced work that was the equal of the School of Paris. Nicholson in particular produced some of the most authentic and original extensions of Mondrian's geometric abstractions. These artists lifted British art from its eccentric and slightly provincial responses to the modern movement and made it a significant part of the overall story of modernism. PMcC

70 WALTER SICKERT

L'Ospedale Civile, Venice, probably 1901
Oil on canvas, 26 x 18½ in (66 x 47 cm)
Gift of Paul Mellon, 1987
First exhibited: Thomas Agnew & Sons, London, *Pictures by W. R. Sickert, A.R.A.,* 1933 (no. 51)
Reference: Baron 1973, 327 (no. 141)

Sickert lived in Venice for several periods during the years 1895–1904, moved easily in the international artistic and literary society that flourished there, and produced a large number of drawings, etchings, and paintings of Venetian subjects. He enjoyed the challenge of treating afresh the famous sights painted by such familiar masters as Canaletto and Turner—as well as by his former mentor Whistler—and brought to them a vision formed in part upon Monet's recent series of paintings of Rouen Cathedral under different conditions of light and atmosphere. Like Monet, he played variations on the theme of the elaborately decorated facade— most often that of St. Mark's, the Doge's Palace, or Santa Maria della Salute—and delighted in rendering the linear, intricate forms of his motif in the most summary and painterly of techniques. The result is more suggestive of memory or imagination than direct observation, depending as much on the richness of Sickert's brushwork and color in their own right as on the beauty of the places they describe.

The Ospedale Civile (city hospital) spans the north side of the Campo S.S. Giovanni e Paolo; the church of that name is on the east side, and the famous Colleoni monument in the center, making the square one of Venice's major tourist attractions. The Ospedale building dates from the later fifteenth century and was originally the Scuola di San Marco, headquarters of one of the city's powerful guild organizations; a statue of the lion of St. Mark dominates the upper part of the entrance bay of the facade. It became a hospital in the early nineteenth century and continues as such today. The facade retains much of its original lavish ornament, including trompe-l'œil reliefs at the first-floor level that create the illusion of arcaded openings into the building.

Sickert painted the Ospedale several times on his first visits to Venice in 1895–96, though in a horizontal format, with the viewpoint further to the left, and including the whole of the facade. The present work, showing the left four of the building's six bays, can be dated on stylistic grounds to a later visit, most likely that of January-July 1901. The view here is from the top of the Ponte Rosso, looking up the Rio dei Mendicanti and including the next bridge north, the Ponte Cavallo. The right edge of the canvas corresponds exactly to the corner of a canalside building that cuts off one's view of the Ospedale from this point. The light is that of late afternoon, with the sun playing brightly on the west side of the building and the facade in shadow. In the distance beyond the Ponte Cavallo are some buildings on the cemetery island of San Michele, which inspired Sickert to exhibit one of his paintings of this subject under the title *From the Hospital to the Grave.*

Though like a French Impressionist painting in its spontaneous-looking brushwork, *L'Ospedale Civile* was probably painted in the artist's studio—perhaps not even in Venice—rather than directly from the motif in true Impressionist fashion. Sickert was disdainful of the idea of a painting as the record of a given place at a given moment and valued highly the technical refinement and imaginative freedom that working in the studio fostered. Instead of on-the-spot observation he relied on sketches and recollections, sometimes on his own earlier paintings of the subject, sometimes on photographs. He owned a collection of photographs of Venetian sites, and—judging by the precise disposition of every element when compared to the actual view, along with the great accuracy of tone but not color—the present work may well have been photographically based.   MW

71 WALTER SICKERT

The Camden Town Murder (also known as *What shall we do about the rent?*), about 1908
Oil on canvas, 10¹⁄₁₆ x 14 in (25.6 x 35.5 cm)
Purchased through the Paul Mellon Fund, 1979
First exhibited: Galerie Bing, Paris, *Trois Peintres Anglais*, 1939 (no. 5)
References: Baron 1973, 348 (no. 269); Baron 1980

This is the kind of painting for which Sickert is best known, its subject from the life of London's working class, its technique fittingly rough and earthy, its tone one of caustic realism, in this case treating the grand artistic tradition of the female nude with a kind of cockney cheek. *The Camden Town Murder* was his primary title for this and at least two other paintings of 1908–9, all of them showing an ungainly nude woman with a clothed man on a bed in a shabby interior. On some level he probably intended this as a jokey reference to the paintings as aesthetic murders, perpetrated as they were in Camden Town, in which accepted ideas of good art and good taste were bloodily savaged. In a more literal sense, however, the title refers to the murder of a prostitute named Emily Dimmock, which took place in the early hours of September 12, 1907. The victim lived and died in Camden Town, which was a seedy district of rented rooms, pubs, eating houses, and music halls in north London. She was found in bed with her throat cut, having apparently been killed in her sleep. The police arrested Robert Wood, a commercial artist; he was tried and acquitted, however, and the crime was never solved. The story was widely reported and discussed, even sensationally illustrated in the popular press, and for a time Camden Town and murder were inseparable in the public mind.

Sickert had a studio on Mornington Crescent in Camden Town and had been painting nudes there, from models who may well have been prostitutes like Dimmock, just a few weeks before the murder took place. When he began painting more nudes in the following year, now in the company of clothed men, the possible implication of such subjects in connection with the murder would have occurred to him and his viewers inevitably. The murder may even have moved him to try such subjects in the first place, and it has been pointed out that his male character in them bears some resemblance to the chief suspect in the Dimmock case, Robert Wood. But the idea that this or either of the other paintings directly represents the murder seems unlikely. Though strangely awkward, the woman's position on the bed is quite unlike Dimmock's as she was found, and there is no blood or any other definite sign of violence about the scene.

Like both of the other paintings called *The Camden Town Murder*, the present work has also been known as *What shall we do about the rent?* (sometimes with "for" instead of "about"). Sickert used the latter title, albeit some twenty years later, when he wrote an inscription on a preparatory sketch.[1] With its suggestion of worries and tensions over money, this puts an altogether more humdrum construction upon the relation of the man and woman; the question might be a line from one of the music-hall songs that Sickert so enjoyed, dealing as they did in the daily pleasures and tribulations of working-class life. On the other hand, since the answer to the question for women in Camden Town was so often going "on the game," it does evoke much the same sordid world—though in less lurid form—as the story of the Camden Town Murder. Both of Sickert's titles enhance his painting's atmosphere of poverty, squalor, and crime, but he surely never intended us to take them at face value. They are part clues to his meaning, part teases aimed at the suggestive viewer. Small, intense, almost furtive, his painting has us looking through a keyhole, getting a glimpse into the intimate lives of people we know nothing about, and speculating as to what kind of story, whether sensational or mundane, they might be living out before us.   MW

1 Baron 1973, 348 (no. 269, study no. 2).

72 SPENCER GORE

Ballet Scene from "On the Sands," 1910
Oil on canvas, 16 x 20 in (40.6 x 50.8 cm)
Purchased through the Paul Mellon Fund, 1983

Reference: Gore and Shone, 20 (no. 10)

Between 1905 and 1912 Spencer Gore painted numerous scenes of music halls. Here he shows a moment from the little-known ballet *On the Sands*, the plot of which centered on the perils of a runaway schoolgirl; the characters ranged from naughty Eton schoolboys to colorful gypsies and sailors, some of whom can be seen on stage in this scene. *On the Sands* was performed in September 1910 at the Alhambra, one of the larger, more elegant music halls in central London. Built in 1883 in Leicester Square, the Alhambra was named after the citadel and palace built at Granada by the Moorish kings in the twelfth century. Every detail, such as the highly gilt piers of the proscenium and the brightly colored, decorative geometric inlays of the balcony boxes, evokes the lush, exotic beauty of such architecture, a style that turn-of-the-century audiences considered magnificently decadent.

Despite its aura of sketchy immediacy and its appearance of having been painted on the spot, the painting was carefully completed in his studio from a series of drawings. Gore was a frequent visitor to the Alhambra balcony; a contemporary remarked that he was "always in the same seat, taking sights with thumb and pencil at the uplifted legs of the ballerinas."[1] Of four known sketches for this composition, two are studies of the figures on stage; the third represents the elaborate architecture of the stage and box facing his seat; and the fourth, the entire composition as it appears in the oil. Clearly he used this last preparatory drawing (squared-up so as to be transferred easily to canvas) to paint the final picture. His meticulous process of working up the painting from a series of sketches lends to the composition a geometric formality that ultimately undermines the overall spontaneity of the scene: the highly patterned surface and the linear definition of the composition seem to immobilize the figures —especially the two dancing

gypsies at center stage—in spite of their shimmering costumes and animated gestures.

Gore preferred to depict the glittering scenes on the stages of the larger, more decorative music halls such as the Alhambra, as opposed to those in the dingier, seamier locales frequented by his mentor and colleague Walter Sickert (who had been dubbed in the 1880s "Painter-in-Ordinary to the London music hall"[2]). Gore's interest in painting theatrical scenes had been influenced by the older painter's fascination with music halls, but he concentrates on the festive, colorful side of the theater. Both artists were drawn to the compositional challenges inherent in two-dimensional representations of events seen onstage and to the strange artificial effects of stage lighting. The work of each has antecedents in Degas's scenes of café-concerts from the 1870s, but unlike Degas and Sickert, Gore tends—as in this image —to capture the hot and vibrant atmosphere of the stage and theater through a speckled, nearly *pointilliste*, type of color and brushwork. Sickert himself admitted that he looked to Gore when trying to observe color in shadows.[3] By the time he painted this picture, Gore had joined Sickert as a leader of a diverse group of painters known as the Fitzroy Street Group, a name referring to their meeting place in one of London's bohemian quarters.

Gore was a remarkable link figure between the splintering factions of the modern art scene of pre-war London. As a leader of the Fitzroy Street Group and later the Camden Town Group, a member of the jury of the New English Art Club, and an exhibitor at Roger Fry's second Post-Impressionist exhibition, he crossed boundaries more freely than any of his contemporaries.
JMA

1 Gore and Shone, 6.
2 Pickvance, 114.
3 Baron and Cormack 1980, xiii.

176

Stanislawa de Karlowska (Mrs. Robert Bevan), about 1913
Oil on canvas, 24⅝₁₆ x 20¼ in (61.8 x 51.5 cm)
Purchased through the Paul Mellon Fund, 1986

Reference: Causey and Thomson, 64 (no. 45)

The Polish artist Stanislawa de Karlowska had been married to Gilman's friend and fellow Camden Town painter Robert Bevan since 1897. A painter of townscapes, interiors, and still lifes, Karlowska showed her work regularly—under her own name—throughout her life: in the exhibitions of the London Group, to which she was elected in 1914, and in 1935 in her one-woman show at the Adams Gallery. But her career was largely overshadowed by that of her husband.

In this portrait of Karlowska, one of four Gilman painted between 1910 and 1919, the artist revels in the expressive power of the paint itself. He exploits the clash of garish colors, busy patterns, and passages of thick impasto with the markedly quiet demeanor and pose of the sitter. More than an investigation of his sitter's character, the work is an exploration of paint and color.

Karlowska's profile position hinders any reading of character into her facial features, largely blocked from view and painted only summarily. Her pose relegates her to a primarily decorative status; her presence becomes analogous to the papered walls that provide the backdrop against which she sits. Her body, face, hair, and clothing allow Gilman to create lively patterns, textures, and juxtapositions of colors that are vehicles for his exploration of the play of light and color. He toys with distinctions of figure and ground, heightening the similarities in pattern and color between the sitter's bright striped chemise and those of the papered surface behind it. Her torso nearly fuses with its backdrop, the vertical stripe on her sleeve echoing the red-, yellow-, and green-dotted stripe on the wall behind her. The overarching verticality of the image is interrupted only by the thick blotches of paint that dot the walls, her sleeve, her hair, and her face. More than a portrait, Gilman's painting resembles a carefully constructed, colorful still-life whose subject happens to be a woman.

Gilman's choice of a profile pose places the image within the tradition of classical portraiture, harking back to busts of rulers on antique coins and to painted portraits of the Renaissance; profile portraits carry the most historical of associations, ultimately referring to the mythic origins of portraiture (which according to the first-century writer Pliny began with the tracing of the shadow of a man's head on a wall). Gilman's modern variation on this ancient theme is to set his profile portrait in an intimate, domestic interior.

Early in his career Gilman had been much influenced by the tonal, atmospheric compositions of Whistler, and around the time of Whistler's memorial exhibition of 1905, he painted a number of portraits evoking this by-then acknowledged modern master. Later Gilman began to exploit un-Whistlerian passages of thick impasto and a high-keyed palette as a means of expression. With this portrait of his friend and colleague, he seems to look back to the contemplative feeling of his Whistlerian paintings—his sitter's quiet attitude and composed demeanor are reminiscent of Whistler's famous painting of his mother—while still employing the charged palette of his mature style.

The founder and leader of the Camden Town Group, Walter Sickert, increasingly found fault with Gilman's use of paint. In 1914 he published an article that berated the younger generation's new fondness for heavy impasto:

> intentional and rugged impasto…so far from producing brilliancy, covers a picture with a grey reticulation and so throws dust in the eyes of the spectator, and serves, to some extent, to veil exaggerations of colour or coarseness of drawing. It is a manner of shouting and gesticulating and does not make for expressiveness and lucidity.[1]

Gilman nevertheless continued in his quest to define his own style and technique. But during the last years of his short life, as if in unwitting response to Sickert's criticism, his handling did become smoother, his surfaces more even, and his colors cooler.   JMA

1 Baron 1979, 67.

Fruit Stall, King's Cross, 1914
Oil on canvas, 25¾ x 22 in (65.4 x 55.9 cm)
Purchased through the Paul Mellon Fund, 1980
First exhibited: Goupil Gallery, 1914 (no. 46)
Reference: Baron and Cormack, 33 (no. 46)

Trained in Paris first as an architect and later as a painter, Ginner was particularly suited to the pictorial exploration of London's streets and squares, a subject he pursued with increasing commitment from 1912 on. In the present picture he cleverly plays off itinerant stalls such as that of the fruit seller at the center against fixed store-fronts, some of whose painted awnings are visible at the right. Framed in the shadow of monumental buildings that tower over the street market on both sides, the central stalls seem to teeter on the brink of collapse, their awnings haphazardly posed and apparently ready to fall with the next strong gust of wind. The piles of vibrantly colored fruit carefully balanced atop wooden crates, themselves perilously poised on the uneven cobblestones, suggest the vitality and transience of the market. The whole scene is anchored, nevertheless, by the pole in the center of the canvas.

More than a glimpse at a moment in the life of workaday London, the painting is a meticulous study in textures, colors, and shapes. Ginner contrasts the lyrical volumes of the heaps of rounded, brightly colored fruit with the strict linearity of the more-or-less monochromatic paving stones and sidewalk. His heavily outlined figures seem fixed in place, each standing immobile, in its own spot, remote from the next. He shows the women from all views: back, profile, and front, each exhibited in turn from left to right. The forms and drapery of their heavy winter dresses and coats, the abstracted features of their faces, and their stiff gestures—especially those of the woman and child at the right, whose poses are nearly identical—are highly sculptural. In its rigidity the scene appears carefully choreographed; it is reminiscent of that frozen instant in the theater after the lights and curtain come up but before the actors move. Through his use of patterns and piled-up forms Ginner constructs a decorative frieze-like composition, one in which any sightline past the scene into the distance remains immutably blocked.

His tight-knit composition forces the viewer to revel in the visual splendor of his technique. In its insistence on form and on the plasticity of the paint, the image is highly self-conscious. Thickly applied in uniform meticulous strokes, the paint becomes an integral part of the composition; it traces Ginner's hand and eye, underlining the fact that this is not a simple, mimetic transcription of the market at King's Cross, but a pictorial rendering of the artist's individual vision of that scene. His technique is busy and robust, like his subject matter, suggesting a sincere, down-to-earth engagement with life's hustle and bustle.

His approach to his urban subjects owes much to the stylistic philosophy, called "Neo-Realism," that he and Harold Gilman developed in the early 1910s. In the manifesto on that subject (which they used as the introduction to their two-man show at Goupil's in 1914), Ginner explained:

> [Neo-Realism] *must interpret that which…ought to lie nearest our hearts, i. e., Life in all its effects, moods and developments. Each age has its landscape, its atmosphere, its cities, its people. Realism, loving Life, Loving its Age, interprets its Epoch by extracting from it the very essence of all it contains…according to the individual temperament…Neo-Realism must be a deliberate and objective transposition of the object under observation, which has for certain specific reasons appealed to the artist's ideal or mood, for self-expression.*[1]

JMA

1 Arts Council of Great Britain, 8.

Self-Portrait, about 1915

Oil on canvas laid on panel, 25⅛ x 18⅛₆ in (63.7 x 46.2 cm)

Purchased through the Paul Mellon Fund, 1982

After the death of her father, Leslie Stephen, in 1904, Vanessa Bell, her two brothers Thoby and Adrian, and her sister Virginia moved from the family home in Kensington to 46 Gordon Square, Bloomsbury. "At last we were free, had rooms of our own and space in which to be alone or to work or to see our friends," she later recalled.[1] Thoby Stephen began to hold regular Thursday evening "at homes," inviting friends from his Cambridge days, and so the Bloomsbury Group began. Besides the Stephens, it would include the painter Duncan Grant; the economist John Maynard Keynes; the art critics Roger Fry and Clive Bell, whom Vanessa would marry in 1907; the publisher and political activist Leonard Woolf, who would marry Virginia; the biographer Lytton Strachey; the novelist David Garnett, and many other peripheral figures.

Free-thinking and free-living, they were and remain a controversial group who would do much, both individually and collectively, to change taste in modern art and literature and to revoke the strictures of Victorian morality in life and thought. The first public manifestation of the new Bloomsbury spirit were the two Post-Impressionist exhibitions organized by Roger Fry in 1910 and 1912. By the time of the second exhibition, British artists, among them Vanessa Bell, were also included. Bloomsbury painting would be forever identified with the various manners of Post-Impressionism.

In her art, her life, her family, and the houses she presided over—particularly Charleston, the Sussex farmhouse which became her and Duncan Grant's final home—Vanessa Bell worked and lived at the center of the Bloomsbury Group. Almost all of the many contemporary accounts of her beauty, presence, and character are colored with a reverential awe and warmth. Her sister Virginia Woolf nicknamed her Dolphin and saw her as "a mixture of Goddess and peasant."[2] Her daughter by Duncan Grant, Angelica Garnett, described her as a Madonna with a sense of humor and went on to elaborate on her "goddess-like" image:

Vanessa had a kind of stoical warmth about her, a monolithic quality that reminded one...of the implacable smile of primitive Aphrodite...Even if she said little, there emanated from her an enormous power, a pungency like the smell of crushed sage.[3]

The date of the *Self-Portrait* is conjectural, but it certainly comes from her best period, in the years before and during World War One. Matisse had dominated the second Post-Impressionist exhibition, and his impact can be clearly felt here in the use of contrasting decorative patterns: the vivid gray-and-white check of her dress against the austere geometry of the background. The crisp modeling of the face may show a passing nod to the Picasso of 1906–7; the Bells owned an important still life of his from this period.

These influences are lightly borne. The force of the composition comes from its originality. Bell shows herself from below, as though the viewer were sitting at her feet. It gives full weight both to the body, treated so attractively and decoratively in the checked dress, and to the head, compressed by the frame but animated by the uneven diagonal line of the background. She is the sensuous and aloof goddess of contemporary descriptions. Her sister once observed that "her pictures do not betray her. Their reticence is inviolable."[4] PMcC

1 Spalding 1983, 49.
2 Rosenbaum, 171.
3 Ibid., 175.
4 Ibid., 172.

At Eleanor: Vanessa Bell, 1915
Oil on canvas, 30½ x 21½ in (65.9 x 55.5 cm)
Purchased through the Paul Mellon Fund, 1982

References: Shone, 118 and 137; Spalding 1997, 170–75

Vanessa Bell found herself falling in love with Duncan Grant steadily throughout 1914. Although he was an avowed and active homosexual, Grant found that he could in some manner return her feelings, and a bond developed which would last for the rest of their lives. In the early spring of 1915 they began living together at Eleanor, a house in West Wittering in Sussex, but there would be complications to the arrangement at the outset.

Grant's portrait of Bell comes from a fraught moment in both their lives. At the end of 1914 Grant had formed an ardent relationship with the young writer David Garnett, which would last several years. Grant and Bell rented Eleanor from John and Mary St. John Hutchinson; he was a leading London barrister, and she had become the mistress of Bell's husband Clive. The Bells' marriage had disintegrated shortly after the birth of their second son, Quentin, in 1910, although they were to retain a close "union of friendship" throughout their lives.

In May 1915 Vanessa Bell wrote to Roger Fry from Eleanor that "it was rather a difficult situation."[1] The strange and disconcerting quality of this portrait, of intimacy and withdrawal, arises from the combination of repose and disquiet in Bell's attitude. The portrait was most likely painted in April, soon after her arrival at Eleanor. Originally the plan was to paint in Henry Tonks's studio in a nearby boathouse, but the unseasonably cold weather had driven them indoors to the dining room of Eleanor. The comfortable chair suggests this domestic setting and not the boathouse. In April Grant fell sick, partly due to the strain of the *ménage à trois* and to the prolonged absence of Garnett in France. Along with the tense personal relationships at Eleanor, the dreadful effects of World War One were beginning to take their toll. Although Bell tried to shut out the war

and refused to read the newspapers, it penetrated deep into their lives. In March the French painter Henri Doucet, a close collaborator of Bloomsbury, was killed in action. In April Rupert Brooke, the poet and Bloomsbury acquaintance, died in the Aegean on his way to Gallipoli.

On a more personal level the uneasiness of the times continued. Virginia Woolf suffered another severe mental breakdown in February 1915, which would last until June of that year. From Roger Fry, her lover between 1911 and 1913, Bell received agonizing and abject letters totally unable to accept that their passionate relationship was over. So the forces of past and present, public and private, gathered around her in the spring of 1915. Small wonder she suffered from severe fatigue and sickness in June of that year.

Grant catches a great deal of this troubled time in Bell's life in his portrait. Her thrown-back head is less languorous than tense at the jaw line and in the slightly arched eyebrows. She stares vacantly into space as though deeply preoccupied within. The gentle, inflected touch of the painting conveys much of Grant's feeling for this withdrawn beauty. The aloofness-intimacy dialogue of the work is masterfully underscored by the contrast of the rich red warmth of her dress and the cool yellow-green stripes of the chair. David Garnett, who was deeply attracted to her and sketched his own portrait of her at the time, remarked: "Her face had a grave beauty in repose: the perfect oval of a sculptured Madonna."[2] PMcC

1 Marler, 177.
2 Spalding 1983, 136.

77 DUNCAN GRANT

In Memoriam: Rupert Brooke, 1915
Oil and collage on panel, 13¼ x 23¼ in (33.6 x 59 cm)
Purchased through the Paul Mellon Fund, 1985

Reference: Spalding 1997, 166–67

Rupert Brooke, the poet and idol of his generation, died of septicemia on April 23, 1915, on his way to Gallipoli. He was buried at night in an olive grove on the island of Skyros. A month later his younger brother Alfred was killed in France. Duncan Grant had known both since childhood, and the double death within the same family brought the terrible effects of the war home to the painter, a committed pacifist and conscientious objector.

Brooke's death took on a national significance. Famous for his beauty as well as his poetry, he had caught the English imagination with a group of sonnets written in 1914 just after the outbreak of World War One. They captured the last moment of heroic idealism before the annihilation of almost an entire generation on the Western Front:

Now, God be thanked Who has matched us with His hour,
*   And caught our youth, and wakened us from sleeping,*
With hand made sure, clear eye, and sharpened power,
*   To turn, as swimmers into cleanness leaping.*[1]

Brooke was twenty-seven when he died, and from the moment of his death he became a symbolic figure of the young and gallant poet and officer struck down in his prime.

Grant gave the memorial tribute to the poet and his brother the form of an abstract painting, as though creating an icon. He sought an image which would transcend the immediate sense of grief and loss and raise itself above the outpouring of sentimental tributes that followed on Brooke's death. Inevitably the image reminds the viewer of a glowing chapel, with the dominating outline of a steeply pitched Gothic roof, against which the bands and blocks of color play. The impersonal qualities of the work make it all the more moving, attempting to give lasting form to personal tragedy.

Both Duncan Grant and Vanessa Bell painted a small group of forward-looking abstract paintings around 1913–14 as a result of their participation in the Omega Workshop initiated by Roger Fry in April 1913. The abstract paintings of Grant and Bell follow closely on their designs for the Workshop and remain some of their most brilliant and original work.

What makes *In Memoriam: Rupert Brooke* so exceptional is that it was the only abstract painting by Grant which carried a specifically symbolic and expressive meaning. Remarkably, the painting was not exhibited for sixty years and remained in the artist's studio until 1975. Its abstract form was the perfect vehicle to assimilate his feelings and attitude towards the poet, for Brooke had an uneasy relationship with the Bloomsbury group. His increasingly tempestuous and temperamental relationships with women, particularly Ka Cox, a friend and intimate of Bloomsbury, alternatively adulating and castigating, led to something of an estrangement and even hostility between Brooke and Bloomsbury at the time of his death. Indeed, Vanessa Bell wrote rather callously to Clive Bell:

I think it's queer how all these people who couldn't stand him alive are driven to talking about the waste and meaninglessness of life by Rupert's death…It's not the first time that a young person has died. He would have been a great popular success and enjoyed himself very much but I can't say I see a great deal beyond his looks.[2]

Duncan Grant, always of a generous spirit, painted *In Memoriam* as a *dona nobis pacem* for his estranged but beautiful and gifted friend.   PMcC

1 Rupert Brooke, "Peace," lines 1–4.
2 Shone, 138.

The Blue Wave, 1917
Oil on canvas, 16 x 20 in (40.6 x 50.8 cm)
Purchased through the Paul Mellon Fund, 1997

Nevinson's painting of a furious wave crashing in on itself is, above all, a haunting and powerful image of war. Executed most likely in early 1917, while he was recuperating in Cornwall from a severe rheumatic fever that had led to his discharge from active service in France, the work reflects both his changing artistic vision and his growing disillusionment with the war raging in Europe.

He uses insistent, repetitive circular forms, loaded brushstrokes, and heavy impasto to evoke the rhythmic movement of the water, which writhes and extends like taut sails to the sky, permitting no escape from its cyclical inundation and violence. Nevinson's abstracted waves bring to mind the image of the unending streams of young men sent to their slaughter at the front. Directly opposed to the celebratory visions of the sea in which marine painters of previous centuries had heralded British military might, this work invites comparison with scenes of sublime destruction and cataclysm, especially the biblical Deluge.

Nevinson's feisty temperament and his attraction to radical movements (he was, after all, the son of a suffragette) had led him to embrace wholeheartedly the European avant-garde movement known as Futurism. Allied closely with Filippo Tommaso Marinetti (they co-published a manifesto of English Futurism in 1914), he had initially considered war an exciting, even necessary manifestation of modernity, declaring boldly in 1915, "this war will be a violent incentive to Futurism, for we believe there is no beauty except in strife, no masterpiece without aggressiveness."[1] But his punishing, even devastating experiences on the front as an ambulance driver,

first with the Red Cross and later as a member of the Royal Army Medical Corps, broke down his optimism and belief in the violence of war. His faith in machines had begun to wane as early as 1915, and the splintered Cubist forms of Futurism he used in his early war paintings infused them with a foreboding atmosphere, conveying his increasing conviction that the war had become "dominated by machines and that men were mere cogs in the mechanism."[2] During his first tour of duty, he transformed his style and his consequent fusing of geometry and naturalism evokes both his growing despair and his awakening respect for human emotion.

Nevinson avoided painting explicit war subjects during his stay in Cornwall, but *The Blue Wave* is arguably the last of his Futurist war paintings. As a subject from nature, one that eschews the glorification of technology—airplanes, engines and the like—the painting reflects his increasing dissatisfaction with the Futurists' praise of machinery as a means to progress. Here the dynamic, repetitive, and abstracted forms of Futurism show not the power of man but instead his impotence before nature. This work stands at the turning point of Nevinson's artistic and theoretical—almost moral—transition from Futurism to the more conventional, emotive, and realistic style he would call his own when he returned to the front as an Official War Artist in the spring of 1917.   JMA

1   Harrison, 123.
2   Nevinson, 87.

79 GWEN JOHN

Young Woman, about 1920
Oil on canvas, 18⅞ x 14¾ in (47.9 x 37.5 cm)
Gift of Paul Mellon, 1993

Reference: Langdale, 163 (no. 101)

Quiet, subdued, and intense, this view of a young woman in an undefined interior exemplifies John's artistic vision in the years around 1920. Since 1915 she had been simplifying her paintings: paring down the details of the setting and monumentalizing her sitters. In this work she presents her model frontally, allowing the young woman to engage the viewer's eyes with her own. Yet, in spite of her open pose and glance, the sitter resists interpretation: she is introspective, impenetrable, and mysterious.

Framed by the corner of the studio, a window of which is visible in the upper right, the model sits as though rooted in place. Her pose, at a slightly oblique angle to the picture plane, is one of quietude and self-containment. Her face, bright under the umbrella of her voluminous hat, and her strong, almost masculine hands folded in her lap with their fingers interlaced, draw the viewer's attention but reveal little of her character. Like a statue, she is inviting yet inert, trapped within the material that has given her form.

Little is known about the model for the present work, although she appears in the majority of John's paintings from this period. She lived near the artist in Meudon, a suburb southwest of Paris. Since her actual name has not come down, she is generally called the "convalescent model," having played such a part in a series of works of the late 1910s. Apparently, she did not always enjoy her task. For John, however, the character and feelings of her models were of no account; painting them was merely "an affair of volumes."[1]

John's technique evolved constantly from her early career as a student at the Slade School in London. Careful and painstaking from the outset, her method was deeply indebted to Whistler, with whom she studied in Paris in 1898. In their evocation of atmosphere by means of subtle tonal juxtapositions, such works as this attest to his enduring influence on her work, even some twenty years after his death. Her abstraction of forms and interest in volumes also reflect her engagement with recent trends in French painting; she was particularly affected by Cézanne's portraits, many of which have a similar compositional structure and setting. In the peculiar brand of tight and intense interiority that marks her painting, however, she was alone.

The charged, emotive atmosphere of her paintings resulted in part from her almost obsessive attention to technique and constant reworkings of subjects. She often painted numerous versions of a pose: this painting, for instance, belongs to a group of works that show the same model alternately wearing a large hat or holding a cat in her lap. John's preoccupation with technique led her to develop her own technical code, which she eventually articulated in notes. In one from around 1930, she elliptically discusses her goals and procedures in making portraits:

> *1. the strange form 2. the pose & proportions*
> *3. the atmosphere & notes the tones 4. the finding*
> *of the forms (the sphere—the hair, the forehead, the cheek,*
> *the eye, the nose, the mouth, the neck, the chin, the torse.)*
> *5. Blobbing 6. the sculpting with the hands.*[2]

The present painting displays the results of this technique: the striking, deliberately "strange" monumentality of the figure conflicts with the small format of the painting, while the thick, dry paint used to sculpt the figure—with the brush and perhaps the hands too—betrays the girl's ostensibly quiet demeanor. As a study of tones and volumes, the painting is ultimately a human still life, the exploration of a compulsive, quiet, and beautiful malaise.   JMA

1 Langdale, 89.
2 Ibid., 21.

80 EDWARD WADSWORTH

Sea-Verge, 1943

Tempera on board, 25 x 35 in (63.5 x 88.9 cm)

Purchased through the Paul Mellon Fund, 1997

Reference: Wadsworth, 374 (no. W/A 240)

Through the careful arrangement of everyday objects to be found on the seashore, Wadsworth creates a mood of strangeness and unease. His painting achieves a dream-like atmosphere, enhanced by the infinities of sea and sky behind, and shows a clear kinship with the international Surrealist movement, although he never exhibited with that group. Painted at the height of World War Two, when history itself was taking horrifyingly Surrealistic turns, the work evokes British fears of a German invasion. The seashore (Wadsworth's favorite source of subject matter since his early career) takes on a new significance and an aura of doom. It is probably no accident that the hanging objects—empty coats, an empty net—suggest a gallows or modern-day Crucifixion.

The allusions to traditional subjects that Wadsworth worked into his modern imagery were given force by a deliberate archaism of technique. From the late 1920s he disdained oil paints and worked in egg tempera. The luminosity of the present work, whose colors seem to emanate from within, results from his use of carefully hand-mixed tempera colors applied thinly over gesso. His nearly *pointilliste* brush strokes combine with the vibrant colors of the tempera to impart an internal light and movement; when used to depict such fixed, immobile objects, this creates an eerie dissonance. His love and respect for this difficult, time-consuming technique stemmed from his early career, when he spent a brief time helping to restore the Mantegna cartoons at Hampton Court, and from his subsequent trips to Italy, where he was awed by the beauties of Giotto, Benozzo Gozzoli, and especially Fra Angelico. By the time the present work was painted, he had become one of the leading experts in Britain on the practice of egg-tempera painting; his lifelong sparring correspondence with Maxwell Armfield was based almost entirely on an ongoing discussion of tempera and its use. Wadsworth's stringent defense of this medium placed him outside the mainstream of contemporary art, although around 1940 officials of the Royal Academy began to approach him with the possiblity of his becoming a member, an honor he regarded with some suspicion.

Despite the respect accorded him by most of his fellow artists and the favor shown him by the Royal Academy, Wadsworth never achieved his patriotic ambition of becoming an Official War Artist. Although the reasons were never officially articulated, it is clear that his name had been consistently omitted from the rosters of war artists because of his personal ties to Germany. In March 1934 his daughter Barbara had married a Bavarian and been forced, by law, to renounce her British citizenship. She and her husband had intended to become naturalized British citizens, but the outbreak of war had prevented this, and in 1940 they had to register as enemy aliens, she in her own country. Wadsworth's fate as an artist became inextricably linked with this event, and he was forever thwarted in his efforts to become a war artist. In 1940 he was officially denied even a sketching permit, a disappointment which affected him both emotionally and artistically. Only two years later, having enlisted the aid of the Duke of Devonshire, was he finally allowed to join the war effort, not as an artist but as a member of the Home Guard.

Seen in the light of his complex relationship with the artistic and political establishments of the early 1940s, *Sea-Verge* conjures not only the sense of overwhelming national unease but also, in its evocation of emptiness, the artist's personal disappointments. The strange suspension of once essential, now disused objects displayed in an airless, frieze-like manner suggests the melancholic stoppage of everyday life that results from war and presents an image of the vestiges of life literally hanging in the balance. JMA

192

81 BEN NICHOLSON

May 1955 (Gwithian), 1955
Oil on canvas, 41¾ x 41¾ (106 x 106 cm)
Gift of Paul Mellon, 1985

Reference: Lynton, 290–91

Ben Nicholson began to enjoy wide international fame in the early 1950s. The British Council under the direction of Lillian Browse ran a vigorous program of exhibitions of contemporary British art abroad, particularly in Europe, and between 1947 and 1960 Nicholson participated in some forty of these. Ironically, his recognition within Britain did not keep pace with his growing fame and success abroad. Although the Tate Gallery gave him a retrospective exhibition in 1955, his solo commercial showings were often unsuccessful, even at the moment when international prizes were showered upon him: the Carnegie Institute Prize in 1952; the Guggenheim International Painting Prize in 1956; and the major foreign artist's prize at the São Paulo Biennale in 1957. A residual prejudice against abstract painting in Britain, allied to a resurgence of realism in post-war British art—alternatively Neo-Romantic and effete or "kitchen sink" and heavy-handed—made Nicholson's reputation relatively embattled. He did, however, have powerful and articulate defenders in Herbert Read and his fellow painter Patrick Heron.

Why Nicholson should have continued to arouse only grudging admiration in Britain at this period is slightly puzzling. From 1949 to 1958, his last years at St. Ives, the picturesque fishing village and artists' colony in Cornwall, he produced a magisterial series of still-life paintings of which *May 1955 (Gwithian)* is a particularly fine example. These pictures are far more approachable than his radically abstract white reliefs of the 1930s or his austerely geometric wartime abstractions. Anybody reasonably familiar with Cubist still lifes would have no difficulty "reading" Nicholson's paintings of the early fifties.

Interestingly, Nicholson himself attributed his interest in still life to his father, the painter William Nicholson:

I owe a lot to my father—especially to his poetic idea and to his still-life theme. That didn't come from Cubism, as some people think, but from my father— not only from what he did as a painter but from the very beautiful striped and spotted jugs and mugs and goblets, and octagonal and hexagonal glass objects which he collected. Having those things throughout the house was an unforgettable early experience for me.[1]

The still-life quality of *May 1955* is fully realized through the interplay of transparent and opaque forms. They have a magical, almost dancing quality, as one motif overlaps and intersects with another. The unsuspected complexity of their relationships in space animates the painting.

The Nicholson still lifes of the 1950s achieved a considerable monumentality. The table in this picture has an architectural resonance, grander and more austere than the drawing and coloring of the still-life motif. The artist claimed that he had always "been interested in the sculptural-architectural approach...But I do not look for massive form...I...like to *chisel out* a form...& there is an excitement for me in chiselling out *flat planes*."[2]

This painting—one of a handsome group of Nicholsons in the Center's collection—combines the sculptural-architectural with an atmospheric quality, as though the still life were bathed in air and light. The Gwithian of the title is a village almost due east of St. Ives and was the site of some of the earliest neolithic remains in Cornwall; *May 1955* echoes these ancient forms. The reference to Gwithian alludes, then, both to the landscape feeling of the work and to the artist's sense of the timeless in art.   PMcC

1   Galería Jorge Mara, n.p.
2   Lewison, 75.

194

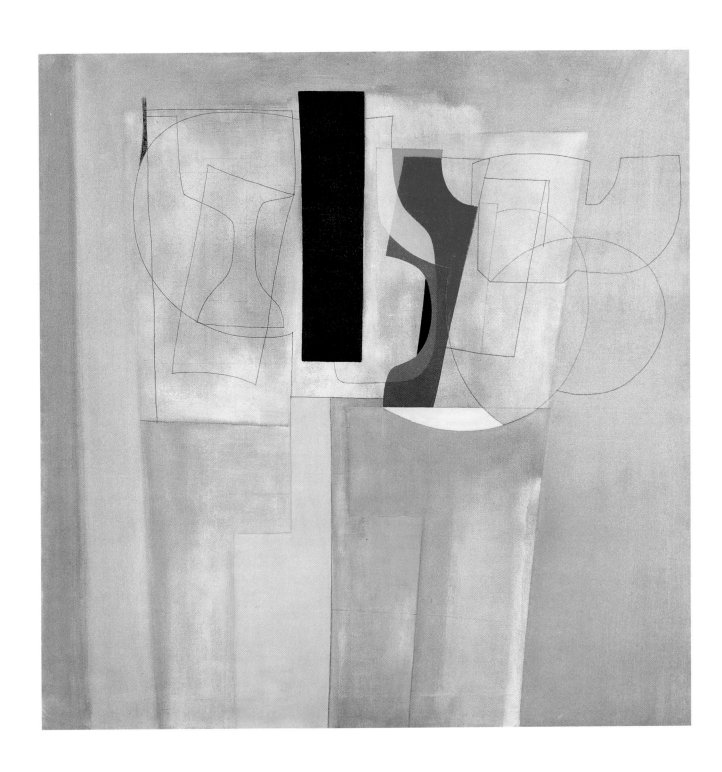

The Artists

Unless otherwise indicated, the portraits of artists are from the collection of the Yale Center for British Art (photography by Richard Caspole).

BATONI, POMPEO (1708–1787). The son of a goldsmith, this Italian artist was initially trained in drawing and engraving but turned to painting in 1727. His training in draftsmanship is evident in the studies of Antique statuary for which he became famous. The work of Annibale Carracci and Raphael clearly influenced him, especially in the luminous coloring and classicizing style of his best work. By the 1740s, in addition to the numerous commissions he received for devotional, mythological, and historical pictures, his contact with British travelers abroad resulted in a flourishing portrait practice. Toward the end of that decade, due to the limited patronage for his history pictures, Batoni concentrated more heavily on portraits for his livelihood. Carefully observed, with a draftsman's accuracy, these brought Batoni wide acclaim across the Continent. The inclusion of antiquities and views of Rome to indicate the cultivated status of his sitters would prove particularly influential upon a later generation of British portraitists. No. 32

Engraving from the Almanacco Pittorico, *Florence, 1792. National Gallery of Art, Washington.*

BEARE, GEORGE (fl. 1743–1749). The work of William Hogarth seems to have had a profound impact upon this talented but little-known provincial portraitist, which has led some to speculate that Beare trained with Hogarth at the St. Martin's Lane Academy in London. By 1746 he was established as a portrait painter in Salisbury. The relatively few works that can be firmly attributed to him show his taste for a robust, earthy palette and his ability to suggest strength of character in his sitters. (No portrait of him is known.) No. 13

BELL, VANESSA (1879–1961). A founding member of the artistic and literary Bloomsbury Group, Bell was a pioneer of the modern movement in Britain. The naturalistic style she developed first under Arthur Cope and later at the Royal Academy Schools shifted markedly after her introduction to Post-Impressionist art and the critic Roger Fry. Sentiment and details were replaced with boldly simplified forms and a non-representational style. As with many of her contemporaries, however, naturalism returned to her art after World War I. Bell is also remembered for her skillful decorative work and involvement with the Omega Workshops. She designed imaginative schemes for domestic interiors and textiles for the consumer market; later, with Duncan Grant, she designed textiles for the Queen Mary ocean liner and book jackets for the Hogarth Press. Bell and Grant employed similar styles during the 1920s and exhibited regularly together with the London Group and the London Artists' Association. After the death of her son in the Spanish Civil War, Bell's art underwent a radical alteration. She became less active in London art circles, spending most of her time at her Sussex farmhouse, Charleston. This retreat became the subject of many of her later paintings, in which richer color and tighter brushwork prevail. No. 75

Detail from a photograph of the artist at Charleston, c. 1922–24. Tate Gallery Archive, London.

BONINGTON, RICHARD PARKES (1802–1828). Had Bonington lived longer, he may well have achieved the status of his friend and associate Eugène Delacroix, with whom he shared similar interests in style and subject matter. Bonington began his training in Calais with Louis Francia and in 1818 moved to Paris to study under Antoine-Jean Gros. With Gros he learned the art of drawing *à la bosse* and the technique of plein-air sketching. The excellence of Bonington's watercolors, the medium for which he is best known today, led Gros to declare the artist a master in his own right. From 1822 to 1824 Bonington traveled throughout France, painting brilliant watercolors of the landscape. He then returned to Paris to further his studies in oil painting. After a trip to London with Delacroix in 1825, which included a visit to West-minster Hall, Sir Samuel Rush Meyrick's famed collection of medieval armor, and a special viewing of the Elgin marbles, both artists worked for a time in a medievalizing and orientalizing style. In 1826 Bonington traveled to Venice, where he discovered the painterly styles and luminous colors of Titian and Veronese. He produced a series of highly original, small-scale fantasy pictures as a result of this trip, which display both his debt to these masters and his own distinctive character as an artist. His promising career was cut short when consumption ended his life at the age of twenty-six. Nos. 56, 58

Mezzotint by J. P. Quilley, after Margaret Carpenter, publ. 1831.

BROWN, FORD MADOX (1821–1893). Though never formally a member of the Pre-Raphaelite Brotherhood, Brown was instrumental in the formation of the group's style, training Dante Gabriel Rossetti and becoming a close associate of John Everett Millais and William Holman Hunt. Born in Calais, he received his first artistic training from European masters in the Low Countries. In 1840 he moved to Paris, where he studied independently, concentrating his attention on paintings by Rembrandt, the Spanish Old Masters, and Eugène Delacroix. While his work from this period is clearly Continental in style, characterized by a dark palette and strong chiaroscuro, the subject matter is often taken from English history. Further travels in the 1840s led to an appreciation of the Italian Old Masters and the contemporary German Nazarenes. The lessons learned from these artists, most importantly a close observation of detail and a clarity of line, color, and light, would prove instrumental in the development of his style and the formation of the Pre-Raphaelite aesthetic. His interest in stained glass and increasing involvement with furniture design in the 1850s fostered the linear and decorative quality of his later art. After settling in north London in 1851, he turned to landscapes and the contemporary social scenes for which he is best known. His last major commission, for twelve large murals in Manchester Town Hall, provided him with his final and greatest opportunity to display his lively historical style in a decorative setting. No. 64

Photograph by W. & D. Downey, 1860s. National Portrait Gallery, London.

CANALETTO (1697–1768). Born Giovanni Antonio Canal, this Venetian artist was first employed as a painter of theatrical scenery, like his father before him. Such work established the skills in perspective and draftsmanship that would define the cityscapes and capriccios to which he turned in the 1720s. Though he spent most of his artistic career in Venice, he worked for about a decade in England, from 1746 to 1755. The foundations for his popularity there had been laid in the 1730s, when his Italian views were widely sought after by British travelers on the Grand Tour. These "pictures for export" were Canaletto's most characteristic, painted on a light background in a calligraphic shorthand of brushstrokes. Under the patronage of Joseph Smith, a collector, banker, and shipping agent, and encouraged by his pictures' popularity with the British, Canaletto quickly established a thriving practice in London, depicting many of that city's best known sites, including Whitehall, the Horse Guards, Westminster Bridge, and the Thames. Though criticized by some for making London look Venetian, his careful observation of England's urban scene, often populated with the lively figures of city life, aided the development of an indigenous school of topographical art. Nos. 22, 23

Engraving by Antonio Visentini, after G. B. Piazzetta, from Prospectus Magni Canalis Venetiarum, Venice, 1735.

CLAUSEN, GEORGE (1852–1944). Said to be the most popular professor at the Royal Academy Schools since Joshua Reynolds, Clausen was largely responsible for bringing Jules Bastien-Lepage's rustic French naturalism to Britain. The son of a Danish interior decorator, Clausen trained initially at the National Art Training School in London and, after obtaining a commission to decorate a door for the painter Edwin Long, received a scholarship to attend the South Kensington School of Art. He later studied in Antwerp, delighting in the fishing villages along the Belgian and Dutch coasts, and in Paris, where he was influenced by the rustic paintings of John Robertson Reid and Léon Lhermitte. Clausen's first encounter with the work of Bastien-Lepage at a show at the Grosvenor Gallery in 1880 proved to be a decisive moment in his career. He admired the artist's simple, rural subject matter and broad painting style and soon adopted a similar approach in his own art. Clausen was a founder-member of the New English Art Club; he exhibited his pictures there and later at the Royal Academy. During World War One he enjoyed success as an official war artist, and later he produced a number of important mural paintings. No. 69

Self-portrait, pen and ink, 1895. National Portrait Gallery, London.

CONSTABLE, JOHN (1776–1837). Although Constable's critical success was uneven during his own lifetime, his landscapes are today recognized as some of the greatest achievements of British art and the artistic equals of Turner's. The son of a gentleman farmer, miller, and merchant from East Bergholt in Suffolk, his career was determined after meeting the connoisseur Sir George Beaumont and the drawing-master John Thomas Smith. Greatly inspired by them, he entered the Royal Academy Schools in 1799. There he copied landscapes by Claude Lorrain, Jacob van Ruisdael, and Richard Wilson, all of whom were to have a great influence on his early paintings. Constable soon broke with the traditions of the picturesque, classically-ordered landscape, however, and sought to observe the world around him (particularly his native Suffolk and, after 1819, Hampstead Heath) in a more direct, "naturalistic" fashion. His deft touch, distinguished by strategically-placed dabs of yellow and white paint, was well suited to suggest the transient qualities of light and atmosphere that so fascinated him. His compositions were based on copious sketches and oil studies made *en plein air* but were not mere topographical records. In fact, they were infused with social, political, religious, and personal meanings that are only today being fully recognized. He exhibited throughout the 1810s, '20s and '30s, receiving mixed reviews from his compatriots. He was admired by some artists in Britain, including Henry Fuseli, but his impact was felt most greatly abroad, and he influenced both the Barbizon School and the Impressionists. Nos. 53, 54, 55, 57, 59

Mezzotint by David Lucas, after Charles Robert Leslie, from Leslie's Memoirs of the Life of John Constable, *London, 1843.*

COPLEY, JOHN SINGLETON (1738–1815). The most talented portraitist in the American colonies before the Revolution, Copley later pursued his artistic career in London. He had an early introduction to the nascent Boston art world through his stepfather Peter Pelham, an engraver of mezzotint portraits. He produced his first oil painting at the age of fifteen and quickly settled into the portrait commissions that offered the primary support for professional artists in the colonies. His earliest work, based on imported mezzotints and painted in an out-of-date British style, already contained the characteristics of his mature art: strong light-dark contrasts, attention to surface pattern, crisp surfaces, and brilliant color. His first professional success in England came with the exhibition of a work at the Society of Artists in 1766, which was commented upon favorably by both Joshua Reynolds and Benjamin West. It was not until the political climate in Boston worsened considerably, however, that Copley left the colonies to settle in London. He arrived there in 1775. Seeking to improve his artistic status, he devoted much of the next two decades to the painting of modern history. No. 39

Soft-ground etching by William Daniell, after George Dance.

DEVIS, ARTHUR (1712–1787). The best-known of a celebrated family of artists, Devis was one of the pioneers of the eighteenth-century conversation piece. Born in Preston, he was apprenticed to the Flemish landscape and sporting artist Peter Tillemans in 1729. After a period of work in his native Lancashire, he established a practice in London in 1742. Capitalizing on the prosperity of the new middle class, he specialized in conversation pieces showing bourgeois families in elegant interiors and parks. While his initial compositions tended to be rather stiff, by the middle of the 1750s he began to imbue his sitters with a greater sense of personality. The treatment of his landscape backgrounds also grew more refined. Nonetheless, Devis's popularity was waning by the 1770s, perhaps due to his unwillingness to join the contemporary reaction against Rococo art, and he was forced to supplement his income by restoration work. No. 11

Self-portrait, oil on canvas, 1742. Harris Museum and Art Gallery, Preston. Photo: North Western Museum and Art Gallery Service, Blackburn.

DOBSON, WILLIAM (1610/11–1646). Arguably the best British-born painter of his generation, Dobson was the immediate successor to van Dyck at the court of Charles I. He trained first under the engraver William Peake and then with the decorative painter Francis Cleyn. It is likely that the latter provided access to Charles I's extensive collections of Continental art, exposing Dobson to the work of Titian, Rubens, and van Dyck. The influence of these artists is clearly felt in Dobson's best portraits, remarkable for their fluid, assured handling of paint and perceptive characterizations. In 1642 the artist followed Charles I to the court established in Oxford during the Civil War. Numerous commissions ensued, although the quality of Dobson's output declined, perhaps due to the difficult wartime circumstances in which he worked. Later he returned to London, where he died in poverty. No. 5

Mezzotint by George White, after a self-portrait.

DYCK, ANTHONY VAN (1599–1641). Van Dyck stands among the finest of Northern Baroque artists and his work for the court of Charles I had a seminal effect upon British painting. Though it was his lifelong ambition to be a history painter, his reputation was made on his portraits. These elegant works, rendered in sweeping, dynamic brushstrokes, would set an ideal for aristocratic portraiture in Britain well into the nineteenth century. An apprentice under Hendrick van Balen in Antwerp, van Dyck showed considerable talent from an early age. By 1618 he had become an assistant in Rubens's shop and adopted much of that artist's technical finesse. After attracting the attention of the Earl of Arundel, he spent a year in England at the court of James I, followed by a trip to Italy in the company of the Countess of Arundel. He remained there for the next six years, primarily in Genoa. After a period in Antwerp he returned to England in 1632, now serving the court of Charles I. He was duly rewarded by the connoisseur king, who had been seeking a personal court artist of international stature, and upon his arrival was named Principal Painter, given a large pension, and knighted. He did not disappoint, his accomplished portraits of the king and his courtiers offering ample visual evidence of the elegance and refinement of Charles I's court. No. 4

Lithograph by William Fairland, after a self-portrait.

FERNELEY, JOHN, SR. (1782–1860). Considered by some the quintessential sporting artist of the Regency and early Victorian periods, Ferneley enjoyed a wide audience through engravings of his work. The son of a master wheelwright, he was encouraged in his artistic ambitions by John, 5th Duke of Rutland. After studying with Benjamin Marshall in London, he set up his principal practice in the foxhunting mecca of Melton Mowbray. There he ran a prolific studio for over fifty years, creating large panoramas of hunt scurries and other compositions celebrating the sporting world. No. 51

Portrait by Henry Johnson, oil on canvas, 1838. National Portrait Gallery, London.

GAINSBOROUGH, THOMAS (1727–1788). One of the greatest European painters of his generation, Gainsborough was the contemporary and rival in Britain of Joshua Reynolds. Best known for his portraits, the fluid brushwork and dignified poses of which delivered precisely the type of elegance demanded by his sitters, Gainsborough achieved considerable success in aristocratic circles. He trained in London under Francis Hayman and the French engraver and draftsman Hubert Gravelot from 1740 to 1748. It is possible that he studied at the St. Martin's Lane Academy as well, becoming acquainted with the works of William Hogarth. He moved his practice to Bath in 1759, where his work was immediately celebrated and sought after by the fashionable set. He continued to exhibit annually at the Society of Artists in London and returned to the capital in 1774. While his portraits have received the most critical attention, his landscapes and rural scenes are equally important, imbued as they are with social and philosophical significance. In his eulogy for Gainsborough, delivered at the Royal Academy in 1788, Reynolds astutely acknowledged their artistic worth and praised his rival with uncommon magnanimity. Nos. 15, 28, 34, 36

Stipple engraving by Francesco Bartolozzi, after a self-portrait, publ. 1798.

GHEERAERTS, MARCUS THE YOUNGER (1561–1635/6). Born in the Netherlands, the son of a well-known painter and engraver, Gheeraerts is best known for portraits commissioned by the court of Elizabeth I. He settled in London with his family by the age of seven and there worked under both his father and his fellow expatriate Lucas de Heere. His mature work shows the iconic poses and richly decorated surfaces that were characteristic of the age, features well known in the work of the contemporary miniaturist Nicholas Hilliard, for example. His sensitivity to sitters' facial expressions and the sweet melancholy that marked his work, however, set him apart from his contemporaries. Although he did enjoy favor with the wife of James I, Anne of Denmark, his style was soon viewed as somewhat naive when compared to that of younger Continental painters such as Paul van Somer and Daniel Mytens. Nevertheless, he continued to receive commissions from scholars and the gentry well into the 1630s. No. 1

Engraving by A. Bannerman, after a self-portrait, from Horace Walpole, Anecdotes of Painting in England, *Strawberry Hill, 1762–71.*

GILMAN, HAROLD (1876–1919). A founding member of the Camden Town Group, Gilman was instrumental in bringing both Post-Impressionist and "Neo-Realist" styles to British art. After a year at Oxford he was forced to leave on account of poor health and began work as a tutor abroad. Upon his return to England in 1896, he enrolled at the Hastings School of Art and later at the Slade School of Art, studying there from 1897 until 1901. A year of travel in Spain introduced him to the work of Velázquez, whose rich tones and expressive handling of paint would prove a considerable influence on his style. Whistler was also a dominant influence at this time. In 1907 Gilman became associated with Walter Sickert, with whom he shared similar artistic interests. The two were instrumental in forming the Camden Town Group in 1911. Gilman's style soon diverged from that of Sickert, however, becoming more formal in composition, stronger in color, and imbued with a sense of intimacy. By 1914 he had openly declared his independence from Sickert, exhibiting with Charles Ginner as a "Neo-Realist." No. 73

Portrait by Walter Sickert, oil on canvas, c. 1912. Tate Gallery, London.

GINNER, CHARLES (1878–1952). Like Gilman, Ginner was a founding member of the Camden Town Group. After sailing around the Mediterranean and the South Atlantic at the age of sixteen, he worked briefly for an engineer and then an architect in Paris. Because his parents disapproved of his interest in the arts, his study of painting was postponed until 1904, when he studied with Paul Gervais at the Académie Vitti in France. Gervais ridiculed Ginner's enthusiasm for van Gogh and his bright palette, prompting him to study at the Ecole des Beaux-Arts for a time. In 1908, through the Allied Artists' Association, he met Harold Gilman and Spencer Gore, contacts he renewed upon settling in London in 1911. In addition to co-founding the Camden Town Group, he was generally active in the pre-war British art scene and involved in both the London and Cumberland Market groups. Ginner's brand of "Neo-Realism" differed from Gilman's in that it privileged personal vision over an exact reportage of the seen world. His mature works, consisting primarily of cityscapes, landscapes, and during the two World Wars harbor and battle scenes, were painted with small, regular touches of thick paint that give his canvases the look of densely worked embroidery. This style, which was clearly indebted to van Gogh, varied little throughout his career. No. 74

Portrait by Malcolm Drummond, oil on board, c. 1911. Southampton City Art Gallery.

GORE, SPENCER (1878–1914). Closely affiliated with the Camden Town Group, Gore was another prominent figure among those early twentieth-century British artists who looked to French Impressionism and Post-Impressionism for stylistic inspiration. He studied at the Slade School of Art in London, where he met and befriended Harold Gilman and Wyndham Lewis. In 1904 Walter Sickert introduced him to the painting technique of Degas, which would have a profound effect upon his early style. Gore was a founding member of the Fitzroy Street Group, coming into contact through that organization with Lucien Pissarro and adopting his Impressionist painting method. Yet after exposure to Roger Fry's ground-breaking Post-Impressionist shows in 1910 and 1912, he broke with Impressionism and in the last years of his short life took up a linear, color-saturated style. No. 72

Photograph, c. 1908. Courtesy of Frederick Gore.

GRANT, DUNCAN (1885–1978). A member of both the Camden Town and Bloomsbury Groups, Grant was at the center of the London avant-garde. Brought up in India, the son of a British soldier, he was encouraged to follow in his father's footsteps but showed no interest and was allowed to pursue a career in the arts instead. In addition to his studies at the Westminster School of Art and the Slade School of Art, he benefited in his youth from a considerable amount of travel abroad. In Paris he gained access to Leo and Gertrude Stein's collection of works by Picasso and Matisse, which left him with a lasting taste for bold color and abstract form. He later worked as a decorator, serving as co-director of the Omega Workshops and completing a number of decorative schemes in collaboration with both his lifelong companion Vanessa Bell and Roger Fry. Grant remained active into the 1970s, his style unchanged, his subject matter often deriving from his frequent travels. Nos. 76, 77

Self-portrait, oil on canvas, c. 1909. National Portrait Gallery, London.

HAYMAN, FRANCIS (1708–1776). An exceptionally versatile figure, Hayman worked as a set decorator, portraitist, history painter, and book illustrator. Apprenticed to the decorative painter Robert Brown in 1718, he found initial employment as a scene painter at Goodman's Fields Theatre and then at Drury Lane. By the end of the 1730s he had begun to accept commissions for conversation pieces and portraits from the burgeoning middle class. He had also begun his lifelong promotion of British history painting, both through his own work and through his campaign for a public art academy. His decorative work continued, most notably with commissions to paint the supper-boxes at Vauxhall Gardens; executed in a loose Rococo style, these comprised genre subjects and scenes from well-known plays. By the 1750s he was also much engaged on book illustrations, including designs for works by Samuel Richardson and William Congreve. A friend and associate of Hogarth, Hayman was a member of the St. Martin's Lane Academy, as well as a founder-member of the Society of Artists and the Royal Academy. Among his pupils the most successful would be Thomas Gainsborough. No. 14

Stipple engraving by Benjamin Reading, after Peter Falconet, publ. 1792.

HOGARTH, WILLIAM (1697–1764). A brilliant satirist, Hogarth was also among the most technically skilled, financially astute, and nationalistic artists of his generation. Much of his subject matter was inspired by his own difficult childhood, marked most strongly by his father's confinement to debtors' prison. After an early apprenticeship to the engraver Ellis Gambel in 1713 and study at the small St. Martin's Lane academy of John Louis Vanderbank and Louis Chéron, he quickly established a career as an engraver of satirical prints. His first attempt at a major painting came in 1728, with his five versions of a scene from John Gay's *The Beggar's Opera*. Combining increasing technical mastery and compositional skill with a sharp eye for social commentary, these set the stage for his brilliant narrative series of the 1730s and 1740s, including *A Rake's Progress* and *Marriage à la Mode*. Hogarth was the first painter in England fully to exploit the market for prints, engraving his own works and thereby lessening his dependence on patrons. In response to rampant piracies of his works, in the 1730s he embarked on a successful campaign for an Act of Parliament that would grant copyrights to engravers. Throughout his life he sought to improve the status of the artist in England and establish a British school of painting that would rival—if not better—those of the Continent. He articulated these desires in theoretical treatises, the most famous of which is *The Analysis of Beauty* (1753). While his genre scenes brought him much attention in his own lifetime and his portraits are today highly praised for their freshness and insight, Hogarth's lifelong ambition of becoming a respected history painter, like his father-in-law Sir James Thornhill, was never realized. Nos. 8, 9, 10

Etching by Samuel Ireland, after the self-portrait in the present volume (no. 9).

JOHN, GWEN (1876–1939). A very private figure, John painted intimate, subtly colored self-portraits and studies of women. She attended the Slade School of Art in 1895 and left for Paris in 1898 to study with Whistler. It was from Whistler that John derived inspiration for the soft, tone-on-tone technique that would define her mature work. Despite the pleas of her brother Augustus, also a painter, she decided to spend the remainder of her career in Paris, making only a few brief trips to London. Initially supporting herself as an artist's model (working for Rodin among others), she was able to establish herself as an artist in her own right by the early 1910s. The delicate touch she brought to her small-scale canvases is seen to effect in her depictions of nuns, a subject inspired by her conversion to Roman Catholicism in 1913, and in her portrayals of young Parisian women. Toward the end of her career an increasing interest in abstraction is evident, along with an emphasis on composition rather than the subject itself. John was always reluctant to display her work in public, and an exhibition at the New Chenil Galleries in London in 1926 was her only solo show. No. 79

*Self-portrait, oil on canvas, c. 1899–1900.
Tate Gallery, London.*

JONGH, CLAUDE DE (before 1600–1663). Dutch by birth and training, de Jongh belonged to a generation of Continental painters who often sought work in Britain. Although he worked in the Netherlands for much of his career, a member of the Utrecht Guild of St. Luke in 1627 and a master by 1633, he is best known for the views of London that resulted from his visits there. These were fairly numerous: his drawings of the city range in date from 1615 to 1628. He would use the drawings as the basis for paintings upon his return to the Netherlands. De Jongh's mature work, rather rough and broad, is closely allied with that of both Jan van Goyen and Esaias van de Velde, while his later forays into Italianate landscapes owe a clear debt to Adam Elsheimer. (No portrait of him is known.) No. 3

LAWRENCE, THOMAS (1769–1830). The successor to Gainsborough and Reynolds as Britain's finest portrait painter, Lawrence was the last in a long line of British artists who could trace their artistic lineage back to van Dyck. He was encouraged from the age of ten to draw portraits of his father's friends in pencil and pastel, entertaining them—and later supporting his financially troubled family—with his precocious talent. In 1787 he spent several months at the Royal Academy, where he received his first formal artistic education. While in London he met Reynolds and was told by him to stop copying the Old Masters and study nature. He chose to devote himself to portraiture, and his early portraits of George III and Queen Charlotte, showing his characteristic fluidity, vividness of color, and flair for composition, firmly established his career in his chosen field. His status as Painter-in-Ordinary to George III led to important commissions from the royal family and from political celebrities and public figures. So great was the demand for his work that by 1800 Lawrence was forced to make considerable use of studio assistants. In 1820 he was elected president of the Royal Academy. Despite this recognition and popularity Lawrence's life was continuously plagued by financial troubles, due in part to his own extravagance. A strong advocate for the formation of national art collections, he was himself an avid and active collector. No. 40

Mezzotint by Samuel Cousins, after a self-portrait, publ. 1830.

LEAR, EDWARD (1812–1888). Best known today for his nonsense rhymes and humorous illustrations, Lear was also a prolific topographical draftsman and painter. Initially self-taught, he began his artistic career as an ornithological illustrator. He began painting landscapes in 1836. A trip to Rome in 1837 inspired in him an insatiable wanderlust, leading to travels on the Continent, throughout the Mediterranean, the Middle East, and India. Despite his delicate health and epilepsy, he would remain abroad for most of the remaining fifty years of his life, returning to England only briefly. The landscapes he produced during these years, notable for their expressive treatment of natural forms and skillful draftsmanship, drew upon both Old Master and contemporary landscape models, the solemn dignity of Claude Lorrain, and the sublime sensibility of Turner. Produced in the studio from his many on-the-spot sketches, his oils were exhibited at the Royal Academy and British Institution in the 1850s and brought him much favorable attention. By the 1860s, however, his circle of patrons had dwindled significantly, and he turned largely to writing for financial support. No. 68

Photograph by McLean, Melhuish & Haes, c. 1860. National Portrait Gallery, London.

LEIGHTON, FREDERIC (1830–1896). Leighton was a central figure in the Victorian art world whose brilliant coloring and inventive compositions brought a new vitality to British Neoclassical painting. With his peripatetic family he traveled throughout Europe as a boy, studying art in Frankfurt, Rome, and Paris. His first critical success came in 1855 with the purchase by Queen Victoria of his *Cimabue's Madonna* from that year's Royal Academy exhibition. Between 1855 and 1859 he perfected his mature style in Paris, combining the painterly effects of Venetian art and the realism of Corot and Daubigny with the exact draftsmanship and historical detail of his earlier works. After several trips to the Near East and North Africa, he was inspired to commission the famous Arab Hall at his house in Holland Park. He became president of the Royal Academy in 1878 and was created a baronet in 1886. His elevation to the peerage in the last year of his life, as Baron Leighton of Stretton, was the first instance in which that honor had been bestowed upon an artist. No. 66

Carte-de-visite by the London Stereoscopic Company, 1860s. National Portrait Gallery, London.

LELY, PETER (1618–1680). The successor to van Dyck, Lely was the most prominent portrait painter in England during the Commonwealth and Restoration periods. Born and trained in the Netherlands, he had established a successful practice in London by the late 1640s. His considerable abilities quickly attracted a large number of influential clients, including several of van Dyck's former patrons. In 1661, following the Restoration of Charles II, he was named Principal Painter to the King. The financial success that accompanied Lely's fame allowed him to live in great style in London's Covent Garden and to assemble one of the finest collections of Continental paintings and drawings in seventeenth-century England. In the later years of his career he ran a flourishing studio, the often mediocre products of which—painted largely by his assistants—failed signally to live up to the technical accomplishment and elegant finesse of his best autograph work. No. 6

Detail from a mezzotint by Isaak Beckett, after a self-portrait.

MARSHALL, BENJAMIN (1768–1835). After a brief apprenticeship to the portraitist Lemuel Francis Abbott, Marshall quickly established his reputation as a painter of sporting subjects with a series of commissions from George, Prince of Wales. Focusing on hunting and horse-racing scenes, he operated a successful practice from his atelier in London from 1795 until 1810. In 1812 he moved his studio to the famous racing center of Newmarket in East Anglia to further impress his patrons with his genuine knowledge of the sport. His impact on the following generation of sporting artists was significant, and both John Ferneley and Abraham Cooper served their apprenticeships under his tutelage. Though Marshall's sporting production has tended to overshadow his accomplished, if occasional, forays into portraiture and landscape, they too are now recognized for their considerable artistic merit. No. 49

Anonymous stipple engraving, publ. 1826.

MARTIN, JOHN (1789–1854). Best known for his dramatic, large-scale canvases of biblical subjects, Martin represented in its most extreme form the Romantic taste for the Sublime. After early apprenticeships to a coachmaker and a glass and ceramics painter, he ventured into the career of a professional artist with small Claudean landscape views. His pictorial ambitions soon climbed to dizzying heights, however, as he developed a penchant for vast canvases depicting lilliputian figures overwhelmed by the enormity of divine and natural forces. His mastery of perspective effects and architectural details contributed to the power of his pictures to draw the viewer in. His subjects were often apocalyptic scenes from biblical or classical sources. His first work in this vein was accepted by the Royal Academy in 1812, firmly establishing his artistic career. After continued success with his large canvases, Martin turned to publishing prints after his own works, mostly mezzotints. No. 61

Stipple engraving by J. Thomson, after W. Derby, publ. 1822.

MERCIER, PHILIPPE (1689 or 1691–1760). Reputedly born in Berlin of French extraction, Mercier is credited wih introducing the conversation piece to Britain. After studying at the Berlin Akademie and traveling in France and England, he found employment at the British court through contacts with the House of Hanover. By 1729 he was Principal Painter to Frederick, Prince of Wales, and by 1730 Keeper of the Prince's Library. While his more formal portraits were rather undistinguished, his informal conversation pictures of the 1720s and 1730s, depicting sitters engaged in leisurely pursuits, were fresh and innovative. This genre would be further developed by William Hogarth and Johann Zoffany. After losing his position in Frederick's court, Mercier moved to York in 1739, where he enjoyed a thriving practice, painting portraits of the local gentry and light-hearted "fancy pictures." Mercier is also remembered for the etchings he made after his own pictures and those of Antoine Watteau, an artist who exerted a strong influence on his work. No. 12

Mezzotint by John Faber, after a self-portrait, 1735.

MILLAIS, JOHN EVERETT (1829–1896). One of the founding members of the Pre-Raphaelite Brotherhood, Millais enjoyed success and popularity throughout his career. He showed remarkable artistic ability from an early age, being the youngest student ever accepted to the Royal Academy Schools. Entering the Academy in 1840 after a brief period at Henry Sass's private art school, he exhibited his first work there in 1846 and received considerable praise. Along with friend and fellow-student William Holman Hunt, however, he soon rebelled against the Academy's notion that art should improve upon nature, the dictum of its founder Joshua Reynolds. Turning against what they perceived as the artificiality of the High Renaissance, they took their inspiration from the period before Raphael and developed a linear, brightly-colored and unidealized style of painting. In 1848, along with another kindred spirit, Dante Gabriel Rossetti, they formed the Pre-Raphaelite Brotherhood. By the 1860s Millais began to abandon the strict tenets of the movement in favor of a less time-consuming, more painterly style, taking his inspiration from Velázquez and eighteenth-century English portraiture. His subject matter also became more accessible and easily likable at this time, catering to popular tastes and sentiments. Millais was a leading figure in the field of wood-engraved book illustration in the 1850s and 1860s, providing blocks for Moxon's edition of Tennyson (1857) and Anthony Trollope's novels. He was created a baronet in 1885 and elected President of the Royal Academy in 1896. Millais died the wealthiest and most celebrated artist of his time. No. 63

Detail from an engraving by D. J. Pound, after a photograph by John & Charles Watkins, c. 1860.

MUNNINGS, ALFRED (1878–1959). Munnings was one of the last of the great British sporting artists, his fluid handling of paint and plein-air naturalism adding new life to that distinguished tradition. He turned to painting after an early career as a lithographic draftsman, taking instruction both in England and at the Académie Julian in Paris. He first tried sporting subjects around 1900 and, after a visit to the Lavenham Horse Fair, developed a lifelong fascination with the horse. He continued to paint landscape and genre scenes as well, concentrating on his native Suffolk countryside. After successful exhibitions in England in the early 1920s, he traveled to the United States for six months and was inundated with society commissions. Though working through a period of radical artistic upheaval, Munnings was a staunch conservative. He made his opposition to modern art, particularly Picasso, a well-known feature of his tenure (1944 to 1949) as president of the Royal Academy. No. 52

Detail from a photograph of the artist at the Newmarket races. Courtesy of the Sir Alfred Munnings Art Museum, Dedham.

NEVINSON, CHRISTOPHER RICHARD WYNNE (1889–1946). With close ties to the Italian avant-garde artist Filippo Tommaso Marinetti, Nevinson was the leading proponent of Futurism in Britain. Although he spent three years at the Slade School of Art in London, it was the Futurist exhibition at the Sackville Gallery in 1912 that would prove decisive for his development. His enthusiasm for the Futurist movement took him to Paris, where he studied at the Académie Julian and the Cercle Russe. Upon his return to London in 1913, he applied the Futurist machine aesthetic of fragmented forms and dynamic movement to depictions of the hustle and bustle of modern London. With the advent of World War One, however, Nevinson's faith in the machine age faded; it was replaced in his later years by a deeper appreciation of the natural world. No. 78

Self-portrait, oil on panel, 1911. Tate Gallery, London.

NICHOLSON, BEN (1894–1982). Closely allied in spirit with the European avant-garde, Nicholson was among the first British artists to experiment with abstraction. He began his artistic training at the Slade School of Art in 1910–11 but did not devote himself seriously to his art until after 1920. While his earliest work was realistic, more in the spirit of Vermeer than any modern artist, he soon fell under the influence of modernism's greatest British champion, Roger Fry. Fry's admiration for the Cubists no doubt led to Nicholson's bold Cubist landscapes and still lifes of the mid- to late-1920s. Travels to Paris exposed him to the work of the Italian Primitives and African tribes, as well as the paintings of Cézanne, Matisse, Picasso, and Braque. By the 1930s he began to develop the style for which he would become internationally known, one that combined abstract form with landscape elements. He studied the works of Miró, Mondrian, and Alexander Calder and was influenced by their non-figurative styles. He produced his first abstract relief in 1933, following this with a series of carved pieces that would mark him at home and abroad as Britain's "most intractable modernist." After 1943 he resided in St. Ives, Cornwall with his second wife, the sculptor Barbara Hepworth, and helped to establish that area as a center for the arts. Among the many honors Nicholson received were the Guggenheim International Painting Prize in 1956 and the Order of Merit in 1968. No. 81

Photograph by Humphrey Spender, c. 1933. National Portrait Gallery, London.

RAMSAY, ALLAN (1713–1784). Ramsay was the leading British portrait painter during the 1740s and 1750s. His early artistic training took place in his native Scotland and in London, where he studied with the Swedish painter Hans Hysing. In 1736 he traveled to Italy, studying under the portraitists Francesco Solimena and Francesco Imperiali. He returned to London the following year and by 1738 had set up a lucrative portrait-painting practice of his own, as well as a summer studio in Edinburgh. After a dramatic early style recalling the Continental Baroque, Ramsay's work became increasingly unaffected and naturalistic. His pictures of the 1750s owe a debt in their delicacy of palette to the French painters Maurice-Quentin de La Tour and Jean-Marc Nattier. His close association with Hogarth is also evident in these portraits, their new directness and candor clearly inspired by that artist. After further trips to Italy and his appointment as court painter to George III (by 1761), Ramsay devoted himself almost entirely to royal commissions. Following an arm injury in 1773, he was less active as an artist and devoted more time to literary endeavors and political pamphleteering. No. 33

Mezzotint by Abraham Wivell, after a self-portrait, publ. 1820.

REYNOLDS, JOSHUA (1723–1792). The nation's most celebrated portraitist and first president of the Royal Academy, Reynolds was arguably the most influential figure in the eighteenth-century British art world. After an apprenticeship to Thomas Hudson and independent work in both Devon and London, he left in 1749 for a period of study in Italy. His two years in Rome led to a deep appreciation of the works of Raphael, Giulio Romano, Tintoretto and, above all, Michelangelo. Fueled by his determination to raise the status of the portrait to that of "high art" (i. e. history painting) and inspired by Michelangelo's "Great style," Reynolds's work on his return to London offered learned allusions to classical art and the Old Masters. He infused Georgian portraiture with an unprecedented sophistication, learnedness, and dignity. His pictures proved immensely popular and would inspire a future generation of portraitists, Henry Raeburn and Thomas Lawrence among them. Reynolds's Italian experience also left an indelible mark on his theories of aesthetics, eloquently delivered in a series of presidential lectures at the Royal Academy. These *Discourses on Art*, delivered to students and Academy members from 1769 to 1790, form the most significant body of art criticism produced in the eighteenth century and are still widely read today. Nos. 35, 37, 38

Mezzotint by Samuel William Reynolds, after a self-portrait, publ. 1821.

ROMNEY, GEORGE (1734–1802). Romney was one of the most successful portraitists of his day, in reputation inferior only to Reynolds and Gainsborough. The son of a cabinetmaker, he was apprenticed to the itinerant painter Christopher Steele in 1755. After setting up a portrait practice of his own in Kendal, he moved to London in 1762. There his career improved considerably, and by the early 1770s his studio was thriving, turning out a prodigious number of society portraits. Although the quality of Romney's later work is uneven, his best oils demonstrate a graceful touch, elegant linearity, and superb coloring. Romney traveled to Rome in 1773, abandoning his lucrative practice to complete his artistic education and pursue his dream of becoming a history painter. There he made numerous sketches after the Antique and the Old Masters and was inspired by both Michelangelo and Raphael. Though influential, his time in Italy was not to have a lasting impact on his art. After returning to London in 1775, he re-established his career by turning again to portraiture. Though never a member of the Royal Academy, he enjoyed enormous success over the next two decades. Poor health forced his virtual retirement from painting in 1796. No. 16

Stipple engraving by William T. Fry, after a self-portrait, publ. 1817.

SANDBY, PAUL (1731–1809). Among the best landscape painters of his generation, Sandby showed his keen sense of light and atmosphere to best advantage in his watercolors and aquatints. Together with his brother, draftsman and architect Thomas Sandby, he found employment in 1747 as a military draftsman for the Board of Ordnance at the Tower of London. That same year he was appointed official draftsman to the Military Survey in Scotland. These early experiences honed his skills in the depiction of landscape, which would be the mainstay of his artistic career. In the 1750s he produced panoramic landscapes and a number of etchings that display his wit and sharp eye for social behavior, as well as an eclectic assimilation of Hogarth, seventeenth-century Dutch art, and the French Rococo. Sandby was active in the burgeoning London art scene, becoming a founding member of both the Society of Artists (1760) and the Royal Academy (1768). Travels through Wales in the 1770s resulted in some of his finest work, a series of aquatints published in 1775 and 1776. Toward the end of his career he painted more oils and a number of watercolors with military themes. His influence on following generations of landscape artists, including both Thomas Girtin and J. M. W. Turner, was undisputed. No. 25

Stipple engraving by D. P. Pariset, after Peter Falconet (drawn 1769).

SCOTT, WILLIAM BELL (1811–1890). Scott's work is closely related to that of the Pre-Raphaelites, owing in part to his close friendship with Dante Gabriel Rossetti. Like his brother, the painter David Scott, he trained at the Trustees' Academy in Edinburgh and learned engraving from his father. In 1837 he went to London, where he was encouraged to become a history painter. Discouraged by the lack of patronage, however, he accepted the Mastership of the Government School of Design at Newcastle upon Tyne in 1843. Among Scott's best known works is his series of large mural paintings at Wallington House, Northumberland, showing scenes from Northumbrian history (begun 1855); these demonstrate the artist's penchant for bright, jewel-like color and historical detail. Scott was also a prolific poet, his verse arguably as rich as his paintings. No. 65

Photograph by W. & D. Downey, 1858. Maas Collection. Photo: National Portrait Gallery, London.

SIBERECHTS, JAN (baptized 1627–c. 1703). Invited to England in 1670 by George Villiers, 2nd Duke of Buckingham, the Dutch-born Siberechts quickly established a thriving career as a landscape painter. He painted hunting scenes and views of country seats, notably Longleat, that reveal a keen interest in the play of light. Though repetitive compositionally, his works are today of great topographical and historical interest. In 1648 he had been made a master of the Guild of St. Luke in Antwerp; his earliest works show the influence of the Dutch Italianates, as well as the inspiration he found in the rustic life of Flanders. His style did not alter significantly upon his arrival in England, and his paintings of the British countryside were clearly informed by a Flemish sensibility. He lived and practiced in England for the remainder of his career, playing a central role in the formation of an indigenous school of landscape painting. No. 7

Engraving by T. Chambars, after Nicolas de Largillière, from Horace Walpole, Anecdotes of Painting in England, *Strawberry Hill, 1762–71.*

SICKERT, WALTER RICHARD (1860–1942). One of the foremost artists active in Britain at the turn of the century, Sickert had a lasting effect upon twentieth-century British art. Born in Germany, the son and grandson of professional artists, he emigrated to Britain with the rest of his family in 1868. After briefly pursuing a career as an actor, he entered the Slade School of Art in London. He left after only a few months to become pupil and studio assistant to James McNeill Whistler. Later his exposure to the work of Degas tempered what he had learned from Whistler, leading him to adopt a stronger palette and extend the range of his subject matter. The resulting series of music-hall scenes are among his best works. In 1889 he exhibited at the London Impressionists exhibition with fellow members of the New English Art Club. For the next thirty years of his prolific career, he continued to refine his technique and explore new themes, working both in London and in Dieppe. He established the Camden Town Group in 1911, and his intimate scenes of working-class life would come to typify Camden Town painting. Always replete with psychological tensions, these and other of Sickert's mature works display his boyhood training as an illustrator, his appreciation of Degas, and his adherence to Whistler's creed that subject was subordinate to treatment. By the 1920s, in addition to teaching and writing extensively on art, Sickert had begun to paint directly from photographs, establishing a working method that has since become widespread in modern art. He was elected ARA in 1924 and RA a decade later, and though he received few other official honors, he lived long enough to know of the major retrospective exhibition of his work held at the National Gallery in London in 1941. Nos. 70, 71

Photograph by George Charles Beresford, 1911. National Portrait Gallery, London.

SOMER, PAUL VAN (1576–1621). Van Somer was one of the leading portraitists at the court of James I. He employed a style that was at once backward-looking and contemporary, somewhere between the iconic Elizabethan portrait and the Continental Baroque of Anthony van Dyck. He received his earliest artistic training in his native Antwerp, perhaps with the same master as his brother, who was a painter, art dealer, and printmaker. By 1604 van Somer was engaged in extensive travels, painting landscapes throughout the Netherlands. He had arrived in England by 1616 and quickly became the favorite of Anne of Denmark, wife of James I. No. 2

Engraving by T. Chambars, after a self-portrait, from Horace Walpole, Anecdotes of Painting in England, *Strawberry Hill, 1762–71.*

STUBBS, GEORGE (1724–1806). The best known British animal painter, his works marked by a keen sense of design and exhaustive knowledge of anatomy, Stubbs ranks along with Gainsborough and Reynolds as one of the most gifted artists of eighteenth-century Britain. Born in Liverpool to a currier and leather-maker, he was almost entirely self-taught. He began his artistic career with a series of etchings to a treatise on midwifery, the result of his anatomical studies at York Hospital in the mid-1740s. In 1754 he made a brief trip to Rome. The classical balance and restraint evident in all his work may be attributed to this visit. By 1756 he had begun his intensive study of the anatomy of the horse. To further his knowledge he worked at a farm in Lincolnshire, where he performed numerous dissections on horses and made scores of drawings and notes. These formed the basis of *The Anatomy of the Horse*, published by the artist with his own engravings in 1766. By this time he had moved to London. There he quickly established a flourishing practice painting portraits of horses, grooms, and owners, the inventive designs of which are testament to his compositional sensitivity. He also began an imaginative series of paintings in which a wild horse falls prey to a lion, a classically inspired theme that he returned to repeatedly and in various techniques. He exhibited at the Royal Academy throughout the last decades of the eighteenth century but declined membership. His work was of profound influence upon the succeeding generation of sporting artists, including James Ward and John Ferneley. Nos. 42, 43, 44–47, 48

Etching by Bretherton, after T. Orde.

TURNER, JOSEPH MALLORD WILLIAM (1775–1851). One of the towering figures of the Romantic age, Turner was both technically brilliant and enormously ambitious, addressing such themes in his work as the fate of empires, the vanity of human endeavor, and the transience of life. He trained at the Royal Academy Schools from the age of fourteen. His earliest works were of architectural subjects, leading him to work briefly as an assistant scene-painter at the Pantheon opera house in London. He later collaborated with Thomas Girtin at the small "academy" of Thomas Monro, copying studies by John Robert Cozens and the topographical painter Edward Dayes. The paintings of this period foreshadow the close observation of nature and loose, atmospheric handling of paint which would come to define Turner's mature landscapes and seascapes. While he was undoubtedly influenced by the Italianate tradition of Claude Lorrain and Nicolas Poussin, he was equally affected by Richard Wilson and the work of northern landscape artists, including Aelbert Cuyp and Jan van Goyen. In the first decade of the nineteenth century Turner expanded his artistic repertoire to include printmaking and poetry. Elected RA in 1802, he became Professor of Perspective to the Academy in 1809. His work of the 1820s and 1830s was dominated by subjects from his travels abroad, beginning with Italy in 1819 and later including France, Switzerland, and Germany. The many oils and watercolors dating from these decades are masterpieces of brilliant coloring and theatrical and sublime composition, exhibiting a remarkably liberated, almost abstract touch. Nos. 30, 31, 60, 62

Soft-ground etching by William Daniell, after George Dance (drawn 1800), publ. 1827.

WADSWORTH, EDWARD (1889–1949). Wadworth's early work is reminiscent of the Post-Impressionists, but he went on to become a central figure in the British Vorticist movement. Raised in a northern industrial environment, his interest in the machine was formed at an early age. He studied engineering in Munich from 1906 to 1907 before winning a scholarship at the Slade School of Art in London. In 1912 he joined the Omega Workshops but left soon after meeting Wyndham Lewis. Influenced by both the Futurists and the musically inspired works of Wassily Kandinsky, he produced paintings for the Rebel Art Centre that revealed his love of maritime themes and aerial views. In 1915 he exhibited at the Vorticist exhibition at the Doré Gallery. He served during World War I in the Royal Naval Volunteer Reserve. A strain of Surrealism entered his later work, which was also marked by an increasingly meticulous attitude towards technique. Selected for the Venice Biennale in 1940, he became an ARA in 1943 and was a founder-member of Unit One, a group dedicated to promoting the spirit of renewal in British art. No. 80

Photograph, c. 1935. Barbara von Bethmann-Hollweg.

WARD, JAMES (1769–1859). A frequent exhibitor at the Royal Academy, Ward was one of the most celebrated animal painters of his era. Initially trained as an engraver, he enjoyed considerable success with mezzotints before turning to oil painting in 1790. His career falls into two periods, with works before 1803 showing the influence of his brother-in-law George Morland and those after this date the influence of Rubens. His reputation was established by his portraits of blood horses and thoroughbreds begun shortly before 1810, the *Sporting Magazine* declaring him in 1811 "the first of English animal painters now living." His distinctive mature style, pairing vigorous brushwork and strong color with dynamic compositions, is quintessentially Romantic. Following the critical failure of his monumental *Waterloo Allegory* (1815–21), commissioned by the British Institution, and a series of personal setbacks, he retired to the country in 1830. The works of his later period often contain moral or religious themes, which were mirrored in his poetry and writings on theology. No. 50

Mezzotint by Ward himself, after John Jackson.

WEST, BENJAMIN (1738–1820). A pioneer of Neoclassicism, the American-born West quickly rose to prominence in the London art world, eventually winning a royal appointment under George III and the presidency of the Royal Academy. After informal training in Philadelphia, as well as a brief stint as a portraitist in New York, he left America in 1760 to study in Italy. Intending to establish himself as a history painter, he became involved with the burgeoning Neoclassical school there, associating with Anton Raffael Mengs and Gavin Hamilton. Settling in London upon his return from Italy in 1763, West's first great critical success came with a commission for a Roman historical picture from the Archbishop of York. The painting so impressed George III that he named West Historical Painter to the King and provided him with an annual stipend of £1,000, freeing the artist from the need to support himself by painting portraits. West was also closely involved with the fledgling Royal Academy, becoming one of its founding members in 1768. He enjoyed unparalleled success as a history painter throughout the 1770s, especially with *The Death of General Wolfe* (1770), a picture that boldly broke with artistic convention by showing a modern history scene in contemporary dress. He was elected president of the Royal Academy on the death of Joshua Reynolds in 1792. Although his republican sympathies cost him his association with the crown, his explorations of Romantic subject matter kept him at the forefront of British art in the early decades of the nineteenth century and ensured him a long and lucrative practice. No. 18

Stipple engraving by Caroline Watson, after Gilbert Stuart, publ. 1785.

WHEATLEY, FRANCIS (1747–1801). Best known in France and Britain for his engraved series of the *Cries of London* (1792–95), Wheatley also produced portraits, conversation pieces, and narrative paintings. He trained at William Shipley's Academy in London, winning a number of prizes for drawing from the Society of Artists in the early 1760s. In 1769, after traveling to the Low Countries, France, and Ireland, he enrolled at the new Royal Academy Schools. In addition to small, full-length portraits, he began painting conversation pieces, closely following the style of Zoffany. Though his works were well-received, he found himself in financial difficulty and was forced to flee to Dublin in 1779 to escape his creditors. In 1783 he returned to London and began work with the print publisher John Boydell. The collaboration led to the publication of numerous engravings of literary and genre subjects after the artist's designs and won him a lasting reputation. In 1791 he was elected RA. Despite this recognition, Wheatley's last years were plagued by poor health and debt. No. 19

Soft-ground etching by William Daniell, after George Dance.

WHISTLER, JAMES ABBOTT McNEILL (1834–1903). Whistler was a leading figure of the Aesthetic Movement whose style broke radically with British contemporary painting. He was born in America but spent his childhood in Russia and England, taking casual art instruction in both countries. After three years at West Point and a position in the drawing division of the U. S. Coast and Geodetic Survey in Washington, DC, he decided to pursue his artistic studies in Paris, where he developed a lifelong appreciation for Velázquez and Courbet, as well as for Rembrandt's etchings. By the 1860s the more favorable reception of his work in Britain led him to settle in Chelsea. There he was introduced to members of the Pre-Raphaelite circle, Dante Gabriel Rossetti and Algernon Swinburne among them. This decade saw the development of his distinctive portrait style, with tonally-balanced compositions executed in thin washes of paint. To underscore his belief that music and art were similar forms of poetic expression, he unconventionally titled his portraits "arrangements" or "harmonies," rather than by the names of the sitters. The same sensibility informed his "nocturnes," night pictures punctuated with small bursts of luminous color. Whistler was a leading figure in the "japoniste" movement, introducing Oriental themes and blue-and-white porcelain frequently into his pictures. One of the great masters of etching, he created a large body of work remarkable for its lightness of touch and depth of expression. Despite the obvious range of his talents, Whistler's rakish personality caused him considerable difficulties with patrons and the public alike. His success was interspersed with periods of bankruptcy and legal disputes, and his last years were spent less in England than abroad. No. 67

Photograph, c. 1864. Glasgow University Library.

WILSON, RICHARD (1713/14–1782). The first great British landscape artist, Wilson enjoyed considerable success with his Claudean views in Italy and at home. Son of a Welsh clergyman, he trained initially as a portrait painter under Thomas Wright in London. After his arrival in Italy in 1750, he soon indulged his natural talent for landscape. Following the path of the Grand Tour aristocrat, he spent the following six years in Italy, sketching and painting ruins, cityscapes, and the surrounding countryside. Their assured sense of composition and atmospheric perspective clearly reminiscent of Claude Lorrain, his views found eager buyers among classically-educated British patrons and collectors. Wilson was an immediate success upon his return home in 1757, helping to found the Society of Artists and the Royal Academy. He expanded his œuvre to include British landscape views, his antiquarian interests leading him to historically significant sites such as Pembroke Castle. While his reputation faded towards the end of his life and his art fell out of favor, he was nevertheless a great influence upon the succeeding generation of landscape painters, Constable and Turner among them. Nos. 21, 24, 26

Stipple engraving by William Bond, after Anton Raffael Mengs, publ. 1812.

WOOTTON, JOHN (c. 1682–1764). The preeminent English sporting artist of the first half of the eighteenth century, Wootton combined a topographical approach to landscape with a taste for classicism. Though primarily known as a horse painter, he never limited himself to that genre alone, and as a result gained both wide-ranging respect and considerable wealth. The details of his early career are unclear, although it is possible that he studied under Jan Wyck in the 1690s. By 1706 he had established a practice in London. His early sporting pictures relied heavily on the Dutch tradition, particularly the works of Philips Wouwerman and Aelbert Cuyp. By the 1730s, however, he had adopted the Claudean conven- tions of the classical landscape, presumably in an attempt to raise the status of sporting art. Wootton attracted a number of wealthy patrons, enabling him to live in style in Cavendish Square from 1727. Though his reputation beyond his own lifetime was short-lived, his elevated brand of sporting art would prove greatly influential upon later generations of artists, including George Stubbs. No. 41

Detail from Gawen Hamilton, A Conversation of Virtuosis…at the Kings Arms (A Club of Artists), *oil on canvas, c. 1735. National Portrait Gallery, London.*

WRIGHT, JOSEPH (1734–1797). One of the foremost painters of the eighteenth century, Wright of Derby (as he was called) was deeply entrenched in the Enlightenment community of scientists and philosophers fascinated with light, color, and other natural phenomena. The son of an attorney, he trained under Thomas Hudson in London in the 1750s, returning to his native Derby to paint portraits of the local gentry and middle classes. While such work would prove the mainstay of his professional life, he is best remembered for dramatic history and genre scenes beginning in the early 1760s, in which the effects of candle- and other types of artificial light figure prominently. The experiments of the Midlands scientific community provided him with subjects through which to explore both pictorial effects and natural phenomena. His studies of light and color continued during his two years' residence in Rome in the mid-1770s, where exposure to the Old Masters and Antique statuary furthered his grasp of classicism. After an unsuccessful attempt to replace Gainsborough as the leading portraitist in Bath, he returned to Derby after 1777. He was the first major British painter to work outside London all his life and to be successful doing so. He was elected ARA in 1781, but disagreements with the Academy kept him from ever being honored with full RA status. Nos. 17, 27, 29

Self-portrait, etching.

ZOFFANY, JOHANN (1733–1810). Arguably the greatest practitioner of the British conversation piece, the German-born Zoffany brought to the genre great technical finesse and a certain theatricality. The son of the Court Cabinetmaker and Architect to the Prince of Thurn and Taxis, he initially worked under the painter and engraver Martin Speer in Regensburg. Travel in Italy in the 1750s brought him opportunity for study and led to an introduction to the Neoclassical painter Anton Raffael Mengs. By the late 1750s he enjoyed the patronage of the Elector of Trier, creating for him a series of palace wall decorations. In 1760 he came to England hoping to establish a career as a decorative painter, but he acquired a taste for conversation pieces while working in the studio of Benjamin Wilson and decided to pursue that genre instead. Wilson introduced him to the actor David Garrick, who commissioned a number of portraits in theatrical garb. Zoffany's technical skill and lively compositions soon brought him to the attention of aristocratic and royal patrons. In the 1760s he completed a number of paintings of the royal family, as well as a group portrait of the members of the newly-founded Royal Academy. Duly impressed with his work, Queen Charlotte sent him to Italy on a commission in 1772. He remained there for the next seven years, his reputation increasing greatly during that time. When he returned to England in 1779, however, he found his style somewhat out of date and the conversation piece no longer in fashion. Owing to the difficulty of obtaining commissions, he decided to seek his fortune in India. He arrived there in 1783 and found enough work among the British and Indian upper classes to return to England in 1789 a very wealthy man. No. 20

Soft-ground etching by William Daniell, after George Dance (drawn 1793), publ. 1814.

Sources

Allen, Brian. *Francis Hayman*. New Haven: Yale University Press, 1987.

—. "Sir Joshua Reynolds' Portrait of the 3rd Earl of Harrington." In *Essays In Honor of Paul Mellon*. Edited by John Wilmerding. Washington: National Gallery of Art, 1986. 11–23.

Arts Council of Great Britain. *Charles Ginner, 1878–1952*. London, 1953.

Baillio, Joseph. *Alfred J. Munnings: Images of the Turf and Field*. New York: Wildenstein, 1983.

Baron, Wendy. *The Camden Town Group*. London: Scolar Press, 1979.

—. *Sickert*. London: Phaidon, 1973.

—. "Sickert and the Camden Town Murder." In *Art at Auction: The Year at Sotheby Parke-Bernet, 1979–1980. 246th Season*. Edited by Joan A. Speers. London, 1980. 71–73.

Baron, Wendy, and Malcolm Cormack. *The Camden Town Group*. New Haven: Yale Center for British Art, 1980.

Beckett, Ronald Brymer. *John Constable's Correspondence*. vol. 6. *The Fishers*. Ipswich: Suffolk Records Society, 1968.

—. *Lely*. London: Routledge and Kegan Paul, 1951.

Bennett, Mary. *Ford Madox Brown, 1821–1893*. Liverpool: Walker Art Gallery, 1964.

—. *Millais*. London: Royal Academy of Arts, 1967.

Bindman, David. *Hogarth*. London: Thames and Hudson, 1981.

Bindman, David, and Scott Wilcox, eds. *"Among the Whores and Thieves": William Hogarth and "The Beggar's Opera."* New Haven: Yale Center for British Art, 1997.

Blake, William. *The Complete Writings of William Blake*. Edited by Geoffrey Keynes. London: Oxford University Press, 1966.

Booth, Stanley. *Sir Alfred Munnings, 1878–1959: An Appreciation of the Artist and a Selection of his Paintings*. London: Philip Wilson for Sotheby's, 1986.

Brenneman, David Andrew. "Thomas Gainsborough's 'Wooded Landscape with Cattle by a Pool,' Art Criticism and the Royal Academy." *Gainsborough's House Review* (1995–96): 37–46.

Brown, David Blayney. *Augustus Wall Callcott*. London: Tate Gallery, 1981.

Burke, Edmund. *The Works of the Right Honourable Edmund Burke*. 6 vols. London, 1906–7.

Butlin, Martin, and Evelyn Joll. *The Paintings of J. M. W. Turner*. Rev. ed. 2 vols. New Haven: Yale University Press, 1984.

Buttery, David. *Canaletto and Warwick Castle*. Sussex: Phillimore, 1992.

Causey, Andrew, and Richard Thomson. *Harold Gilman, 1876–1919*. London: Arts Council of Great Britain, 1981.

Clark, Anthony M. *Pompeo Batoni: A Complete Catalogue of His Works with an Introductory Text*. Edited and prepared for publication by Edgar Peters Bowron. New York: New York University Press, 1985.

Constable, W. G. *Richard Wilson*. Cambridge: Harvard University, 1953.

Constable, W. G., and J. G. Links. *Canaletto: Giovanni Antonio Canal, 1697–1768*. 2nd rev. ed. 2 vols. Oxford: Clarendon Press, 1976.

Cormack, Malcolm. "Constable's 'Stratford Mill.'" In *Essays In Honor of Paul Mellon*. Edited by John Wilmerding. Washington: National Gallery of Art, 1986. 71–83.

—. "In Detail: Constable's *Hadleigh Castle*." *Portfolio* (Summer 1980): 36–41.

—. "'The Dort': Some Further Observations," *Turner Studies* 2, no. 2 (Winter 1983): 37–39.

—. *The Paintings of Thomas Gainsborough*. Cambridge: Cambridge University Press, 1991.

Cunnington, C. Willett and Phillis. *Handbook of English Costume in the Eighteenth Century*. London: Faber and Faber, 1957.

Deuchar, Stephen. *Sporting Art in Eighteenth-Century England: A Social and Political History*. New Haven: Yale University Press, 1988.

The Dictionary of National Biography. 66 vols. Edited by Leslie Stephen. London, 1885–1901.

D'Oench, Ellen. *The Conversation Piece: Arthur Devis and His Contemporaries*. New Haven: Yale Center for British Art, 1980.

Egerton, Judy. *Sport in Art and Books: The Paul Mellon Collection. British Sporting and Animal Paintings, 1655–1867*. London: Tate Gallery, 1978.

—. "Four Shooting Paintings by George Stubbs." In *Essays In Honor of Paul Mellon*. Edited by John Wilmerding. Washington: National Gallery of Art, 1986. 85–95.

—. *George Stubbs, 1724–1806*. London: Tate Gallery Publications for the Tate Gallery and the Yale Center for British Art, 1984.

—. *Wright of Derby*. London: Tate Gallery, 1990.

Erffa, Helmut von, and Allen Staley. *The Paintings of Benjamin West*. New Haven: Yale University Press, 1986.

Feaver, William. *The Art of John Martin*. Oxford: Clarendon Press, 1975.

Galería Jorge Mara. *Ben Nicholson*. Madrid, 1995.

Garlick, Kenneth. *Sir Thomas Lawrence: A Complete Catalogue of the Oil Paintings*. Oxford: Phaidon, 1989.

Gore, Frederick, and Richard Shone. *Spencer Frederick Gore (1878–1914)*. London: Anthony d'Offay, 1983.

Graves, Algernon. *The Royal Academy: A Complete Dictionary*. 8 vols. London, 1905–6.

Graves, Algernon, and William Vine Cronin. *A History of the Works of Sir Joshua Reynolds, PRA*. 4 vols. London, 1899–1901.

Grundy, Cecil R. *James Ward, RA: His Life and Works, with a Catalogue of His Engravings and Pictures*. London, 1909.

Harrison, Charles. *English Art and Modernism, 1900–1939*. 2d ed. New Haven: Yale University Press, 1994.

Hawes, Louis. "Constable's *Hadleigh Castle* and British Romantic Ruin Painting." *Art Bulletin* 65, no. 3 (September 1983): 455–70.

Hayes, John T. "Claude de Jongh." *Burlington Magazine* 634, no. 98 (January 1956): 3–11.

—. *Gainsborough: Paintings and Drawings*. London: Phaidon, 1975.

—. *The Landscape Paintings of Thomas Gainsborough: A Critical Text and Catalogue Raisonné*. 2 vols. Ithaca: Cornell University Press, 1982.

Hearn, Karen, ed. *Dynasties: Painting in Tudor and Jacobean England, 1530–1630*. London: Tate Publishing, 1995.

Hogarth, William. *The Analysis of Beauty*. Edited with an introduction by Joseph Burke. Oxford: Clarendon Press, 1955.

Ingamells, John, and Robert Raines. " A Catalogue of the Paintings, Drawings and Etchings of Philip Mercier." *Walpole Society* 46 (1976–78): 1–70.

Langdale, Cecily. *Gwen John*. New Haven: Yale University Press, 1987.

Larsen, Erik. *The Paintings of Anthony van Dyck*. 2 vols. Freren, Germany: Luca Verlag, 1988.

Leslie, Charles Robert. *Memoirs of the Life of John Constable*. London, 1843.

Leveson-Gower, Lord Granville. *Private Correspondence, 1781 to 1821*. 2 vols. London, 1916.

Levey, Michael. *Sir Thomas Lawrence, 1769–1830*. London: National Portrait Gallery, 1979.

Lewison, Jeremy. *Ben Nicholson*. London: Tate Gallery, 1993.

Lynton, Norbert. *Ben Nicholson*. Oxford: Phaidon, 1993.

MacClintock, Dorcas. "Queen Charlotte's Zebra." *Discovery* 23, no. 1 (1992): 3–9.

Marler, Regina, ed. *The Selected Letters of Vanessa Bell*. New York: Pantheon, 1993.

Mellon, Paul, with John Baskett. *Reflections in a Silver Spoon: A Memoir*. New York: William Morrow, 1992.

Millar, Oliver. "Marcus Gheeraerts the Younger; A Sequel through Inscriptions." *Burlington Magazine* 105, no. 729 (December 1963): 533–40.

—. *Sir Peter Lely, 1618–1680*. London: National Portrait Gallery, 1978.

Neff, Emily Ballew, with an essay by William L. Pressly. *John Singleton Copley in England*. Houston: Museum of Fine Arts, 1995.

Nevinson, C. R. W. *Paint and Prejudice*. London: Methuen, 1937.

Nicolson, Benedict. *Joseph Wright of Derby: Painter of Light*. 2 vols. London: Paul Mellon Foundation for British Art, 1968.

Noakes, Aubrey. *Ben Marshall, 1767–1835*. Leigh-on-Sea: F. Lewis, 1978.

Noakes, Vivien. *Edward Lear, 1812–1888*. London: Royal Academy of Arts, 1985.

Noon, Patrick. "Richard Parkes Bonington: 'Fish Market, Boulogne.'" In *Essays In Honor of Paul Mellon*. Edited by John Wilmerding. Washington: National Gallery of Art, 1986. 239–53.

—. *Richard Parkes Bonington: "On the Pleasure of Painting."* New Haven: Yale University Press, 1991.

Ormond, Leonée, and Richard Ormond. *Lord Leighton*. New Haven and London: Yale University Press, 1975.

Parris, Leslie, and Ian Fleming-Williams. *Constable*. London: Tate Gallery, 1991.

Pater, Walter. *The Renaissance: Studies in Art and Poetry*. London, 1910.

Paulson, Ronald. *Hogarth: His Life, Art, and Times*. 2 vols. New Haven: Yale University Press, 1971.

Penny, Nicholas, ed. *Reynolds*. London: Royal Academy of Arts, 1986.

Pickvance, Ronald. "The Magic of the Halls and Sickert." *Apollo* 76 (January 1962): 107–15.

Prown, Jules David. "Benjamin West's Family Picture: A Nativity in Hammersmith." In *Essays In Honor of Paul Mellon*. Edited by John Wilmerding. Washington: National Gallery of Art, 1986. 269–87.

—. *John Singleton Copley*. Cambridge: Harvard University Press, 1966.

Reynolds, Graham. *The Early Paintings and Drawings of John Constable*. 2 vols. New Haven: Yale University Press, 1996.

—. *The Later Paintings and Drawings of John Constable*. 2 vols. New Haven: Yale University Press, 1984.

Reynolds, Joshua. *Discourses on Art*. Edited by Robert R. Wark. New Haven: Yale University Press, 1997.

Ribeiro, Aileen. *The Art of Dress: Fashion in England and France, 1750 to 1820*. New Haven: Yale University Press, 1995.

Rogers, Malcolm. *William Dobson, 1611–1646*. London: National Portrait Gallery, 1983.

Romney, The Rev. *Memoirs of the Life and Works of George Romney.* London, 1830.

Rosenbaum, S. P., ed. *The Bloomsbury Group.* London: Croom Helm, 1975.

Rosenthal, Michael. *Constable: The Painter and His Landscape.* New Haven: Yale University Press, 1983.

Royal Academy of Arts. *Frederic Leighton, 1830–1896.* London, 1996.

Shanes, Eric. "The True Subject of a Major Late Painting by J. M. W. Turner Identified." *Burlington Magazine* 126 (May 1984): 284–88.

Shawe-Taylor, Desmond. *The Georgians: Eighteenth-Century Portraiture and Society.* London: Barrie and Jenkins, 1990.

Shone, Richard. *Bloomsbury Portraits.* Oxford: Phaidon, 1993.

Smart, Alastair. *Allan Ramsay, 1713–1784.* Edinburgh: Scottish National Portrait Gallery, 1992.

—. *Allan Ramsay: Painter, Essayist, and Man of the Enlightenment.* New Haven: Yale University Press, 1992.

Solkin, David. *Richard Wilson: The Landscape of Reaction.* London: Tate Gallery, 1982.

Spalding, Frances. *Duncan Grant.* London: Chatto and Windus, 1997.

—. *Vanessa Bell.* London: Weidenfeld and Nicolson, 1983.

Strong, Roy C. *The English Icon: Elizabethan and Jacobean Portraiture.* London: Paul Mellon Foundation for British Art, 1969.

Surry, Nigel. *George Beare.* Chichester: Pallant House, 1989.

Tate Gallery. *The Pre-Raphaelites.* Edited by Leslie Parris. London, 1984.

Tattersall, Bruce. *Stubbs and Wedgwood: Unique Alliance between Artist and Potter.* London: Tate Gallery, 1974.

Vertue, George. *Note Books.* 6 vols. Oxford: Oxford University Press for the Walpole Society, 1930–55.

Wadsworth, Barbara. *Edward Wadsworth: A Painter's Life.* Salisbury: Michael Russell, 1989.

Walker, John. "Hogarth's Painting *The Beggar's Opera*: Cast and Audience at the First Night." In *Essays In Honor of Paul Mellon.* Edited by John Wilmerding. Washington: National Gallery of Art, 1986. 363–80.

Walpole, Horace. *Anecdotes of Painting in England.* New Haven: Yale University Press, 1937.

Ward, Humphry, and W. Roberts, eds. *Romney: A Biographical and Critical Essay, with a Catalogue Raisonné of His Works.* 2 vols. London, 1904.

Waterhouse, Ellis. *Gainsborough.* London: Hulton, 1958.

—. *Reynolds.* London, 1941.

Webster, Mary. *Francis Wheatley.* London: Paul Mellon Foundation for British Art, 1970.

—. *Johan Zoffany, 1733–1810.* London: National Portrait Gallery, 1976.

Whistler, James McNeill. *The Gentle Art of Making Enemies.* London and New York, 1890.

White, Christopher. "The Portrait of Mountjoy Blount, 1st Earl of Newport by Sir Anthony van Dyck." In *Essays In Honor of Paul Mellon.* Edited by John Wilmerding. Washington: National Gallery of Art, 1986. 383–87.

Woodall, Mary, ed. *Letters of Thomas Gainsborough.* Rev. ed. Greenwich, Connecticut: New York Graphic Society, 1963.

Yale Center for British Art. *The Art of Paul Sandby.* New Haven, 1985.

—. *Country Houses in Great Britain.* New Haven, 1979.

Young, Andrew McLaren, et al. *The Paintings of James McNeill Whistler.* 2 vols. New Haven: Yale University Press, 1980.